RADICAL
ECUMENICITY

RADICAL ECUMENICITY

Pursuing Unity and Continuity
after John Howard Yoder

EDITED BY JOHN C. NUGENT

Abilene Christian University Press

Abilene, Texas

Radical Ecumenicity:
Pursuing Unity and Continuity after John Howard Yoder

Copyright 2010 by Abilene Christian University Press

Edited by John C. Nugent

ISBN 978-0-89112-042-1
LCCN 2010002380

Printed in the United States of America

LIBRARY OF CONGRESS CATALOGING-IN-PUBLICATION DATA
Radical ecumenicity : pursuing unity and continuity after John Howard Yoder / edited by John C. Nugent.
    p. cm.
ISBN 978-0-89112-042-1
1. Yoder, John Howard--Congresses. 2. Christian union--Congresses. 3. Continuity of the church--
Congresses. 4. Restoration movement (Christianity)--Congresses. I. Nugent, John C., 1973-
BX2.R33 2010
230'.97092--dc22

                                                                        2010002380

Cover design by Jennette Munger
Interior text design by Sandy Armstrong

For information contact:
Abilene Christian University Press
1626 Campus Court
Abilene, Texas 79699-9138

1-877-816-4455 toll free
www.abilenechristianuniversitypress.com

10 11 12 13 14 15 / 7 6 5 4 3 2 1

CONTENTS

ACKNOWLEDGEMENTS

Whatever positive impact *Radical Ecumenicity* makes is due to the collaborative efforts of a host of persons to whom I am deeply grateful. The conference from which this book came would never have happened without the hospitality of Englewood Christian Church—especially Chris Smith and Mike Bowling—and the financial support of Delta Community Christian Church and Abilene Christian University Press. Likewise, the stimulating conversations that typified this gathering were made possible by our three guest Yoder scholars—Craig Carter, Gayle Gerber Koontz, and Mark Thiessen Nation—who went above and beyond expectations to engage conference participants in robust ecumenical dialogue not only during their allotted sessions, but throughout the conference.

I am also grateful to John Howard Yoder's daughter, Martha Yoder Maust, for attending this conference, enriching our conversations, and granting permission to include two of her father's essays in this collection; and to Leonard Allen and Heidi Nobles of Abilene Christian University Press for taking such a keen interest in this project and for working so graciously and patiently with a first-time editor like myself. Finally, I thank my wife Beth for supporting and encouraging me throughout this endeavor.

John C. Nugent

Contributors

Lee C. Camp is Associate Professor of Theology and Ethics at Lipscomb University in Nashville, Tennessee. His graduate education includes degrees from Abilene Christian University (M.A., M.Div.) and the University of Notre Dame (M.A., Ph.D.). At Notre Dame, Lee was one of John Yoder's last graduate students. He is the author of *Mere Discipleship: Radical Christianity in a Rebellious World*, and the host and creator of "Tokens," online at www.TokensShow.com.

Craig A. Carter is Professor of Religious Studies at Tyndale University College & Seminary in Toronto, Ontario and Theologian-in-Residence at Westney Heights Baptist Church in Ajax, Ontario. He earned his doctorate degree at the University of Toronto and specializes in Systematic Theology and Christian Ethics. He is the author of *The Politics of the Cross: The Theology and Social Ethics of John Howard Yoder* (Brazos, 2001) and *Rethinking Christ and Culture: A Post-Christendom Perspective* (Brazos, 2007).

Joe R. Jones is Professor Emeritus of Theology and Ethics at Christian Theological Seminary. Receiving his Ph.D. in Philosophical Theology from Yale University, he has had a long career in theological education and served as Visiting Professor of Theology at Yale Divinity School in 2005/2006. Recently published texts include *A Grammar of Christian Faith: Systematic Explorations in Christian Life and Doctrine*, 2 vols. (Rowman & Littlefield, 2002) and *On Being the Church of Jesus Christ in Tumultuous Times* (Cascade Books, 2005).

Paul J. Kissling is Professor of Old Testament and Biblical Languages and Research Director for TCMI Institute, a non-traditional format graduate seminary educating Christian leaders in Eastern Europe and Central Asia. His Ph.D. is in Hebrew Bible from the University of Sheffield under David Clines. He is the author of four books and numerous chapters and articles, the co-editor of the *College Press NIV Commentary Old Testament*, and a founding editorial board member of *Stone-Campbell Journal*.

Gayle Gerber Koontz is Professor of Theology and Ethics at the Associated Mennonite Biblical Seminary in Elkhart, Indiana, where she currently teaches a course on the theological legacy of John Howard Yoder. Her doctoral thesis compared the implications for religious pluralism of the theological ethics of Yoder and H. Richard Niebuhr. She is co-editor of *A Mind Patient and Untamed: Assessing John Howard Yoder's Contributions to Theology, Ethics, and Peacemaking* (Cascadia, 2004).

Mark Thiessen Nation is Professor of Theology at Eastern Mennonite Seminary in Harrisonburg, Virginia, and holds a Ph.D. from Fuller Theological Seminary. Mark is the author of more than two dozen articles and the editor or co-editor of six books, many of which pertain to Yoder's work. He has written *John Howard Yoder: Mennonite Patience, Evangelical Witness, Catholic Convictions* (Eerdmans, 2006) and co-authored *Reasoning Together: A Conversation on Homosexuality* (Herald Press, 2008).

John C. Nugent is Professor of Old Testament at Great Lakes Christian College in Lansing, Michigan. His Ph.D. is from Calvin Theological Seminary where he wrote a dissertation on Yoder's appropriation of the Old Testament for ecclesiology. He holds additional graduate degrees from Duke Divinity School (Th.M.) and Emmanuel School of Religion (M.Div.). John has published articles in books, academic journals, and popular level magazines and regularly writes Bible lesson commentaries for Standard Publishing.

Branson Parler is Assistant Professor of Theological Studies at Kuyper College in Grand Rapids, Michigan. He received his M.A. from the Institute for Christian Studies in Toronto, and he is currently a Ph.D. candidate at Calvin Theological Seminary, where he is writing his dissertation on Yoder's thought on Christ, creation, and culture. His essay "John Howard Yoder and the Politics of Creation" appears in *Power and Practices: Engaging the Work of John Howard Yoder* (Herald Press, 2009).

Introduction

John Howard Yoder, Radical Ecumenicity, and the Stone-Campbell Tradition

John C. Nugent

In the spring of 2009 a group of scholars, ministers, and laity associated with the Stone-Campbell Movement gathered in Indianapolis, Indiana to discuss the significance of John Howard Yoder's work.[1] This was the first time adherents to a particular tradition outside of Yoder's Mennonite heritage had gathered for this purpose.[2] The meeting was enriched by the participation of three leading Yoder scholars from beyond Stone-Campbell circles—Craig A. Carter (Baptist), Gayle Gerber Koontz (Mennonite), and Mark Thiessen Nation (Mennonite)—as well as the gracious presence of Yoder's daughter, Martha Yoder Maust.[3] Over the course of a weekend, this group of self-professed Yoder sympathizers engaged one another in rigorous dialogue about the core substance of Yoder's work, contested issues in Yoder studies, and the practical implications of Yoder's thought for both Stone-Campbell churches and the broader Christian tradition. *Radical Ecumenicity: Pursuing Unity and Continuity after John Howard Yoder* brings together six papers from this gathering, two later submissions by Stone-Campbell scholars, and two of Yoder's lesser known essays that are particularly relevant to the themes of this collection.

It is fitting that constituents of the Stone-Campbell tradition would engage Yoder since he routinely engaged them by name throughout his writings.[4] He regarded their heritage as one of the most important intellectual developments of the nineteenth century, a creative and culturally astute unity movement, and a kindred spirit regarding free-church eccle-siology, peace witness, restoration, and renewal. Furthermore, throughout his prolific career Yoder provided in-depth analysis of themes that were central to Stone-Campbell thought. He wrote critically yet sympathetically about ecumenism,[5] restitutionism,[6] creedalism,[7] traditionalism,[8] and most of all pacifism,[9] which formerly was important to Stone-Campbell thought. Yoder worked tirelessly to debunk caricatures of the convictions that res-torationists, Mennonites, and other Free Church traditions have held with relation to these topics. He also exposed the worst manifestations of these convictions and challenged Free Church thinkers to articulate their posi-tions in ways that are clear, consistent, biblical, and historically disciplined. Yoder engaged members of these churches not in order to make them Mennonites but to make them better Disciples, Baptists, and so forth.

Though the essays of this volume were not originally written with an eye toward a common theme, they nevertheless address two promi-nent themes in the Stone-Campbell tradition, unity and continuity, albeit in a Yoderian key. Though Stone-Campbellites have often pursued unity by shunning particularity (whether creedal or confessional) and by unit-ing around common practices (whether baptism or the Lord's Supper), Yoder recognized the limitations of such approaches and advocated unity across particular traditions by way of robust and patient dialogue. Though Campbellites have attempted to maintain continuity with the early church, especially in ecclesial structure and practice, Yoder stressed the need for continuity with Old Testament Israel, the New Testament church, and wider Christian history. Yoder's work thus offers an ecumenical pos-ture that is radical in its peace-church perspective, in its appeal to deep Christian roots, and in its thoroughgoing commitment to dialogue.

The first three essays of *Radical Ecumenicity* help to position this col-lection insofar as they introduce the reader to the ecclesial context of this collection, the pacifist standpoint of Yoder's writings, and the ecumenical posture that pervades his life's work. Lee C. Camp, a Church of Christ scholar who studied under Yoder and who has written an informative exposition of Christian practices from a Yoderian perspective,[10] leads this collection in chapter one with an autobiographical reflection on the significance of Yoder's work for two themes that are central to the Stone-Campbell tra-dition: unity and restoration. In so doing, Camp furnishes both a helpful window into the life of one of the three branches of the Stone-Campbell

Movement and a general sense of how Yoder's careful thought might guide this tradition through the identity crisis that has befallen the Churches of Christ in recent years.

Yoder is most known for his pacifist stance as expressed in his popular work *The Politics of Jesus.*[11] Unfortunately, Yoder's pacifism is often misunderstood by those whose exposure to him is limited to that single work. Those who are unfamiliar with Yoder's wider corpus or who strive to better understand the substance of his stance will therefore greatly benefit from Mennonite scholar Mark Thiessen Nation's contribution to this collection. In chapter two, Nation draws upon his intimate acquaintance with Yoder's voluminous writings to provide a holistic account of Yoder's pacifism that fills the various gaps that surface when one reads only one or two of his works. Nation's essay thus situates both new and experienced readers of Yoder to grasp the substance of the essays to follow.

In chapter three, Gayle Gerber Koontz makes a valuable contribution to all who are ecumenically minded by outlining Yoder's ecumenical theology and practice. With the familiarity that comes from teaching alongside Yoder and scouring unpublished records of his life and thought, Koontz helpfully sketches Yoder's ecumenical thought. Through her detailed personal account, Koontz allows Yoder to teach us that neither unity without integrity nor fellowship without conversation is worthy of Christ's prayer that his followers be one. In this relentlessly ecumenical pursuit, Yoder is truer to the spirit of Stone and Campbell than the vast majority of contemporary Stone-Campbellites, thereby setting a formidable ecumenical example for members of all ecclesial traditions.

The remaining essays that engage Yoder's work showcase his radically ecumenical approach as it pertains to specific issues. Baptist theologian and Yoder scholar Craig A. Carter leads this group in chapter four with a provocative essay engaging conflicting receptions of Yoder's thought. After briefly sketching the rich theological contours of Yoder's pacifism, Carter critiques two representative liberal appropriations of Yoder's pacifism and submits six possible strategies for freeing Yoder's thought from ecumenically-debilitating liberal captivity. Carter challenges readers to consider whether Yoder's project has what it takes to remain ecumenically viable.

Seasoned Disciples theologian Joe R. Jones follows in chapter five with a passionate plea for the various branches of the Stone-Campbell tradition to embrace and confess trinitarian orthodoxy. Picking up the continuity thread in Yoder's thought, Jones argues that adherents to this tradition have been particularly vulnerable to American individualism and blind patriotism because their discipleship is not properly rooted in holistic trinitarian thought. This is not to say that all traditions that espouse trinitarian thought avoid nationalistic trappings. Jones therefore challenges believers from all ecclesial traditions to apprehend the radical dimensions of discipleship that necessarily follow from trinitarian orthodoxy. Though Jones upholds Yoder as exemplary in this regard, he challenges readers to push farther than Yoder in orthodoxy and orthopraxis.

Historically, Stone-Campbell thought has downplayed continuity not only with orthodox Christian tradition but also with the church's deep Old Testament roots. In chapter six, Paul J. Kissling, an Old Testament scholar among the Christian Churches, showcases Yoder's serious engagement of the Old Testament with attention to its ecclesial relevance. Kissling does not, however, concur with every aspect of Yoder's interpretation of the Old Testament. He thus enumerates several problems in Yoder's narration and proposes how it may be strengthened by the insights of recent Bible scholars so as to better support Yoder's own ethical, theological, and ecclesial vision.

Throughout his career, Yoder espoused a vision of public theology that he believed had great ecumenical potential. One component of that theology is Yoder's vision of vocation—a vision that Yoder alluded to throughout his writings but never set forth in detail. In chapter seven, Christian Church theologian and ethicist John C. Nugent draws from a wide sampling of Yoder's writings to provide a holistic account of his doctrine of vocation. He then evaluates the viability of Yoder's contributions as a means of uniting Christians from various traditions around a post-Christendom view of vocation.

Though Yoder strove to be ecumenical, his work on the sacraments tends to alienate even those who are highly sympathetic with his larger theological and ethical agenda. This is one area, it is believed, where Yoder's Free Church commitments drove him into a sectarian cul-de-sac. Branson Parler disagrees, refusing to see Yoder as a low-church despiser of the sacraments who reduced them to mere social processes. Instead, Parler argues in chapter eight that Yoder sought to dismantle the problematic dualism between liturgy and ethics and to expand traditional views of the sacraments to include their oft-neglected social and publicly accessible dimensions.

The final two essays in this collection were written by Yoder himself and have been reprinted here by permission of Martha Yoder Maust and Evangel Press. The purpose for their inclusion is twofold: it makes easily accessible two important works to which scholars have not paid sufficient attention precisely because of their inaccessibility, and it gives readers who are not familiar with Yoder's work a firsthand appreciation of how he approached matters of ecclesial unity and continuity.

"The Ecumenical Movement and the Faithful Church" is a pamphlet Yoder produced in 1958 bringing together a series of short articles from the *Gospel Herald*.[12] In his informative biography of Yoder, Mark Thiessen Nation furnishes a substantial background and overview of its contents, so I will not repeat that work here.[13] It is important, however, to heed Nation's observation that this piece "presents the heart of Yoder's views on ecumenism, views that remained substantially unaltered for the next four decades." Likely due to its considerable size (originally 43 pages) and its in-house nature (geared toward Mennonites), Yoder did not deem it appropriate to include this piece in his well-known collection of ecumenical essays, *The Royal Priesthood*.[14] Since one cannot fully grasp Yoder's ecumenical convictions without taking into account this early treatise, we were eager to heed Nation's suggestion to include it in this collection.

In 1967 Yoder presented the essay, "Is There Historical Development of Theological Thought," at the Eighth Mennonite World Conference, a gathering in Amsterdam attended by over 6,000 Mennonites from thirty different countries.[15] Though the proceedings of this conference were printed shortly thereafter in the United States by Evangel Press, Yoder's contribution has received little attention. The present volume's emphasis on continuity therefore provides an ideal opportunity to bring it forward. The brief introduction to follow sketches the substance of this piece and makes clear why, for Yoder and for us, the pursuits of continuity and unity cannot be separated.

Yoder begins this essay with a sampling of Johannine passages indicating that the church is headed for change, yet bound to retain its identity with its past confession. He then poses the provocative question that occupies the balance of his essay: "How now can we work in a theologically responsible way with the apparently contradictory concepts of continuity and change?" He then recognizes that how one answers this question immediately poses an ecumenical dilemma. When multiple traditions seek to discuss their conflicting convictions about following Jesus Christ and these traditions have themselves undergone change throughout their various histories—changes that they attribute to the Holy Spirit's work among them—then they have passed the point of being able to ask, "Is there a development of doctrine worked by the Holy Spirit?" This question is not eluded by traditions that commit to preserving the early Christian legacy by repeating biblical words because, Yoder observed, "to say the same thing in a different place or time is to say something different."[16]

Having skillfully diagnosed the ecumenical problem of continuity and change, Yoder offers a brief typology of possible ways to relate them, all of which he finds lacking. Perhaps the way forward, he suggests, is not a general principle but a particular procedure. Rather than find or make a way around the ecumenical conundrum, Yoder commends resources within Free Church ecclesiology for forging a way through it. In doing so, Yoder has not solved the problem of continuity and change—least of all from the perspective of those beyond Free Church circles—yet in masterfully elucidating the ecumenical challenge and provoking Free Church thinkers to confront the realities of historical development in a proactive way (rather than deny them), he moves estranged parties closer together and provides practical resources for more fruitful dialogue.

It is in this same spirit, then, that we are pleased to offer this collection of essays. We trust that this offering will prove helpful to Stone-Campbellites who have yet to perceive the relevance of Yoder's thought to our tradition, to Yoder scholars seeking to keep up with the latest in Yoder scholarship, and to all unity-minded believers seeking to learn along with us from Yoder's radically-ecumenical perspective.

Endnotes

[1] This gathering, "John Howard Yoder and the Stone-Campbell Churches," was hosted by Englewood Christian Church and sponsored by Delta Community Christian Church (Lansing, Michigan) and Abilene Christian University Press. The conference was born out of conversations between members of the aforementioned congregations at an annual Ekklesia Project conference in Chicago, Illinois. By design, this conference was relatively small. The aim was to gather persons from within the Stone-Campbell heritage who were already highly conversant with Yoder studies. The conference organizers were pleasantly surprised to find over fifty persons who identified themselves as such, even if only half were able to attend this event (28 participated, including our guests).

[2] The Stone-Campbell Movement, also known as the Restoration Movement, gained momentum on the American frontiers in the early 1800s. Church leaders from several traditions began breaking from what they perceived to be the shackles of their various heritages (e.g., Elias Smith and Abner Jones of the New England Baptists; James O'Kelly of the Methodist tradition; and Alexander Campbell and Barton W. Stone of the Presbyterian heritage). Though each emphasized different aspects, a common call for Christian unity emerged. It was thought that denominational barriers would fall if all Christians would drop distinctively sectarian labels, abandon creeds as tests for fellowship, focus on essentials, deemphasize non-essentials, and rally around the New Testament Scriptures for guidance in all matters of faith and ecclesiology. Barton W. Stone and Alexander Campbell were two of the most well-known influential leaders. Around 1831-32, these men and their churches united to form one movement or "denomination in protest." This unity lasted less than a century. In 1906, the most conservative branch first split off. Twenty years later an additional fissure emerged in what remained and, by the late 1960s, there were three separate branches: the Christian Church (Disciples of Christ), the Independent Christian Churches, and the Churches of Christ. The Disciples are the closest to mainstream Protestantism and have adopted many of its denominational structures and superstructures. The Churches of Christ, often distinguished by their non-instrumental services, most adamantly seek to restore primitive Christian practices. The Independent Christian Churches typically regard themselves as moderates though they vary greatly on issues of theology and ecclesial practice. In recent years these various branches have drawn more closely together. This is reflected by the recent founding of the *Stone-Campbell Journal* and its concomitant annual "Stone-Campbell Journal Conference"—a joint venture that has gone far to bring scholars within the movement into closer conversation with one another. The Yoder conference was partly intended to further this ecumenical spirit as members of all three branches were present. Cf. Leroy Garrett, *The Stone-Campbell Movement: The Story of the American Restoration Movement*, rev. ed. (Joplin, MO: College Press, 1994); and *The Encyclopedia of the Stone-Campbell Movement*, eds. Douglas Foster, et al (Grand Rapids: Eerdmans, 2005).

[3] The work of these three scholars furnishes a helpful introduction to Yoder's thought. See Craig A. Carter, *Politics of the Cross: The Theology and Social Ethics of John Howard Yoder* (Grand Rapids: Brazos, 2001); Gayle Gerber Koontz, co-editor with Ben C. Ollenburger, *A Mind Patient and Untamed: Assessing John Howard Yoder's Contributions to Theology, Ethics, and Peacemaking* (Telford, PA: Cascadia, 2004); and Mark Thiessen Nation, *John Howard Yoder: Mennonite Patience, Evangelical Witness, Catholic Convictions* (Grand Rapids: Eerdmans, 2005).

[4] Yoder discusses the Stone-Campbell Movement at length in *Christian Attitudes to War, Peace, and Revolution*, eds. Theodore J. Koontz and Andy Alexis-Baker (Grand Rapids: Brazos, 2009), 256-259, 268, an edited edition of *Christian Attitudes to War, Peace, and Revolution: A Companion to Bainton* (Elkhart, IN: Goshen Biblical Seminary, 1983), which is a compendium of study resources based on taped lectures of Yoder's seminary course instruction. Additional references include "Anabaptism and History," in *The Priestly Kingdom: Social Ethics as Gospel* (Eugene, OR: Wipf and Stock, 2000), 131-133; "Another 'Free Church' Perspective on Baptist Ecumenism," in *The Royal Priesthood: Essays Ecclesiological and Ecumenical*, ed. Michael G. Cartwright (Scottdale, PA: Herald Press, 1998), 266, 268, 271-272, and 274; "Apostle's Apology Revisited," in *The New Way of Jesus: Essays Presented to Howard Charles*, ed. William Klassen (Newton, KS: Faith and Life Press, 1980), 116; "Believers Church and the Arms Race," in *For the Nations: Essays Public and Evangelical* (Grand Rapids: Eerdmans, 1997), 148, fn. 2; "Believers' Church: Global Perspectives," in *The Believers' Church in Canada: Addresses and Papers from the*

Study Conference in Winnipeg, May 15-18, 1978, ed. Jarold K. Zeman and Walter Klassen (The Baptist Federation of Canada and Mennonite Central Committee [Canada], 1979), 6; "Binding and Loosing," in *Royal Priesthood*, 352; *Body Politics: Five Practices of the Christian Community Before the Watching World* (Nashville, TN: Discipleship Resources, 1992), 10, 59-60, and 82, fn. 20; "Civil Religion in America," in *Priestly Kingdom*, 181; "Church and State according to the Free Church Tradition," in *On Earth Peace: Discussions on War/Peace Issues between Friends, Mennonites, Brethren, and European Churches, 1935-75*, ed. Donald F. Durnbaugh (Elgin, IL: Brethren Press, 1978), 280; "The Disavowal of Constantine: An Alternative Perspective on Interfaith Dialogue," in *Royal Priesthood*, 246-247; "Free Church Ecumenical Style," in *Royal Priesthood*, 235; "Free Church Syndrome," in *Within the Perfection of Christ: Essays on Peace and the Nature of the Church* (Evangel Press and Brethren in Christ Historical Society, 1990), 171; "'Free Church' Perspective on Baptism, Eucharist and Ministry," in *Royal Priesthood*, 279-80; "Catholicity in Search of Location," in *Royal Priesthood*, 320-321; *The Fullness of Christ: Paul's Vision of Universal Ministry* (Elgin, IL: Brethren Press, 1987), 85, 88, 95, and 105, fn. 2; "Hermeneutics of Peoplehood," in *Priestly Kingdom*, 197, fn. 2 and 198, fn. 8; "Historiography as a Ministry to Renewal," *Brethren Life and Thought* 43 (1997): 222; "Introduction," in *Priestly Kingdom*, 5; "Kingdom as Social Ethics," in *Priestly Kingdom*, 204, fn. 11; "Orientation in Midstream: A Response to the Responses," in *Freedom and Discipleship: Liberation Theology from an Anabaptist Perspective*, ed. Daniel S. Schipani (Maryknoll, NY: Orbis Books, 1989), 161 and 164; "Paradigmatic Public Role of God's People," in *For the Nations*, 20-21; "Power Equation, the Place of Jesus, and the Politics of King," in *For the Nations*, 140; "Radical Reformation Ethics in Ecumenical Perspective," in *Priestly Kingdom*, 106 and 122; "Restitution of the Church: An Alternative Perspective on Christian History," in *Jewish-Christian Schism Revisited*, 135; "Thinking Theologically from a Free Church Perspective," in *Doing Theology in Today's World: Essays in Honor of Kenneth S. Kantzer*, eds. John D. Woodbridge and Thomas Edward McComiskey (Grand Rapids: Zondervan, 1991), 254 and 263, fn. 4; "Unique Role of the Historic Peace Churches," *Brethren Life and Thought* 14, no. 3 (1969): 137; "Utility of Being Misunderstood," in *To Hear the Word* (Eugene, OR: Wipf & Stock, 2001), 52, fn. 41; "War as a Moral Problem in the Early Church: The Historian's Hermeneutical Assumptions," in *The Pacifist Impulse in Historical Perspective*, eds. Harvey L. Dick and Peter Brock (Toronto: University of Toronto Press, 1996), 94.

[5] For a representative sampling, see Yoder "A 'Free Church' Perspective on Baptism, Eucharist and Ministry," in *Royal Priesthood*, 277-288; "A 'Peace Church' Perspective on Covenanting," *Ecumenical Review* 38 (Jul 1986): 318-321; "Another 'Free Church' Perspective on Baptist Ecumenism," in *Royal Priesthood*, 262-276; "Calling a Council for Peace," *Ecumenical Trends* 15 (Nov 1986): 157-160; "Catholicity in Search of Location," in *Royal Priesthood*, 300-320; "Could There Be a Baptist Bishop?" *Ecumenical Trends* 9 (Jul/Aug 1980): 104-107; "The Disavowal of Constantine: An Alternative Perspective on Interfaith Dialogue," in *Royal Priesthood*, 242-261; *The Ecumenical Movement and the Faithful Church*, included in the present volume; "The Free Church Ecumenical Style," in *Royal Priesthood*, 231-241; "The Imperative of Christian Unity," in *Royal Priesthood*, 289-299; "The Nature of the Unity We Seek: A Historic Free Church View," in *Royal Priesthood*, 221-230; "On Christian Unity: The Way from Below," *Pro Ecclesia* 9, no. 2 (Spring 2000): 165-183; and "Radical Reformation Ethics in Ecumenical Perspective," in *Priestly Kingdom*, 105-122.

[6] Yoder engages restitutionism sporadically through many of his writings, but some of the most substantial engagements include "Anabaptism and History," in *Priestly Kingdom*, 123-134; "Biblicism and the Church," with David A. Shank, *Concern Pamphlet #2*

(Scottdale, PA: By Concern, 721 Walnut Avenue, 1955), recently reprinted in Virgil Vogt, ed., *The Roots of Concern: Writings on Anabaptist Renewal 1952-1957* (Eugene, OR: Cascade Books, 2009), 67-101; *Fullness of Christ: Paul's Vision of Universal Ministry*, 85-105; "Is There Historical Development of Theological Thought?," included in the present volume; "The Kingdom as Social Ethic," in *Priestly Kingdom*, 86-88, "Primitivism in the Radical Reformation: Strengths and Weaknesses," in *The Primitive Church in the Modern World*, ed. Richard T. Hughes (Urbana and Chicago: University of Illinois Press, 1995), 74-97; "The Restitution of the Church: An Alternative Perspective on Christian History," in *The Jewish-Christian Schism Revisited*, eds. Michael G. Cartwright and Peter Ochs (Grand Rapids: Eerdmans, 2003), 133-143; "Thinking Theologically from a Free Church Perspective," in *Doing Theology in Today's World: Essays in Honor of Kenneth S. Kantzer*, eds. John D. Woodbridge and Thomas Edward McComiskey (Grand Rapids: Zondervan, 1991), 251-265; and "Your Hope is Too Small," in *He Came Preaching Peace*, 126-127 and 130.

[7] Yoder engages the slogan "no creed but the Bible" in "Thinking Theologically from a Free Church Perspective," in *Doing Theology in Today's World*, 256-257; and "The Free Church Ecumenical Style," in *Royal Priesthood*, 238. He discusses the early ecumenical creeds in *Preface to Theology: Christology and Theological Method* (Grand Rapids: Brazos, 2002), chs. 7-9, esp. 222-223.

[8] Though the above sources in which Yoder engages "restitutionism" often convey his view of tradition, he discusses it most thoroughly in "The Authority of Tradition," in *Priestly Kingdom*, 63-79. Yoder discusses the unique role of founding fathers in various Christian traditions, including his own, in "Ambivalence of the Appeal to the Fathers," in *Practiced in the Presence: Essays in Honor of T. Canby Jones*, eds. D. Neil Snarr and Daniel L. Smith-Christopher (Richmond, IN: Friends United Press, 1994), 245-255.

[9] For a helpful summary of the pacifist stance of Alexander Campbell, cf. Craig Watts, *Disciple of Peace: Alexander Campbell on Pacifism, Violence and the State* (Indianapolis: Doulos Christou Press, 2005). For an account of how the Churches of Christ left this position behind, see Michael Casey, "From Religious Outsiders to Insiders: The Rise and Fall of Pacifism in the Churches of Christ," *Journal of Church and State* 44, no. 3 (Summer 2002): 455-475. Yoder's thoughts on pacifism permeate his massive literary corpus. Mark Thiessen Nation's essay in this volume provides an excellent introduction. For a sense of the scope of Yoder's writings on this topic (and others), see Nation's *A Comprehensive Bibliography of the Writings of John Howard Yoder* (Goshen, IN: Mennonite Historical Society, 1997).

[10] Lee C. Camp, *Mere Discipleship: Radical Christianity in a Rebellious World*, 2d ed. (Grand Rapids: Brazos, 2008).

[11] Yoder, *The Politics of Jesus*, 2d ed. (Grand Rapids: Eerdmans, 1994; original ed., 1972).

[12] *Gospel Herald* published parts 1-6 in 1957 in the following issues: Jan 15, 22, 29 and Feb 5, 12, and 19.

[13] Nation, *John Howard Yoder: Mennonite Patience, Evangelical Witness, Catholic Convictions* (Grand Rapids: Eerdmans, 2006), 78-88.

[14] Ibid., 78-79, fn. 3.

[15] The theme of this gathering was "The Witness of the Holy Spirit," which followed from the previous gathering's theme "The Lordship of Christ" (1962, Kitchener, Ontario, Canada). For details concerning this conference, see *The Witness of the Holy Spirit: Proceedings of the Eighth Mennonite World Conference* (Napanee, IN: Evangel Press, 1967), III-XI. Yoder's contribution, "Is There Historical Development of Theological Thought," appears in this same volume, 379-388.

[16] Yoder, "Is There Historical Development," 226 in present volume.

Chapter One

RESTORATION AND UNITY IN THE WORK
OF JOHN HOWARD YODER

LEE C. CAMP

After a weekend fishing expedition, I teased professor Yoder about the rural corner I had discovered in Elkhart county, Indiana, where three Mennonite churches are all located within a stone's throw from one another.[1] On one side of the corner stands an old order Mennonite church, which does not permit use of automobiles by its members; on the other side stood a meeting house for more liberal adherents, who drive black automobiles; and back behind these stood the church for those who had sold out to the "world," driving vehicles painted in a variety of colors.[2]

My gloating over this instance of Christian splintering was, I admit, depraved, and depraved not simply because division among Christians ought never be taken lightly. It was depraved because my gloating grew out of a "rejoicing in evil" which draws attention away from one's own failures: the lack of unity among those three Mennonite congregations allowed me to observe smugly that my own tradition in the Churches of Christ was not alone in its difficulties in "restoring New Testament Christianity."

The Mennonites are of significance to those in the Stone-Campbell Movement for our shared historical agenda: attempting to take seriously the witness of the New Testament as the ground and basis for Christian faith and practice. That constructive agenda generally carries with it a starting point of critique, the claim that numerous contemporary practices of Christianity have missed the original intention of the gospel. Like many in Churches of Christ, the Mennonites have sought—and claimed—to be neither Protestant nor Catholic; and this distinction has proven to be more than mere exclusivistic rhetoric. Instead, a number of scholars in the late twentieth century have observed that groups like the Mennonites and Churches of Christ constitute a "third-way," an ecclesiology so significantly different from both historically Protestant and Catholic models as to merit discussion as a serious alternative.[3] Out of such a shared agenda, it is not surprising then that someone like David Lipscomb would voice his deep respect and admiration for those of the Mennonite faith.[4]

Here I would like to sketch briefly some of the difficulties encountered by my own tradition in the Churches of Christ in our efforts to "restore New Testament Christianity," and then sketch how the Mennonite John Yoder, speaking out of a fellow Believers Church tradition, has helped me address those difficulties; further, I suggest that he can provide some clues for us to move ahead in our much discussed "identity crisis" in the Churches of Christ.

The Stone-Campbell Restoration and Unity Agenda

Contemporary Churches of Christ emerged from a nineteenth-century effort by such religious reformers as Alexander Campbell and Barton W. Stone. Stone and Campbell sought to effect unity among the warring Christian factions on the untamed western frontier. Alexander's father, Thomas, suggested a remedy for such divisiveness in his *Declaration and Address*, which is considered by historians of the ecumenical movement as a "famous apologia for Christian unity."[5] Many Christians of that day were "tired and sick of the bitter jarrings and janglings of a party spirit, [and] we would desire to be at rest; and, were it possible, we would also desire to adopt and recommend such measures, as would give rest to our brethren throughout all the churches: as would restore unity, peace, and purity, to the whole Church of God."[6]

How could Christians attain this admirable goal? By rejecting "human opinions and the inventions of men as of any authority, or as having any place in the Church of God,"[7] by rejecting all human creeds and simply returning to the text of the New Testament alone as sole authority. Refusing to engage in arguments over opinions, the "Divine word alone" must replace speculation and human teaching, taking the Holy Spirit alone as guide, and taking Christ alone for salvation. Thus Campbell and friends rejected any practice or teaching not backed by a "Thus saith the Lord, either in express terms, or by approved precedent." Christians must "conform to the model and adopt the practice of the primitive Church," a model and practice "expressly exhibited in the New Testament." The elder Campbell believed the evils of a sectarian spirit could be "remedied," and the glory of God extolled, by "exhibit[ing] a complete conformity to the apostolic Church" and "willingly conform[ing] to the original pattern laid down in the New Testament."[8] Thus the Campbells adopted what later interpreters call a "patternistic" approach to restoration: through restoring the patterns of worship and church polity found in the New Testament, all of divided Christendom could be unified upon a common platform.[9]

Subsequent history illustrates the difficulties attendant to such an endeavor. In particular, the basic hermeneutical assumptions appeared naïve: "no creed but the Bible" may be a powerful aphorism, but it could not do away with the complexities of biblical interpretation. (As a matter of fact, the aphorism often became a means of denial, a way to pretend that one does not bring presuppositions and assumptions to the task of interpretation.) Instead of bringing about unity, attempts to restore the "pattern" of the New Testament yielded (at least among the right wing of the movement) an increasingly hostile exclusivism. By the 1860s, the influential Moses Lard pronounced what became orthodoxy for mainline, early twentieth-century Churches of Christ: "I mean to say distinctly and emphatically that Martin Luther, if not immersed, was not a Christian. . . . If a man can be a Christian without immersion, let the fact be shown; or if a man can or may commune without being a Christian, let the fact be shown. I deny both. Immovably I stand here. But I shall be told that this is Phariseeism, that it is exclusivism. Be it so; if it be true . . . then am I so far the defendant of Phariseeism and exclusivism."[10]

By the time of the 1906 U.S. religious census, the unity movement was officially divided, to paint in broad strokes, into two predominant streams: the "liberal" Disciples of Christ and the "conservative" Churches of Christ. The Disciples increasingly focused upon unity and debunked the motif of "restoration." By the 1960s, the Disciples split again between the "Independent Christian Church" and the "Christian Church (Disciples of Christ)." The Churches of Christ, on the other hand, focused upon a patternistic "restoration," and often employed rhetoric of condemnation against those who failed to read the Bible in the same way they did. Having inherited

Alexander Campbell's Scottish Common Sense philosophy and an epistemology informed by John Locke, the conservatives remained convinced of the perspicuity of Scripture, and thus charged that it was the liberals who were actually the ones guilty of dividing the body of Christ by refusing to submit to the "clear teaching" of Scripture. They claimed, for example, since the New Testament authorizes neither the use of instruments of music in worship nor the participation in para-church institutions such as missionary societies, accepting such practices destroys the unity of the body of Christ.

Churches of Christ have continued to fragment over various issues. Like the Mennonites, various issues have arisen that appear incidental if not trivial to outsiders and yet become points of serious division, if not "breaking of fellowship." The most well-known directory of a cappella Churches of Christ documents issues ranging from the number of cups used in communion to whether a church may corporately support an orphanage out of its treasury.[11] The arguments reach comic (though tragic) proportions, epitomized in the (possibly apocryphal) anecdote[12] of a woman of some means in a Church of Christ near Valparaiso, Indiana who generously donated land and funds with which a local congregation might erect a church building. When the workmen began installing the baptistery in which immersions (following the New Testament pattern) were to take place, the benefactor objected: the baptistery must not be built higher than the floor level of the church auditorium, since the Scriptures record that for the purpose of baptism Philip and the Ethiopian eunuch "went down into the water" (Acts 8:38). Thus, upon this supposedly sturdy exegetical foundation, the woman registered her objection: the baptistery must be built lower than floor level, in order to observe the pattern dictated in the Scriptures. When several members of the church pointed out that steps would be built to allow the candidate for immersion to ascend to a small landing at the top of the baptistery and thence descend into the waters, she conceded the proposed arrangement as having legitimate New Testament authority. While such an anecdote does not do justice to the well-intentioned and serious exegetical work of many prominent leaders in Churches of Christ, the anecdote is nonetheless telling: it may tell more of the painful truth than we would like to admit.

Cues from Yoder

If one is raised—as I was—in the midst of patternistic bickering, one becomes rather convinced that one's religious neighbors haven't a snow-ball's-chance-in-hell of escaping eternal torment, whether Baptist, Methodist, or Presbyterian. And the Catholics are, of course, the source of how Christendom all went wrong in the first place. Convinced of this as a sometimes too serious high-schooler, my world was quite transformed when my undergraduate Greek professor introduced me to the gospel according to Saint Paul. A gospel of grace was actually good news after all. Paul's correspondence with the Galatians and the Romans helped assuage my incessant pangs of guilt and transformed my practice of Christianity. Perhaps God was not so patternistic after all. Perhaps the New Testament was not intended to serve as an exact blueprint to be emulated in every detail of church polity, the slightest variance with which could condemn one's soul to hell, but a message of God's forgiveness, a message of the expiation of guilt, and of the personal love of God for me and other individuals.

I had become, I suppose, something more akin to an "evangelical." But in short order, Leonard Allen at Abilene Christian University introduced me to Yoder's work. Yoder, in turn, helped me recover the "gospel" that underlay those—to me—traditional categories of "restoration" and "unity."

Restoration

Due to our patternistic proclivities, Yoder said on at least one occasion that Churches of Christ had discredited the notion of "restoration of New Testament Christianity." Given the narrow agenda in which polemical issues became the end-all-and-be-all of salvation, issues to which our allegedly ahistorical readings of Scripture led us, many—myself included—are tempted to forsake altogether any notion of "restoration." Indeed, this is what some among the Disciples of Christ have argued should occur.

But an otherwise helpful construct should not be discarded because some abuse it, and so Yoder did not want to throw the proverbial baby out with the bathwater. The "radical reformation" vision, argued Yoder, is a coherent, faithful, and catholic viewpoint. Our task is not a rejection of all "tradition,"[13] but rather correcting tradition when the tradition has moved away from the canonical witness to the nature of the Lordship of Christ.[14] Unfaithfulness *has* occurred at various points in Christian history, and "restitution" provides a cogent model for making sense of the shape of that infidelity. Christians say they believe that Jesus is Lord, and this claim is the ground upon which a restitutionist claim must stand.[15]

Thus, a return to "primitive Christianity" need not be a naive endeavor, is not fundamentalist, and is not "world-denying." In fact, Ernst Troeltsch and H. Richard Niebuhr notwithstanding, "primitive" Christianity, it turns out, is not concerned with withdrawing from "culture" or "society" in anticipation of an other-worldly redemption, but about the inbreaking of God's reign so that those elements of history which have rejected the rule of God might be reconciled to the God of Creation. The gospel is *For the Nations*, proclaimed the title of Yoder's last book published before his death.[16] Those of us who confess the Lordship of Christ are those called to participate in the redemption occurring even now, creatively emulating the kind of politics in which Jesus himself engaged. Thus Christianity should be "evangelical," as Yoder liked to say, and had said early on in his *Original Revolution*: "evangelical" not in the sense of adherence to some particular set of doctrines (though that has its place, he noted). Neither is the gospel in its original context primarily about attaining confidence in the face of one's mortality (though that has importance, too). The gospel is to be "evangelical" in that Christians are bearers of the good news of the reconciliation of all things to God: in Christ, peace has come.[17] The church, then, serves as bearer of that good news, and embodies the reconciliation that has occurred in Christ, thus emulating *The Politics of Jesus*. To put it differently, "grace" is not just about pardon, but power, power to embody a ministry of reconciliation. Without forsaking our heritage as a people committed to recovering "New Testament Christianity," Yoder then points us to a different way to envision that task which is more faithful to Scripture.[18]

Unity

As noted previously, our history in Churches of Christ appears to indicate empirically that "restoration" and "unity" cannot be happy bedfellows. Given this experience, my feeling is that some scholars within Churches of Christ who are aware of Yoder are hesitant to place much stock in his work. Wary of the exclusivism to which our patternism historically led us, they have no desire to be relegated any longer to any theological backwaters. Might not the Mennonite Yoder just lead us into another sectarian swamp?[19] I was amused, for example, by a colleague of mine at Notre Dame who had had no exposure to Yoder's work; this colleague is a "back-slidden" member of the Churches of Christ, having grown so weary of our infighting that he left us. He came one day to inform me that after having begun to read Yoder he began having Church of Christ nightmares again. The restoration impulse in Yoder brought back all his old fears. But as already indicated, Yoder conceived "restoration" not as patternistic emulation of the New Testament, but as a return to the gospel of reconciliation. Reconceived in this way, "restoration" becomes again a means to realize the "unity" already given in Christ. Given this, "restoration" cannot be so narrowly exclusivistic, and it is clear from Yoder's writings that he had no desire to pursue an agenda of withdrawal.

He, along with the H. Richard Niebuhr of *The Meaning of Revelation*, was profoundly aware of the historical contingency of all our knowing.[20] This, of course, makes humility a virtue. But against Niebuhr, Yoder contended that humility could not become the ultimate virtue for the Christian scholar, as the Niebuhr of *Christ and Culture* appears to assert,[21] and as many superficial approaches to ecumenism purport. Instead, the primitivist impulse to discount the authority of any figure to dictate the meaning of a text correctly surmises that the will of God is knowable (that is, by a community gathered in the Holy Spirit). But the will of God which Yoder believed he knew in Christ was not an arrogant, presumptuous claim to infallibility—a danger some of us in Churches of Christ fear when we hear people talking seriously about "restoration of New Testament Christianity."[22] Indeed, it is at the heart of the Believers Church tradition that a human claim to infallibility is part and parcel of the very corruption of Christianity.[23]

Instead, the word of God in Christ was God speaking peace, was reconciliation, was the appearance of the new creation. Christian unity does not result, then, from theological flabbiness, by not taking differences seriously, but by practicing discipleship. There are ecclesiological lines to be drawn, and they should be drawn around those who voluntarily submit to the Lordship of Christ.[24] But this does not result in consigning others to hell, or to an exclusivistic discounting of the claims of others (again, as many in the "left-wing" of Churches of Christ fear). The "free-church" emphasis upon discipleship can (and must) continue to be concerned with the unity of all those who claim to follow Christ because discipleship entails walking in the footsteps of him who died to reconcile all people to God, and thereby all people to one another. Thus Yoder did not talk about unity by embracing the method apparently suggested by some ecumenical movements, that of not taking theological convictions seriously. Instead, he sought unity because his deepest theological convictions were rooted in the reconciliation which God has brought about in Jesus Christ.

And so, just as the means of participating in the kingdom of God is Suffering Servanthood, the way to Christian unity is the same. That means unity will likely not be effected through a magisterial top-down conception, but from the grass-roots up[25]; and it also means that unity cannot come from discounting one another's sensibilities or thinking that one opinion is as good as another.[26]

Besides witnessing in his writings this emphasis upon walking in the way of the cross as a means to embodying the unity given in Christ, I witnessed this in his day-to-day work as a Mennonite scholar in a Roman Catholic university. Even though he believed the Just War tradition fundamentally flawed and unfaithful to the gospel, he was the one who took the tradition so seriously that he knew it better than many of its adherents, and was willing to concede that more lives might be saved by Notre Dame ROTC trainees taking the tradition seriously than through getting them to embrace his pacifism.[27] Or again, he was the one, in spite of the fact that relics are not the hottest theological fad in Mennonite circles, who pointed out to the Catholics at Notre Dame that the 1700th anniversary of saint and martyr Marcellus was nearing, whose bones allegedly lie under the high altar in Sacred Heart basilica, the church at the heart of the campus. (Marcellus, a Christian and Roman centurion, was put to death when he renounced his military oath of allegiance because, claimed Marcellus in his own defense, "it is not fitting for a Christian man who serves Christ the Lord to serve human powers."[28])

Just as he took other people's claims seriously, so he encouraged his students. On the one hand, he encouraged a number of us to attend an Acton Institute Conference so that we might better understand how conservative U.S. politics and economics, done in the name of Christ, works. Similarly, Yoder assigned a book by Jerry Falwell, in all seriousness, to a colleague of mine[29] in a directed reading course. On the other hand, he had undergraduate classes at Notre Dame, often full of conservative Catholic students, read the vituperative Tolstoy[30] and watch the film *Gandhi*.

Yoder's emphasis upon dialog as an emulation of the ministry of Christ is epitomized by my encounter with him one day after I had been asked by my local church's preacher to deliver a sermon on the "ethic of Jesus," utilizing those subversive "sermon on the plain" texts from Luke 6. The audience for the sermon was to be our now non-pacifist, oftentimes militantly pro-America, Church of Christ. Somewhat nervous about the reaction I might receive from a few of our occasionally contentious veterans, I asked Yoder one day after class whether he had any homiletical or strategic suggestions. Propped up on his crutches, looking down at the floor in silence, he thought momentarily and then responded, shaking his unkempt head-full of hair, and his long, untrimmed gray beard, "No, no—just be reconciling."[31]

I witnessed there "restoration" and "unity" being held together.

Moving Ahead

So how might such claims help us in Churches of Christ, in the midst of our much-discussed "identity crisis"? Yoder first led me to take seriously my own tradition, and one finds there some surprising treasures that may have been hidden from view. One finds, for example, that Stone and Campbell both, in their own way, envisioned a life of discipleship as pre-eminent, trumping even their own interpretations of practices as significant as baptism. Campbell, whose emphasis upon "restoration of the Ancient Gospel" and "restoration of the Ancient Order" could appear—and often was—particularly exclusivistic, nonetheless submitted his own interpretation of baptism to the more ultimate criterion of Christian discipleship. So in his well-known "Lunenburg letter," Campbell claimed, "Should I find one [baptized as an infant] more intelligent in the Christian Scriptures, more spiritually-minded and more devoted to the Lord than . . . one immersed on a profession of the ancient faith, I could not hesitate a moment in giving the preference of my heart to him that loveth most. Did I act otherwise, I would be a pure sectarian, a Pharisee among Christians."[32]

With Campbell, then, one's willingness and efforts to submit all things to the Lordship of Christ is the basis for a common cause, and not one's personal interpretation of even an important doctrine and practice. Barton Stone similarly proclaimed that "none of us are disposed to make our notions of baptism, however well founded, a bar of christian fellowship. We acknowledge all to be brethren, who believe and obey the Saviour, and, who walking in the Spirit, bear his holy image; yet, in the meekness of Christ, we labor to convince such of their duty in submitting to every ordinance of the Lord."[33] For Stone and Campbell (and others of their day), there was much room for dialog among those who obviously sought to submit their lives to the Lordship of Christ; and there was much room for fellowship, while not discounting significant differences, which should be discussed and even constructively argued about.

There is here in the early restorationist leaders—the "patternistic" tone of their notions of restoration notwithstanding—something which Yoder repeatedly stated: the gospel cannot be a set of "doctrines" or "propositional truths" which can be separated from ethics.[34] "Doctrine" and "ethics" are always, and must be, two sides of the same coin. We have not been called merely to *believe* certain things; we have been called to receive the gift of a new way of life, an alternative community, the peaceable kingdom.

The increasingly narrow focus upon a "patternistic" conception of restoration in the twentieth century allowed Churches of Christ to separate doctrine and ethics. Or perhaps it is more accurate to say that our doctrinal focus left us with a fragmented and compartmentalized ethic. So one should not be surprised to find in the historical work of Mike Casey[35] or Richard Hughes[36] that Churches of Christ moved away from radical ethical commitments which many of its leaders held in the nineteenth century. Those unaware of the history might find the contrasts between the end of the twentieth century and the beginning of the nineteenth shocking. Long before the rumblings of a Civil War which would lead to the emancipation of African slaves, Joseph Thomas reported in 1812 that the Stoneite Christians in Kentucky had begun to free their slaves: "The Christians of these parts *abhor* the idea of *slavery*, and some of them have almost tho't that they who hold to slavery cannot be a Christian."[37] But by the 1960s, most publications in our racially segregated movement had practically nothing to say about issues of civil rights.[38] Further, in the middle of the twentieth century, our churches and journals could impose the expectation of precise *doctrinal* correctness with regard to baptism "unto the remission of sins," while simultaneously accepting the *practice* of *segregated* baptisteries: people of "color" were to be baptized in their own baptisteries, not in "white" baptisteries.[39] Such separation of doctrine and ethics is a frightening oversight—or perhaps more, a frightening example of forthright unfaithfulness—especially given that Paul's discussion of baptism in Galatians makes explicit that the putting on of Christ in baptism leads to a dissolution of all those social barriers that led to estrangement and alienation between peoples: there is for the one baptized "neither Jew nor Greek," "slave nor free," "male nor female" (3:27-28).

A similar contrast is found with the issue of warfare. In spite of some current canons that suggest Campbell could not sustain a social ethic, an examination of his views of warfare suggests otherwise: in the opening issue of the 1823 *Christian Baptist*, he scoffed at the "glaring inconsistency" of the "christian general" with his ten thousand soldiers and "chaplain at his elbow," preaching the gospel of good will, exhorting his soldiers to kill and maim, with Bible in one hand and a sword in the other, making widows and orphans through their violence, and calling upon God in their prayers to give them valiant victory.[40] And in spite of the various adjustments and changes in Campbell's viewpoint during his long career, he maintained a theological and philosophical critique of warfare, developing the critique most fully in his 1848 "Address on War,"[41] and lamenting as an aged editor the onset of the Civil War in 1861.[42] A return to taking seriously the Lordship of Jesus Christ—who proclaimed that we should love our enemies, not kill them—could never, for Campbell, legitimate Christian participation in the wars of the nation-states.

But by the 1940s this widely shared nineteenth century pacifism was cast aside as irrelevant. The prominent preacher Foy E. Wallace Jr. decried those among his fellowship who stood up as conscientious objectors in the face of the threat of Hitler. Wallace called any CO who selected alternative service or a prison sentence instead of military service "a freak speciman [sic.] of humanity," having a "dwarfed conscience." Wallace further accused the COs of making "murderers out of noble sons in army camps who bravely give their all in the defense . . . of the nation." By the time of the Vietnam War, pacifist sentiment among mainline Churches of Christ had "almost entirely vanished from the fellowship" according to Mike Casey, and was little considered a legitimate option.[43]

Yoder notes the strangeness of such claims, especially among those who employ the rhetoric of Christian unity: "No doctrine of Christian unity has yet explained why it should be more serious for Christians to disagree about the relative merits of episcopal, synodocal, or congregational polity than for them to accept, under formal protest but with no real intention to object effectively, to prepare for, and to carry out if necessary, mass killing of other Christians at the call of their respective governments."[44] Discussing "restoration" and "unity," then, must necessarily draw us back to issues we have tended to marginalize, if not simply ignore.

It could be, then, that there are those among both the "progressives" and the "conservatives" in Churches of Christ who continue to miss the point of a fuller, more biblical notion of restoration: ongoing arguments over issues of church polity, over style of worship, over "fellowshipping" this group or that—these discussions all have their place, but they currently remain too high on the priority list. We have been called—as Yoder helps us see, and as the early generations of the restoration movement understood—to be about the business of participating in the peaceable kingdom of God, the rule of God that has come in human history over all human rebellion. Let us not miss this call because of a too narrow conception of what it means to be "faithful to New Testament Christianity."

Conceiving restoration in such a way, we will be helped in at least two ways. First, this call to be a part of the story of the people of God is a vision of restoration that transcends the Enlightenment rationalism which originally served as the context which gave birth to our movement. This call to restoration thus escapes many of the difficulties arising from the "post-modern" ethos of our day and allows our tradition to continue to bear faithful witness to the good news in a new and different cultural context. Second, we will continue to discover disciples in many different denominations who are themselves seeking to be faithful to just such a New Testament Christianity, and we may thus find ourselves participating in God's ongoing work of effecting reconciliation and unity. That is, we may find ourselves able to hold together restoration and unity after all.

Endnotes

[1] John Yoder was, prior to his death, my initial dissertation advisor at the University of Notre Dame. A version of this paper was first presented in January 1999 at the Society of Christian Ethics on a panel of former Notre Dame students of John Yoder, in memory of his work and scholarship. The panel occurred just after the first anniversary of his death (December 1997). Each of us discussed the impact that Yoder's life and scholarship had had upon our own faith and scholarship. The paper was subsequently published as "Restoration and Unity in the Work of John Howard Yoder," *Restoration Quarterly* 44 (January 2002): 1-14, and is reprinted here, with some editing, by permission of the editor.

[2] Or so characterized my friend who pointed out the three churches to me. I'm aware, of course, that the differences run more deeply than my superficial presentation suggests.

[3] For example, see Donald F. Durnbaugh, *The Believers' Church: The History and Character of Radical Protestantism* (Scottdale, PA: Herald Press, 1985); George Huntston Williams, *The Radical Reformation*, 3d. ed., Sixteenth Century Essays and Studies, Volume XV (Philadelphia: Westminster Press, 1962; 3d. ed., Kirksville, MO: Sixteenth Century Journal Publishers, 1992); Franklin H. Littell, *The Anabaptist View of the Church: A Study in the Origins of Sectarian Protestantism*, 2d. ed. (Boston: Beacon Hill Press, 1958); James Leo Garrett, Jr., ed., *The Concept of the Believers' Church* (Scottdale, PA: Herald Press, 1969); James W. McClendon, *Ethics*, Volume 1, *Systematic Theology* (Nashville: Abingdon Press, 1986); John Howard Yoder, "The Believers' Church Conferences in Historical Perspective," *Mennonite Quarterly Review* 45/1 (January 1991): 5-19.

[4] See Robert E. Hooper, *Crying in the Wilderness: A Biography of David Lipscomb* (Nashville: David Lipscomb College, 1979), 98, 111, and 122. Hooper, however, inaccurately characterizes Mennonites (as do many, influenced by H. Richard Niebuhr's unhelpful typology in his *Christ and Culture*) as a group "who almost totally withdrew from any worldly involvement," 98.

[5] See Don Herbert Yoder, "Christian Unity in Nineteenth Century America," in *A History of the Ecumenical Movement*, eds. R. Rouse and S.C. Neill, 2 volumes (Philadelphia: Westminster, 1967), 1:237. On the *Declaration and Address,* see also Thomas H. Olbricht and Hans Rollman, eds., *The Quest for Christian Unity, Peace, and Purity in Thomas Campbell's Declaration and Address: Text and Studies*, ATLA Monograph Series, no. 46 (Lanham, MD: Scarecrow Press, 2000); and Hiram J. Lester, "The Disciple Birthday—A Disciple Passover," *Discipliana* 44, no. 4 (Winter 1984): 51-54.

[6] "Declaration and Address," in Olbricht and Rollman, 5.

[7] Ibid.

[8] Ibid., 76, 92, 93, and 85.

[9] Thus the pages of Alexander Campbell's *Millennial Harbinger*, which he edited beginning in 1830, are filled with debates, for example, over the nature of church government (the New Testament, he concluded, only authorizes congregational authority structures), or the nature and mode of baptism (adult, believer baptism, practiced as immersion is the New Testament pattern, he concluded).

[10] Moses Lard, "Do the Unimmersed Commune?" *Lard's Quarterly* 1 (September 1863): 44.

[11] Mac Lynn, *Churches of Christ in the United States* (Nashville: 21st Century Christian, 2000). Lynn provides ten different designations for practices and beliefs that could be an issue of "fellowship."

[12] Related to me by Ward Sullivan, former long-time elder in the Donmoyer Avenue Church of Christ, South Bend, Indiana. Though the account bears some marks of myth, such exegetical moves are not uncommon.

[13] And indeed, such a thing is not possible in the first place. Tradition, culture, and history are the warp and woof in which the gospel is inseparably lived and embodied.

[14] As Gary Holloway has suggested was true of Alexander Campbell. See Holloway, "Both Catholic and Protestant: Alexander Campbell and Tradition," *Christian Studies* 11:2 (1991): 31-40.

[15] Yoder, *Priestly Kingdom*, 1-12; "The Nature of the Unity We Seek: A Historic Free Church View," in *Royal Priesthood: Essays Ecclesiological and Ecumenical*, ed. Michael G. Cartwright (Grand Rapids: Eerdmans, 1994), 225; and "The Free Church Ecumenical Style," 238.

[16] Yoder, *For the Nations: Essays Evangelical and Public* (Grand Rapids: Eerdmans, 1997). The title appears to be a not-too-veiled critique of the rhetoric of Hauerwas, who

had previously published *Against the Nations* (Notre Dame, IN: University of Notre Dame Press, 1992).

[17] See, e.g., Yoder, "The Original Revolution," in *For the Nations*, 165-179.

[18] Yoder, *The Politics of Jesus*, 2d. ed. (Grand Rapids: Eerdmans, 1994).

[19] I overhead one conversation, for example, in which a colleague from my Churches of Christ seminary remarked that he did not want us to revert to a withdrawalist stance with the likes of Yoder. He was actually discussing more immediately the work of Hauerwas, and lumped Yoder in with the latter. There are, however, significant differences between the two, and they ought not be conflated. A most obvious example is the use of rhetoric, though I think this to be more than simply a difference in personalities, but rooted in Yoder's emphasis upon dialog as root and ground of reconciliation, as discussed below. Another example is Hauerwas' publicly stated reservations regarding the notion of a "Believers Church," with its emphasis upon the voluntary nature of faith.

[20] See, e.g., Yoder, "'But We Do See Jesus': The Particularity of Incarnation and the Universality of Truth," in *Priestly Kingdom*, 46-62.

[21] See Yoder, "How H. Richard Niebuhr Reasoned: A Critique of *Christ and Culture*," in Glen H. Stassen, D.M. Yeager, and Yoder, *Authentic Transformation: A New Vision of Christ and Culture* (Nashville: Abingdon Press, 1996), 31-89.

[22] This is because the most conservative among us speak as if their patternistic reasoning is indeed infallible, unaware of the historical nature of their reasoning.

[23] Cf. Yoder, *Priestly Kingdom*, 5. In "The Disavowal of Constantine: An Alternative Perspective on Interfaith Dialogue" in *Royal Priesthood*, 251, Yoder addressed this issue in the context of dialog between different faiths. Since Constantine, Yoder asserts, the Christian church is conceived as "indefectible." But for dialog to be fruitful, each of the various parties must bring a stance of repentance. Instead of asserting, "We still think we are right, but you may be right, too," or "Yes, that is a wrong idea, but that is not what we really meant," ecumenical dialog could take on a completely different tenor if Christians said, "We were wrong. The picture you have been given of Jesus by the Empire, by the Crusades, by struggles over the holy sites, and by wars in the name of the 'Christian West' is not only something to forget but something to forgive. We are not merely outgrowing it, as if it had been acceptable at the time: we disavow it and repent of it. It was wrong even when it seemed to us to be going well. We want our repentance to be not mere remorse but a new mind issuing in a new way—*metanoia*." Thus the church must be willing to confess fallibility. "The capacity for, or in fact the demand for, self-critique is part of what must be shared with people of other faiths and ideologies."
It is worth noting, too, that in James Wm. McClendon's three-volume systematic theology (one of the few systematic works that takes as its starting point the Believers Church or "baptist" tradition), he insists that the two "constitutive rules" for guiding the "struggle" of theology are "the principle of fallibility," (*Ethics*, 45), and "trying all things" (*Ethics*, 46).

[24] Yoder, *Priestly Kingdom*, 10-12.

[25] Yoder, "The Free Church Ecumenical Style," in *Royal Priesthood*. Many ecumenical efforts, claims Yoder, typically assume a magisterial conception of the church—i.e., "church" is seen as "a structure of governments" for administering preaching and sacraments, or some other set of common goals. "In this context of mainstream ecumenism it is taken for granted that the nature of the unity we seek among denominations is analogous to the nature of the unity that we think we already have within a given denomination. Then the unity of Christians is a unity of church governments." But there are more serious theological differences *within* denominations, which should be the concern of ecumenical efforts: differences between "rich and poor, between liberal and conservative, between

races, between east and west," which must be first addressed by talking to the people within the local congregation and to the congregation across the street (232-234).

[26] Yoder, "The Nature of the Unity We Seek," in *Royal Priesthood*, 230.

[27] As I heard him once say. I asked him once, though, whether this was not conceding too much. Does not this approach, I queried, fail to take the Just War adherents to task for their unfaithfulness? As I recall he pointed, in his response, to the practice itself of taking the Just War tradition seriously, as if this was itself an embodiment of the ministry of reconciliation. For example, he claims elsewhere that reconciliation "must *begin at the point of offense*," taking seriously past difficulties and points of contention, and addressing them. "There is then about the search for unity an element of repentance and openness, rather than negotiation from fixed positions or representation of entrenched constituencies" ("The Free Church Ecumenical Style," in *Royal Priesthood,* 240).

[28] To my knowledge, Yoder's attempts to have this event commemorated in a meaningful fashion were unfruitful in any official or institutional sense. However, in honor of both Yoder and Marcellus, I took my freshman theology seminar to the basilica and there read to them the account of Marcellus' martyrdom before pointing out the location of his relics beneath the altar, as well as noting that according to the account preserved by P. T. Ruinart, *Acta Martyrum* (Ratisbon: G. Josephi Manz, 1859) [see translation by Samuel Kapustin reprinted in Albert Marrin, *War and the Christian Conscience* (Chicago: Regnery, 1971), 40-45], the day of our meeting there in the basilica (November 3, 1998) marked the 1700th anniversary of Marcellus' death.

[29] Recounted by Joe Cappizi.

[30] In one class session, for which the assigned reading had been from Tolstoy, Yoder asked for initial reactions to the assignment. A student opened up the discussion with "I didn't know Tolstoy was a heretic," thereby discounting whatever Tolstoy might have had to say. Though Yoder responded in a non-threatening way—as I recall, he simply stated that we should go on, in spite of the fact that he had been excommunicated by the church, and see what we might learn from him—he looked as if he had been personally insulted, and stunned to see someone so readily discounted.

[31] My wife Laura often and graciously reminds me of this story.

[32] *Millennial Harbinger* (1837): 412. See discussion by Gary Holloway, "Not the Only Christians: Campbell on Exclusivism and Legalism," *Christian Studies* 15 (1995-96): 46-54.

[33] Barton Stone, *The Christian Messenger* 4, no. 9 (Aug 1830): 201.

[34] This is James McClendon's point in starting his systematic theology with *Ethics* instead of the more traditional ordering of systematic theologies. See chapter 1 of *Ethics* where he articulates this notion at some length.

[35] Michael Casey, "From Pacifism to Patriotism: The Emergence of Civil Religion in the Churches of Christ During World War I," *Mennonite Quarterly Review* 66 (July 1992): 376-90; cf. "Warriors Against War: The Pacifists of the Churches of Christ in World War II," *Restoration Quarterly* 35 (1993): 159-174; and "Churches of Christ and World War II Civilian Public Service," in *Proclaim Peace: Christian Pacifism from Unexpected Quarters*, eds. Theron F. Schlabach and Richard T. Hughes (Chicago: University of Illinois Press, 1997), 97-114.

[36] Richard Hughes, *Reviving the Ancient Faith: The Story of Churches of Christ in America* (1996; new edition, Abilene, TX: Abilene Christian University Press, 2007).

[37] Joseph Thomas, *The Travels and Gospel Labors of Joseph Thomas* (Winchester, VA: n.p., 1812), 56. Cited in Hughes, 271.

[38] Hughes, ch. 12.

[39] See, for example, Carl Spain's account of the uproar caused by such a baptism in his ACU lecture, "Modern Challenges to Christian Morals," in *Christian Faith in the Modern*

World: The Abilene Christian College Annual Bible Lectures 1960 (Abilene Christian College Students Exchange, 1960), 198-231. Reproduced at http://www.mun.ca/rels/restmov/texts/race/haymes15.html.

[40] Campbell, "The Christian Religion," *Christian Baptist* 1 (1823): 18.

[41] Campbell, "An Address on War," *Millennial Harbinger* 3d ser., 5 (July 1848): 361-386.

[42] Campbell, "Wars and Rumors of War," *Millennial Harbinger* 5th ser., 4 (June 1861): 344-348.

[43] See citations in Michael Casey, "Warriors Against War," 159-174. Casey also notes, for further examples, that Wallace's brother, Cled, likewise dubbed the writings of the pacifists as "idiotic drivel" and "patriotic rot." Another key figure, G. C. Brewer, preacher and editor of the influential *Gospel Advocate*, proclaimed in a speech to the American Legion that "I, for one, am ready to give the last drop of blood in my veins in the cause my forefathers fought and died for."

[44] Yoder, "The Nature of the Unity We Seek: A Historic Free Church View," in *Royal Priesthood*, 227. Yoder continues: "This observation does not necessarily drive one to pacifism. It does mean, however, that to take seriously the fact of Christian unity as given would revolutionize the positions of those Christians who argue the necessity of war, as a last resort, for the defense of order. None of the arguments that justify morally the participation of Christians in war can justify their participation *on both sides* of a war. ... If Christians in the Allied nations were right in accepting war because the defeat of Hitler was necessary for the defense of order, then for the same reason all Christians in Germany should have been conscientious objectors." So, Yoder concludes, if one wants the Just War tradition to be taken seriously, then one must take steps to make it effective. He develops this latter observation more fully in his *When War Is Unjust: Being Honest in Just War Thinking*, rev. ed. (Maryknoll, NY: Orbis, 1996).

CHAPTER TWO

THE POLITICS OF YODER REGARDING *THE POLITICS OF JESUS*
Recovering the Implicit in Yoder's Holistic Theology for Pacifism

MARK THIESSEN NATION

This essay can be seen in several ways. On the most basic level it has a two-fold purpose. First, I want to name the strategy or politics of John Howard Yoder in his writing of what came to be his signature work, *The Politics of Jesus.*[1] In an essay published one year before *The Politics of Jesus* was originally published, Yoder said, "Anabaptism was intended in the 16th century as a corrective. It never claimed to be more than 'the rest of the Reformation.'"[2] Likewise Yoder saw himself in *The Politics of Jesus* as offering a corrective. He saw himself as recovering the "social-political-ethical" dimensions of the gospel of Jesus Christ, dimensions which too often, at the beginning of the 1970s, were filtered out of the New Testament witness.[3] Yoder said very specifically, for instance, in his chapter on justification by grace through faith: "In view of the corrective intent of the present argument it should be reiterated that my purpose is not to reverse a prior error by claiming that justification is *only* social. I am objecting to a particular polemical application of the traditional doctrine, which used it to *exclude* the ethical and social dimensions."[4] If we do not take Yoder seriously at this point—and note that he is offering a corrective—then we may in fact "reverse a prior error." We may forget his intention and thus confuse his *corrective* emphases in *The Politics of Jesus* with the whole of what Yoder would have to say about the gospel of Jesus Christ. Once we are aware of Yoder's strategy then we will realize the need to read more broadly in

Yoder's writings in order to acquire his holistic, biblically rooted theology thereby recovering what is often only implicit in *The Politics of Jesus*. Thus I have named the second purpose of this essay and the one to which most attention will be given. Once we see Yoder's holistic theology, the provocative and creative work in *The Politics of Jesus* seems richer and even more compelling as an articulation of Jesus' claims upon the social (or "political") existence of all who call themselves by his name.

Many of the readers of this essay may have read Yoder's most influential and well-known book, *The Politics of Jesus*. If you have, that may be helpful. However, that book is difficult; many find its multi-layered argument complex and difficult to comprehend. Moreover, my experience tells me not only that many do not fully grasp the argument of the book, but they seriously misunderstand it. There are various reasons for that. At least one of them is that many readers have not fully understood Yoder's use of the word "politics" in the title. Obviously the word is intended to be centrally defined by Jesus, but it also needs to be seen as necessarily rooted in the confessions and the life of the Christian community (as distinct from the world beyond the church). Without both of these connections, the word "politics" in the title can easily lead the reader astray. Though I hope this essay provides a framework for reading *The Politics of Jesus*, it is not intended as a summary of that book.[5] Rather, its purpose is to provide a synopsis of Yoder's overall theology, especially as it relates to pacifism. The place where Yoder himself attempted to do this, briefly and straightforwardly, is in *Nevertheless*, a book in which he describes twenty-nine different types of pacifism.[6] There, in Chapter 19, entitled "The Pacifism of the Messianic Community," Yoder outlines his own position.[7] But it is barely more than an outline, slightly less than five pages and written partly in reference to the other twenty-eight types of pacifism he discusses in the book. There he says about his own approach: "To say that this is the pacifism of the *messianic* community is to affirm its dependence upon the confession that Jesus is Christ and that Jesus Christ is Lord. To say that Jesus is the Messiah is to say that in him are fulfilled the expectations of God's people regarding the coming one in whom God's will would perfectly be done. Therefore, in the person and work of Jesus, in his teachings and his passion, this kind of pacifism finds its rootage, and in his resurrection it finds its enablement."[8] In what follows I will elaborate on this brief characterization, drawing from *Nevertheless*, as well as other writings by Yoder.

Thus I will name what was vital for his own theological position regarding that dimension of discipleship that is expressed through concretely loving enemies in the midst of a sinful and often violent world (i.e., pacifism).

The Person of Jesus

For Yoder there is nothing more crucial for getting theology and ethics right than naming the centrality of Jesus.[9] Jesus is the Word of God made flesh.[10] Jesus is also the Messiah and thus was seen as the fulfillment of expectations regarding the redemption (including the political redemption) of the people of Israel within the context of first-century Judaism.[11] Yoder names this crucial centrality in varied and compelling ways. Sometimes he does this by reflecting on the person and work of Jesus. As he puts it in *The Politics of Jesus*, "Ethics as well as 'theology' . . . must . . . be rooted in revelation, not alone in speculation, nor in a self-interpreting 'situation.' . . . This will of God is affirmatively, concretely knowable in the person and ministry of Jesus."[12]

First, then, the person of Jesus. Among the many different types of pacifism Yoder has named in *Nevertheless*, he says that it is his own "position for which the person of Jesus is indispensable." He continues, "It is the only one of these positions which would lose its substance if Jesus were not Christ and would lose its foundation if Jesus Christ were not Lord."[13] Connecting his own approach to classic orthodox theology, Yoder claimed in *The Politics of Jesus* that "the view of Jesus being proposed here is more radically Nicene and Chalcedonian than other views. I do not here advocate an unheard-of modern understanding of Jesus. I ask rather that the implications of what the church has always said about Jesus as Word of the Father, as true God and true Man, be taken more seriously, as relevant to our social problems, than ever before."[14]

As Yoder had said earlier in the same book, the language of incarnation in Christian theology is precisely an attempt to name the reality "that God broke through the borders of our standard definition of what is human, and gave a new, formative definition in Jesus."[15] Moreover, the development of the language of "trinity" by the early church is an acknowledgement "that language must be found and definitions created so that Christians, who believe in only one God, can affirm that God is most adequately and bindingly known in Jesus."[16] This is a claim regarding "revelation" says Yoder. This revelation has a particular character. It "has come to us not on a tablet of stone chiseled by the finger of God alone on Sinai, or from the mouth of a prophet or an oracle. Instead, the telling has come in the full humanity of a unique and complete human being."[17] For it is centrally Jesus of Nazareth, Jesus the Christ who reveals to us "the nature and will of God."[18] Yoder attempts to lay out the most salient particulars of this revelation in Jesus— at least as regards a social ethic—in *The Politics of Jesus*. Toward the beginning of this book Yoder suggests "that the ministry and the claims of Jesus are best understood as presenting to hearers and readers not the avoidance of political options, but one particular social-political-ethical option."[19] Having taken the reader through most strands of New Testament thought (along with a glance at the Old Testament), Yoder concludes, "A social style characterized by the creation of a new community and the rejection of violence of any kind is the theme of New Testament proclamation from beginning to end, from right to left. The cross of Christ is the model of Christian social efficacy, the power of God for those who believe."[20]

This characterization of the New Testament, not surprisingly, is connected to the claim that all Christians are called to follow Jesus. However, Yoder also wants to make it clear that following Jesus is not about some "moralism" or a "preoccupation with never making a mistake."[21] Rather, we are called to be "participants in the human experience, that particular way of living for God in the world and being used as instruments of the living of God in the world, which the Bible calls *agapē* or cross."[22] Yoder here is echoing the emphases of his teacher, Karl Barth, when he says that *our* "living for God" is also the "living of God" in the world—thus the God we know through the person of Jesus is still manifest in the present body of Christ.

By the early 1980s, Yoder was at times strategically employing postmodern terminology, acknowledging that "reality always was pluralistic and relativistic, that is, historical. The idea that it could be otherwise was itself an illusion laid on us by Greek ontology language, Roman sovereignty language, and other borrowings from the . . . rulers of Europe."[23] We should neither shy away from a world that sees truth claims as historically particular nor allow ourselves to be captive to any "isms" within this world, including relativism. Within this conceptual world we may, and as Christians should, continue to confess Jesus as Lord of the world and invite others to repent and to accept his Lordship. We should not imagine, however, that the gospel of Jesus Christ was ever really some form of an abstract claim regarding absolute truth, a claim outside of the relativities of history or to be employed coercively. Rather, the gospel was fundamentally the announcement of the Word of God made flesh in a particular man from Nazareth who embodied what many have heard as good news—a message which beckons us to follow this Messiah, this Savior. "The real issue," said Yoder, "is not whether Jesus can make sense in a world far from Galilee, but whether—when he meets us in our world, as he does in fact—we want to follow him. We don't have to, as they didn't then. That we don't have to is the profoundest proof of his condescension, and thereby of his glory."[24]

The Work of Jesus

Next we turn to "the work of Jesus." Yoder wanted to make it clear that it is through the life, death, and resurrection of Jesus that we receive the gift of Christ's "salvation as restored communion and consequently restored capacity to obedience."[25] Or as he puts it elsewhere, "To say that the kingdom of God is at hand, that the new world is on the way, is first of all to anchor our thoughts in the priority of grace."[26] He reminds us that "the call to follow Jesus is a call addressed to all people. But the standards by which such a life is guided are not cut to the measure of persons in general. That pattern of life can be clearly perceived—to say nothing of being even modestly and partially lived—only through that reorientation of the personality and its expression which Jesus and his first followers called repentance and new birth."[27]

Thus we can see that, for Yoder, it is God's salvation that makes it possible for us to be "participants in the human experience, that particular way of living for God in the world and being used as instruments of the living of God in the world."[28] "In the believers' church stream of church history," said Yoder, "we find that it is important to keep in view God's call to discipleship and the wholeness of salvation, which is not simply something done for us 'out there,' but is done to us and through us."[29] It is partly the emphasis on the need for the salvation made possible through the work of Jesus that led Yoder to distinguish his own approach from what he referred to as liberal approaches. As he put it in one of his early essays,

> The traditional liberal thought in ethics did fail, in large part,
> to take sin seriously enough, and thus did tend to see the ade-
> quate ethical fulfillment of the requirements of love as a simple

possibility. This sort of perfectionism contradicts both history and Christian doctrine. . . . Biblical perfectionism affirms not a simple possibility of achieving love in history, but a *crucial* possibility of participating in the victory of Christ over the effects of sin in the world. Obedience for the [Christian] thus involves the cross, and the presence of sin has been worked into ethics, without either undermining the integrity of ethics as part of a valid theology or cheapening the work of redemption. This perfectionism of the cross is therefore not optimistic about either the world's or the Christian's goodness; it dares simply share the Bible's own confidence that with God all things are possible. . . .

As the cross becomes meaningful in the New Testament only in relation to the resurrection and to Pentecost, so in [Christian] ethics is forgiving grace rightly understood only in the context of empowering grace. Interpreting justification by faith as a ratification for conscious compromise with the presence of sin is what Paul calls sinning "that grace may abound"; what Bonhoeffer called "cheap grace." The Biblical perfectionist refuses to flatten God's goodness into mere forgiving mercy. [The disciple] experiences redemption as a brand-new dimension of possibility for discipleship given the [one made new] through his [or her] participation in the body of the risen Lord, and knowing the reality of this new life [the disciple] refuses to spiritualize or to eschatologize it out of the realm of [their] earthly living and doing. This also is the grace of God, that we may walk in newness of life.[30]

In this early essay, Yoder began by affirming the need to take sin seriously joined to an awareness that embodying love is no simple possibility because of inherent human capacity. Not only is there no reason to be optimistic about the fallen world, said Yoder, there is also no reason to be optimistic about Christian goodness. It is because of the cross and resurrection, the coming of the Holy Spirit, forgiving and empowering grace, redemption and new life in Christ—and *only* because of these—that Christians may know the new possibility for discipleship and boldly claim that "with God all things are possible."[31]

One of the key theological themes by which Yoder signals—from the 1950s to the 1990s—that peace, Christianly understood, is not mostly about human agency is that of eschatology. Yoder names this near the beginning of his writing career in his poignant essay, "Peace without Eschatology," in which he clearly distinguishes his own position from liberal pacifist positions which communicated that peacemaking was all (or mostly) about human agency.[32] This essay originated in 1954, while Yoder was engaged in ecumenical discussions in Western Europe, and quite deliberately the year the World Council of Churches was also focusing on the theme of "Christ, the Hope of the World."[33] Human actions, says Yoder, are to be seen in light of final goals or ultimate hopes: "'Peace' describes the pacifist's hope, the goal in the light of which Christians act, the character of Christian actions, the ultimate divine certainty that lets the Christian position make sense; it does not describe the external appearance or the observable results of Christian behavior. This is what we mean by eschatology: a hope that, defying present frustration, defines a present position in terms of the yet unseen goal that gives it meaning."[34]

More than three decades later, in his presidential address to the Society of Christian Ethics as well as in two subsequent essays, Yoder elected to emphasize the connections, as one essay has it, between "Ethics and Eschatology."[35] In fact, in this latter essay, distinguishing his approach from biblical scholar John J. Collins, Yoder importantly comments, "To say simply, as Collins does, that 'apocalypse is validated by the ethics it sustains' would be a wrongly reductionistic horizontalism. It would be self-defeating, since the vision will only support the ethos if the seer considers God and the revelation to be real."[36] We must not lose the point here. Yoder has specifically, in 1990, distanced himself from the perspective that would utilize apocalyptic or eschatological thought *only* because it validates a particular ethic. He refers to this approach as "reductionistic horizontalism" and aligns himself with the biblical author who "considers God and the revelation to be real."

The way Yoder sometimes made his point about eschatology and human agency was to invoke the vital importance of the power of the resurrection. For instance, to make sure that no one confuses the argument of *The Politics of Jesus* with an argument for a liberal program to change the world or to acquire our own ends through the employment of nonviolence, he ends with a chapter on the final book of the New Testament, "The Revelation of John." Here he reminds all readers that what he has described throughout this book is really "the war of the Lamb," not our war. John the revelator attempts to reassure his readers that, in the midst of suffering, those who are followers of Jesus can trust that Jesus Christ, the Lamb that was slaughtered, will finally triumph over evil. In order to do that, the author of Revelation employs apocalyptic language. Through his vivid language this writer shows, as Yoder puts it, that "the relationship between the obedience of God's people and the triumph of God's cause is not a relationship of cause and effect but one of cross and resurrection."[37] Or put differently, "the triumph of the right, although it is assured, is sure because of the power of the resurrection and not because of any relation of causes and effects."[38] Perhaps this was Yoder's way of reaffirming what he had said earlier in an unpublished 1964 lecture: "The resurrection is . . . the Nile of the Bible . . . . It is the center around which all the rest of the biblical message rotates, from which all the rest of the message draws its significance and authority, then it is also God's word to us . . . that the center of our history is that same event."[39]

I hope the last few paragraphs on the work of Christ have accomplished several things. First, I hope I have demonstrated that Yoder meant what he said in a footnote in *The Politics of Jesus*: "In view of the corrective intent of the present argument it should be reiterated that my purpose is not to reverse a prior error by claiming that justification [by grace through faith] is *only* social."[40] As I have shown above, he believed that we make a serious mistake if we ignore our need for redemption, including personal transformation through Christ. Second, however much Yoder may have emphasized the social dimensions of the gospel, he never intended for us to imagine that we can engage in what he referred to as "reductionistic horizontalism." God's redemptive work in Christ *matters* and is real. It matters for us as individuals and it matters for God's redemptive work in the world (especially through the redemptive community, the church). Since Yoder believed that the social (and properly understood, "political") emphases were mostly ignored in theological writings prior to the early 1970s, they became the burden of *The Politics of Jesus*.[41] Drawing on what were then recent biblical and theological studies, Yoder wanted to show some of the ways the person and work of Christ matter for the redemption of the world. He did this by pointing to the New Testament portrayal of the coming of the kingdom of God, the way in which money was to be shared, Christ overcoming the principalities and powers, the reconciliation of Jews and Gentiles, and the call to an embodiment of faithfulness by communities of disciples. These were important correctives, correctives that have influenced many. Then I would say, "1972 is not 2010." Of course knowing what to say when requires contextual discernment. But I at least wonder if, in the early twenty-first century, many Christians influenced by Yoder (or similar views) are not in fact committing the very reverse error (of social reductionism) that Yoder wanted to avoid (which is not to argue for a return to the error of seeing the relevance of Jesus only in terms of individualistic pietism).[42]

The Messianic Community

Next we turn to Yoder's emphasis on the "messianic community." It is important as we begin this discussion to start where Yoder started: "To say that this is the pacifism of the *messianic* community is to affirm its dependence upon the confession that Jesus is Christ and that Jesus Christ is Lord."[43] To circle back to earlier affirmations, this is a reminder that we don't begin a discussion of Christian community by focusing only on human agency. This is a community dependent upon God, the God of Israel, the God made flesh in Jesus of Nazareth. This God has graciously redeemed us, made us into a community who together worship and serve him. Trust, hope, and faithfulness find their rootage in this particular God.

Being reminded through worship that our life together is truly about God's presence with us leads us to see that our worship—our life together as a church community—cultivates an alternative consciousness: "Another view of what the world is like is kept alive by narration and celebration which fly in the face of some of the 'apparent' lessons of 'realism.'"[44] Yoder expounds upon this elsewhere, saying, "Because we are in this alternative community we see things other people don't see, we notice things they don't notice, we make connections they haven't seen. But it does more than that. It enables perseverance, it motivates, it protects us from the erratic and the impulsive. We live with one another the maintenance of the language that gives meaning to our countercultural identity."[45] That is to say, our life together is comprised of "a covenanting group of men and women who instruct one another, forgive one another, bear one another's burdens, and reinforce one another's witness."[46] This community provides mutual support and accountability.

It is also the case that this "alternative community discharges a modeling mission. The church is called to be now what the world is called to be ultimately."[47] In fact, "the existence of a human community dedicated in common to a new and publicly scandalous enemy-loving way of life is itself a new social datum."[48] And because the existence of this community is a result of the "priority of God's grace," we are emboldened to say that the practices of the church "are actions of God, in and with, through and under what men and women do."[49] Thus it is important to realize that the Christian community, empowered by the Holy Spirit, exists as a witness to the gospel of Jesus Christ. And it is precisely in giving this witness— embodying love for neighbors and even enemies—that this community gives its life for a society.[50] As this community gives its life for the world around us, we still must nurture the identity of this community because "only a continuing community dedicated to a deviant value system can change the world."[51]

The Relationship between Church and World

But the question remains for many readers of Yoder: How do we bring about changes in the world beyond the church?[52] For Yoder, before we can begin to address this set of issues we must be straight on some fundamental theological matters—matters implied by what has already been stated but that nonetheless may get lost. First, Yoder wants us to see that "the need is not, as some current popularizers would suggest, for most Christians to get out of the church and into the world. They have been in the world all the time. The trouble is that they have been *of* the world too. The need is for what they do in the world to be different because they are Christian; to be a reflection not merely of their restored self-confidence nor of their power to set the course of society but of the social novelty of the covenant of grace."[53]

Second, and related to the first, we must acknowledge the visibility of both the church and the world. Many are aware of Yoder's views about "Constantinianism."[54] What has not often received enough attention in many of these discussions is the following claim by Yoder: "The most pertinent fact about the new state of things after Constantine and Augustine is not that Christians were no longer persecuted and began to be privileged, nor that emperors built churches and presided over ecumenical deliberations about the Trinity; what matters is that the two visible realities, church and world, were fused."[55] Yoder believed it was of fundamental importance to retain the distinction between these two visible realities. "The 'world' must return in our theology to the place that God's patience has given it in history. The 'world' is neither all nature nor all humanity nor all 'culture'; it is *structured unbelief*, rebellion taking with it a fragment of what should have been the Order of the Kingdom."[56] Similarly, "over against this 'world' the church is visible; identified by baptism, discipline, morality, and martyrdom."[57] Or as he put it elsewhere, "if the church is visible in that these people keep their promises, love their enemies, enjoy their neighbors, and tell the truth, as others do not, this may communicate to the world something of the reconciling, i.e., the community-creating, love of God."[58]

This is related, third, to Yoder's conviction that "biblically the meaning of history is carried first of all, and on behalf of all others, by the believing community."[59] Following from this set of beliefs are several other convictions. (1) Christian ethics is for Christians.[60] This in some ways logically follows from everything I have said to this point. If Jesus and the church matter crucially for understanding biblical pacifism, then such pacifism is not fully intelligible apart from the particulars to which these claims point. We cannot really understand redemption, faithfulness, or an embodied love that would be willing to die rather than kill unless we have adequately grasped the fullness of the gospel of Jesus Christ. (2) This point is intricately connected to Yoder's caution that "the short-circuited means used to 'Christianize' 'responsibly' the world in some easier way than by the gospel [has] had the effect of dechristianizing the Occident and demonizing paganism."[61] (3) Next is the affirmation that distinguishes Yoder's approach from similar (often social gospel) approaches, namely that "the church's responsibility to and for the world is first and always to be the church."[62] (4) The fourth ramification that warrants attention is the scandalous conclusion that "there may well be certain functions in a given society which that society in its unbelief considers necessary, and which the unbelief renders necessary, in which Christians will not be called to participate."[63] Putting the same point positively, Yoder said that Christians should practice "conscientious participation" in societal life.[64] This is another way of stating Yoder's concern that Christians see that "the need is for what they do in the world to be different *because* they are Christian," that is, "to be a reflection ... of the social novelty of the covenant of grace."[65]

The Church as Polis, a Polis for the Sake of the World

Some will undoubtedly still be left unsatisfied. In some ways that is as it should be. Why? Negatively put, because many have imagined Yoder to be a Rauschenbusch-type social gospeler, moving directly from theological claims (e.g., about the kingdom of God) to progressive social causes. Because of the church's centrality as distinct from the world, Yoder refuses to fit such categorizations. Positively put, for Yoder it is imperative that our hope be placed in the Lordship of Christ; that we realize the central role for the people of God within God's work in the world (thus our first "politics" is the politics of Jesus);[66] that we not confuse church and world; that we have patience to allow the world to be the world; and that we not place undue trust in the effectiveness of our own efforts for peace and justice. Lesslie Newbigin names this concern brilliantly:

> It remains central to the missionary calling of the church that the gospel calls for a radical conversion of heart and mind, and a full commitment to the life of a community which is identified with the Kingdom, but is properly *the sign and foretaste of the kingdom*. When we set Kingdom issues against church issues, we are always in danger of defining the Kingdom in terms of some contemporary ideology and not in terms of the manifestation of the Kingdom in the incarnate, crucified, and risen Jesus. The apocalyptic strand in the teaching of the New Testament cannot be removed without destroying the strength of the whole. There is no straight line from the politics of this world, from the programs and projects in which we invest our energies, to the Kingdom of God. The holy city is a gift from God, coming from above. . . . The church exists as a sign and foretaste of the gift that is promised; in all its members it is called to act now in the light of the promised future: that is its proper this-worldliness. But the church maintains at its heart, through the word and sacraments of the gospel, its witness to a reality which is not of this world. Only the church can give that witness.[67]

If we are clear on all of this—perhaps especially that "the church's responsibility to and for the world is first and always to be the church"—then we are free to engage in creative efforts to bring about social and political changes beyond the believing community.[68] As we do such work, we should always remember the temptations of most societies to be inattentive or at least under-attentive to the poor, the marginalized, and the strangers among us, and to be violently attentive to the present enemies of their nation.[69] For those Christians actively engaged in such activities, we should be vigilant to realize the temptation to let our hearts, minds, and souls be captive to communities and ideologies which are, in significant respects, alien to the gospel and the body of Christ.[70]

And then? Yoder saw involvement in the world beyond the faith community as something that needs to be discerned contextually and can quite appropriately be thought about in various terms (as long as what has already been named is kept clearly alive through the convictions and practices of Christian communities). Through the early 1960s, borrowing from ecumenical conversations, Yoder used the term "middle axioms" as a way of naming how to address the larger culture. "These concepts," Yoder said, "will translate into meaningful and concrete terms the general relevance of the lordship of Christ for a given social ethical issue. They mediate between the general principles of Christological ethics and the concrete problems of political application."[71] Though Yoder borrowed this terminology that was in use at the time for his own purposes, one should keep in mind that Yoder never used this term after the early 1960s. It appears that he had either abandoned the term or found better ways to discuss Christian social ethical engagement beyond the church community. One of the more creative and illuminating ways he did this was to offer reflections directly on what it means to be a "believing community" in relation to the world.[72]

Yoder's most consistent way of framing this set of issues, however, was something he borrowed from Karl Barth. He puts it this way in *The Christian Witness to the State*:

> In modern usage the application of the term *political* to the state rather than to the church is so well established that it cannot be combated. It leads to a distortion, however, for in biblical thought the church is properly a political entity, a *polis*. In both biblical languages the word *church* (*qahal, ekklesia*) refers originally to a deliberative assembly of the body politic. Though the disparagement of the cultic and the priestly elements in the old covenant has gone too far in some recent theology, it does remain true that biblical language about Christ and the church is more political (kingdom, Messiah, New Jerusalem, *politeuma*) than cultic. In this

root sense, therefore, the church is more truly political, i.e., a truer, more properly ordered community, than is the state.[73]

In a footnote at the end of this claim, Yoder says two important things. He indicates that this claim is related to the writing of *The Politics of Jesus*, and he credits Barth with this idea, saying, "Karl Barth has advocated a method of 'analogy' for relating church ethics derived from a faith commitment to the lower standards applicable to the civil community."[74] Over the next thirty years Yoder wrote numerous essays and one book that attempted to articulate what this looks like.[75] A number of things seem clear to me about this approach. First, Yoder never really imagined that he had arrived at the "best" way to articulate the theological bridge from the church as *polis* (i.e., the politics of Jesus) to the church's serving, witnessing, and ministering in those other realms of politics beyond the faith community. Second, he simply kept making fresh attempts to articulate ways of thinking about these relationships. Third, because some efforts were more successful than others—and none was fully successful—if one is really to come close to understanding Yoder's approach to this set of issues, one needs to read a number of his writings. Fourth, because he utilized this Barthian approach so frequently, we can only conclude that he preferred it to others.[76] Fifth, and finally, Yoder may have preferred the Barthian approach because it expresses the need to serve the world while keeping one of his central, and most offensive, convictions clear: "the church's responsibility to and for the world is first and always to be the church."[77]

Let me close where I began, with Yoder's own summary of his position. Perhaps my exposition will have made Yoder's brief summary even richer in meaning: "To say that this is the pacifism of the *messianic* community is to affirm its dependence upon the confession that Jesus is Christ and that Jesus Christ is Lord. To say that Jesus is the Messiah is to say that in him are fulfilled the expectations of God's people regarding the coming one in whom God's will would perfectly be done. Therefore, in the person and work of Jesus, in his teachings and his passion, this kind of pacifism finds its rootage, and in his resurrection it finds its enablement."[78] Yoder concludes his description of his own position as follows:

This position is closer than the others [described in *Nevertheless*] to the idiom of the Bible and to the core affirmations of the Christian faith. It reckons seriously with the hopelessness of the world as it stands and yet affirms a gospel of hope. It shares the integrity of the principled views [described earlier] without their withdrawal from history. It includes the practical concern of the programmatic views [which focus on the effectiveness of nonviolent strategies] without placing its hope there. After all, the invocation of violence to support any cause is also a messianism. Any national sense of mission claims implicitly to be a saving community. One cannot avoid either messianism or the claim to chosen peoplehood by setting Jesus or his methods aside. One only casts the aura of election around lesser causes.[79]

Endnotes

[1] John Howard Yoder, *The Politics of Jesus*, 2d ed. (Grand Rapids: Eerdmans, 1994; original ed., 1972). All references will be to the second edition.

[2] Yoder, "The Recovery of the Anabaptist Vision," *Concern* 18 (July 1971): 22. It is intriguing to me that Yoder said this. I think this statement is a fair assessment of, for instance, the 1527 Schleitheim confession of faith. That is, it was a statement offered as a "corrective," not attempting to deal with the whole of the Christian faith. However, certain sixteenth-century Anabaptist writers, such as Menno Simons, were attempting to be holistic in their articulation of the Christian faith. Numerous essays by Egil Grislis on Menno published in the 1980s and 1990s confirm this about Menno.

[3] This is one way to read the whole book. However, the focus on the filtering is most obvious in chapters one and six of *The Politics of Jesus*.

[4] Yoder, *Politics of Jesus*, 215, fn. 2, original emphases. Cf. also 226.

[5] I have done so previously in *John Howard Yoder: Mennonite Patience, Evangelical Witness, Catholic Convictions* (Grand Rapids: Eerdmans, 2006), ch. 4.

[6] Yoder, *Nevertheless: Varieties of Religious Pacifism*, rev. and expanded ed. (Scottdale, PA: Herald Press, 1992; original edition 1971). All references to this book will be to the 1992 edition.

[7] Ibid., 133-138.

[8] Ibid., 133-134, original emphasis.

[9] This is evident in many of Yoder's writings. He names this in an interesting, provocative, and somewhat postmodern way in "'But We Do See Jesus': The Particularity of Incarnation and the Universality of Truth," in *The Priestly Kingdom* (Notre Dame, IN: University of Notre Dame Press, 1984), 46-62 and 199.

[10] See, e.g., Yoder's reflections on the prologue to the Gospel of John in "Glory in a Tent," in *He Came Preaching Peace* (Scottdale, PA: Herald Press, 1985), 69-88.

[11] In addition to *Politics of Jesus*, see Yoder, *The Original Revolution*, rev. ed. (Scottdale, PA: Herald Press, 1977), chs. 1-4. See my foreword in the 2003 reprint. It is remarkable to me how Yoder's schema for interpreting Jesus within the context of first-century Judaism, articulated in the title essay in *The Original Revolution*, comports with N. T. Wright's major writings on Jesus.

[12] Yoder, *Politics of Jesus*, 233.

[13] Yoder, *Nevertheless*, 134. See the fuller statement of the same point in *Politics of Jesus*, 237.

[14] Yoder, *Politics of Jesus*, 102.

[15] Ibid., 99.

[16] Ibid.

[17] Yoder, *Nevertheless*, 134. Yoder also claims numerous times in his writings that his convictions about Jesus fit within the orthodox Christian claim that Jesus was fully human and fully divine. I have named this more fully in an unpublished lecture, "Mending Fences & Finding Grace: Regarding Christology and Divine Agency in Yoder's Thought," presented May 26, 2007, at the conference, "Inheriting John Howard Yoder," Toronto Mennonite Theological Centre.

[18] Yoder, *Nevertheless*, 134.

[19] Yoder, *Politics of Jesus*, 11. In relation specifically to the ministry of Jesus, the current scholar who has most confirmed Yoder's reading is N. T. Wright. Specifically in relation to the question of violence, see Richard B. Hays, "Victory over Violence: The Significance of N. T. Wright's Jesus for New Testament Ethics," in *Jesus & the Restoration of Israel: A Critical Assessment of N. T. Wright's Jesus and the Victory of God*, ed. Carey C. Newman (Downers Grove, IL: InterVarsity Press, 1999), 142-158 and 313.

[20] Yoder, *Politics of Jesus*, 242. It might be noted that in chapter seven, "The Disciple of Christ and the Way of Jesus," Yoder offers a rich summary of many of the dimensions of the call to discipleship in the New Testament. In his widely acclaimed book, *The Moral Vision of the New Testament* (San Francisco: HarperSanFrancisco, 1996), Richard Hays offers strong praise for Yoder's careful and thorough work in this book (239-253).

[21] Yoder, *Nevertheless*, 135. Regarding this charge also see Yoder, "'Patience' as Method in Moral Reasoning: Is an Ethic of Discipleship 'Absolute'?" in *The Wisdom of the Cross: Essays in Honor of John Howard Yoder*, ed. Stanley Hauerwas, Chris K. Huebner, Harry J. Huebner, and Mark Thiessen Nation (Grand Rapids: Eerdmans, 1999; reprinted, Wipf & Stock, 2005), 24-42.

[22] Yoder, *Nevertheless*, 135.

[23] Yoder, "'But We Do See Jesus,'" in *Priestly Kingdom*, 59.

[24] Ibid., 62. Another essay in which Yoder even more fully articulates his own views of the claims of the gospel in a postmodern world is "On Not Being Ashamed of the Gospel: Particularity, Pluralism, and Validation," *Faith and Philosophy* 9 (July 1992): 285-300.

[25] Yoder, *Preface to Theology: Christology and Theological Method*, ed. Stanley Hauerwas and Alex Sider (Grand Rapids: Brazos Press, 2002), 312.

[26] Yoder, "Why Ecclesiology Is Social Ethics," in *The Royal Priesthood: Essays Ecclesiological and Ecumenical*, ed. Michael G. Cartwright (Grand Rapids: Eerdmans, 1994; reprinted, Herald Press, 1998), 104.

[27] Yoder, *Nevertheless*, 136.

[28] Ibid., 135.

[29] Yoder, *Preface to Theology*, 289. For a discussion of salvation that seems consistent with Yoder's, see N. T. Wright, *Surprised by Hope: Rethinking Heaven, the Resurrection, and the Mission of the Church* (New York: HarperOne, 2008), 189ff. I would also point to the important work by Michael Gorman on Paul, which also offers reflections on salvation quite consistent with Yoder's.

[30] Yoder, "The Anabaptist Dissent: The Logic of the Place of the Disciple in Society," *Concern: A Pamphlet Series* 1 (June 1954): 58-61, original emphasis. My slight alterations to the quote are alterations I imagine Yoder would have made later in his life. This essay was recently reprinted in Virgil Vogt, ed., *The Roots of Concern: Writings on Anabaptist Renewal 1952-1957* (Eugene, OR: Cascade Books, 2009), 29-43.

[31] There are various, more recent essays where Yoder named the spiritual resources needed for faithful discipleship. See, e.g., *The Christian Witness to the State* (Newton, KS: Faith and Life Press, 1964; third printing, with updated footnotes, 1977; reprinted, Herald Press, 2002), 29; "Why Ecclesiology Is Social Ethics," in *Royal Priesthood*, 116; and "The Constantinian Sources of Western Social Ethics," in *Priestly Kingdom*, 139.

[32] This 1954 essay was first published as a pamphlet in 1961, with a foreword by Dietrich Bonhoeffer's good friend, Franz Hildebrandt. Now see Yoder, "If Christ Is Truly Lord," in *The Original Revolution*, with a foreword by Mark Thiessen Nation (Scottdale, PA: Herald Press, 2003; original 1971), 52-84; and "Peace without Eschatology," in *Royal Priesthood*, 143-167.

[33] Yoder, "Peace without Eschatology," in *Royal Priesthood*, 145, fn. 1.

[34] Ibid., 145. One can see, in this 1954 essay, not only the attempt to connect with World Council of Churches conversations but also with debates shaped by the thought of Reinhold Niebuhr. Those contexts should be kept in mind. See Yoder's 1966 essay, "Christ, the Hope of the World," in *Original Revolution* (1971/1977/2003), 140-176 and 182-183. This essay, also on eschatology, is shaped more by engagement with the mid-1960s revolutionary contexts of Latin America. It should also be kept in mind that Yoder was happy to reprint both of these essays in the 1994 collection *Royal Priesthood*.

[35] Yoder, "To Serve Our God and to Rule the World," in *Royal Priesthood*, 127-140 [original 1988]; "Armaments and Eschatology," *Studies in Christian Ethics* 1/1 (1988): 43-61; and "Ethics and Eschatology," *Ex Auditu* 6 (1990): 119-128.

[36] Yoder, "Ethics and Eschatology," 126.

[37] Yoder, *Politics of Jesus*, 232. This final chapter is a profound meditation on Yoder's claim that his understanding of theological pacifism challenges the notion that effectiveness can be central—even through nonviolent means.

[38] Ibid. Yoder is slightly more positive and nuanced in *Nevertheless*, where he says, "[My position] reckons seriously with the hopelessness of the world as it stands and yet affirms a gospel of hope. It shares the integrity of the principled views [named in the book], without their withdrawal from history. It includes the practical concerns of the programmatic views [which emphasize the effectiveness of nonviolent strategies] without placing its hope there" (137).

[39] Yoder, "Faith Is Resurrection," Christian Life Week Lectures, Bethel College, January 1964, unpublished manuscript (18). Located in author's files.

[40] Yoder, *Politics of Jesus*, 215, fn. 2, original emphasis.

[41] N. T. Wright has been making similar arguments now for a couple of decades. For one of his latest offerings, see *Surprised by Hope*, esp. 189-295.

[42] Commenting on recent studies of Paul, Luke Timothy Johnson raises this sort of question in "Reading Romans," *Christian Century* (January 15, 2008): 32-36.

[43] Yoder, *Nevertheless*, 133, original emphasis.

[44] Yoder, "The Kingdom as Social Ethic," in *Priestly Kingdom*, 94.

[45] Yoder, "The Believers Church and the Arms Race," in *For the Nations: Essays Public & Evangelical* (Grand Rapids: Eerdmans, 1997; reprinted, Wipf & Stock, 2002), 153.

[46] Yoder, *Nevertheless*, 135.

[47] Yoder, "The Kingdom as Social Ethic," in *Priestly Kingdom*, 92.

[48] Yoder, *Nevertheless*, 136.

[49] Yoder, *Body Politics*, 72-73. For a rich discussion of this way of viewing worship, see Bernd Wannenwetsch, *Political Worship: Ethics for Christian Citizens* (Oxford: Oxford University Press, 2004). See my review of the book in *The Mennonite Quarterly Review* (April 2008): 333-335.

[50] Yoder, *Nevertheless*, 135.

[51] Ibid., 136.

[52] One of the most insightful discussions I have seen of this subject, one dependent very much on Yoder, is Bryan Stone, *Evangelism: The Theology and Practice of Christian Witness* (Grand Rapids: Brazos Press, 2007), 175-221.

[53] Yoder, "A People in the World," in *Royal Priesthood*, 80, original emphasis. John C. Nugent's account of Yoder's views on vocation within this volume is important for understanding the quote I have just given, as it applies to ordinary Christians in their daily lives.

[54] For Yoder's own fullest statement, see "The Constantinian Sources of Western Social Ethics," in *Priestly Kingdom*, 135-147 and 209-212. One of the problems is that many who would criticize "Constantinianism"—or even more, "the religious right"—are not equally aware of how captive many of us are to modernity. On this, see Bryan Stone, *Evangelism after Christendom*, 131-170 (also see his lucid account of "The Constantinian Story," 115-130).

[55] Yoder, "The Otherness of the Church," in *Royal Priesthood*, 57.

[56] Ibid., 62, original emphasis.

[57] Ibid., 56.

[58] Yoder, "A People in the World," in *Royal Priesthood*, 81. Early in his writing career, Yoder often referred to this visibility of the church as the call to be distinctive or different. In a footnote to the 1994 version of this essay, Yoder offered the following reflections on this: "A few decades' observation of the debate on this point suggests that 'specific' would be better than 'distinctive' or 'different.' To be 'specific' is to belong to one's species, to befit one's kind. That will not always involve being different, although the cases where it 'makes a difference' will be the decisive ones" ("A People in the World," 81, fn. 19). For a longer discussion, see Yoder, "On Not Being Ashamed of the Gospel," 294.

[59] Yoder, "Why Ecclesiology Is Social Ethics," in *Royal Priesthood*, 118. He goes on to say, "This theme is so fundamental in the biblical witness, and since Constantine is so scandalous for many of us, that it must be a major theme within this essay" (118). Yoder also reflects on this claim in "Otherness of the Church," in *Royal Priesthood*. Cf. also Gerhard Lohfink, *Jesus and Community*, trans. John P. Galvin (Philadelphia: Fortress Press, 1984); Gerhard Lohfink, *Does God Need the Church?: Toward a Theology of the People of God*, trans. Linda M. Maloney (Collegeville, MN: Liturgical Press, 1999); and Christopher J. H. Wright, *The Mission of God* (Downers Grove, IL: InterVarsity Press, 2006).

[60] Yoder, "Otherness of the Church," in *Royal Priesthood*, 62; see also Yoder, "Why Ecclesiology Is Social Ethics," in *Royal Priesthood*, 116.

[61] Yoder, "Otherness of the Church," in *Royal Priesthood*, 61.

[62] Ibid., 61.

[63] Ibid., 63.

[64] Yoder, *Christian Witness to the State*, 20.

[65] Yoder, "A People in the World," in *Royal Priesthood*, 80, emphasis mine.

[66] Already in his early work, *The Christian Witness to the State*, Yoder said, "in biblical thought the church is properly a political entity, a *polis*" (18). *The Politics of Jesus* is really a book-length exposition of this claim. Arne Rasmusson picked up on this claim and provided a wonderful exposition of its contemporary significance in *The Church as Polis* (Notre Dame, IN: University of Notre Dame Press, 1995).

[67] Lesslie Newbigin, *Signs Amid the Rubble: The Purposes of God in Human History*, ed. Geoffrey Wainwright (Grand Rapids: Eerdmans, 2002), 106, emphasis mine. This captures in a nutshell the distinction between Yoder's writings and some of the more recent writings of Jim Wallis and Brian McLaren.

[68] Yoder, "Otherness of the Church," in *Royal Priesthood*, 61.

[69] Yoder, *Christian Witness to the State*, 41ff.

[70] See my essay in which I attempt to reflect on this set of issues: "The First Word Christians Have to Say about Violence Is 'Church': On Bonhoeffer, Baptists, and Becoming a Peace Church," in *Faithfulness & Fortitude: In Conversation with the Theological Ethics of Stanley Hauerwas*, ed. Mark Thiessen Nation and Samuel Wells (Edinburgh: T & T Clark, 2000), 83-115. John Webster has also written some helpful essays as reminders to keep the gospel of Jesus Christ central as we give a social witness. Cf. "The Church as Witnessing Community," *Scottish Bulletin of Evangelical Theology* 21 (2003): 21-33; and "Christ, Church and Reconciliation," in *Church and Word* (Edinburgh: T & T Clark, 2001), 211-230.

[71] Yoder, *Christian Witness to the State*, 32-33. Yoder has a lengthy footnote in which he further elaborates on the meaning of the term. Perhaps especially important for contemporary purposes is the reminder that he saw these middle axioms as mediating "between the norms of faith and the situation conditioned by unbelief" (33, fn. 3). Yoder connects middle axioms to reflections on contemporary issues in the late 1950s in *Christian Witness to the State*, 35.

[72] The two chief examples here would be the 1967 address, "A People in the World" (*Royal Priesthood*, 65-101) and the 1978 lecture, "The Believers Church and the Arms Race" (*For the Nations*, 148-161). Cf. also "The Kingdom as Social Ethics," in *Priestly Kingdom*, 80-101 and 201-202; and Yoder's set of eight "Christian Life Week Lectures," at Bethel College, Kansas, in 1964.

[73] Yoder, *Christian Witness to the State*, 17-18. Yoder indicates his own shift to using the word "political" primarily for the Christian community in a footnote to the 1994 reprinting of a 1954 essay: "Peace without Eschatology," in *Royal Priesthood*, 147, fn. 3.

[74] Yoder, *Christian Witness to the State*, 18, fn. 2. This book was originally published in 1964. A third printing had been issued by 1977. Although this printing does not indicate it has been revised, the footnotes have been updated, thus the possibility of referencing *The Politics of Jesus*.

[75] See the various relevant sections of the first half and most of the essays in the second half in Yoder, *Karl Barth and the Problem of War and Other Essays on Barth*, ed. Mark Thiessen Nation (Eugene, Ore.: Cascade Books, 2003). Cf. also "The Hermeneutics of Peoplehood" and "The Christian Case for Democracy," in *Priestly Kingdom*; "Why Ecclesiology Is Social Ethics" and "Sacrament as Social Process" in *Royal Priesthood*; the first two essays in *For the Nations*; and *Body Politics*. These are simply the most obvious examples. One could find echoes of this approach many other places in Yoder's writings. Branson Parler, in this volume, has given a very good account of Yoder's theological understanding of the liturgical life of the church as it relates to daily living.

[76] I have come to believe not only that Yoder's instinct to borrow from Barth is correct but that many who have divorced ethics from theology or social action from worship need reminders that Barth can offer. Among secondary sources I would mention Eberhard Busch, *Barth* (Nashville: Abingdon Press, 2008); idem, *The Great Passion: An Introduction to Karl Barth's Theology* (Grand Rapids: Eerdmans, 2004); idem, *Karl Barth: His Life from Letters and Autobiographical Texts* (Philadelphia: Fortress Press, 1976); and books by John Webster, Joseph Mangina, and George Hunsinger.

[77] Yoder, "Otherness of the Church," in *Royal Priesthood*, 61. By now, some may be saying that Yoder's approach does indeed fit H. Richard Niebuhr's characterization of "Christ against culture." This term is taken from Niebuhr's influential book, *Christ and Culture* (New York: Harper & Row, 1951). However, it is hard to know how such a dualistic notion can fit the man who, at the beginning of his career, wrote *Christian Witness to the State* and continued to write on ways to think about constructive engagement with the world until his untimely death in 1997. Anyone who continues to wonder

should, among other things, read Yoder, "How H. Richard Niebuhr Reasoned: A Critique of *Christ and Culture*," in *Authentic Transformation: A New Vision of Christ and Culture* (Nashville: Abingdon Press, 1996), 31-89 and 271-284; Philip D. Kenneson, *Beyond Sectarianism: Re-Imagining Church and World* (Harrisburg, PA: Trinity Press International, 1999; reprinted, Wipf & Stock); Craig A. Carter, *Rethinking Christ and Culture: A Post-Christendom Perspective* (Grand Rapids: Brazos Press, 2006); and Mark Thiessen Nation, *John Howard Yoder: Mennonite Patience, Evangelical Witness, Catholic Convictions*. All of these works challenge such notions.

[78] Yoder, *Nevertheless*, 133-134, original emphasis.

[79] Ibid., 138-139.

Chapter Three

Unity with Integrity
John H. Yoder's Ecumenical Theology and Practice

Gayle Gerber Koontz

What might John Howard Yoder have to say to a would-be unity movement? As a guest in an ongoing conversation about the meaning of Christian unity among those who stand in the Stone-Campbell tradition, this question is not mine to answer.[1] But Yoder does offer substantive theological reflection on church unity from the perspective of a particular "free church" perspective, a perspective which might fruitfully interact with the insight and experience of different branches of the Stone-Campbell Movement.

In general, Yoder's understanding of interchurch relations can be characterized by *ecumenical integrity* and *unity of fellowship in conversation*.[2] Both his theology and his practice reflected the joining of the conviction that God was in Christ reconciling the world to God's self and the subsequent gift of the ongoing ministry of reconciliation to those who receive this good news in Christ. These convictions grounded a passion for engaging in relationships across denominational and theological boundaries as well as a responsibility to testify with integrity to the understanding of the gospel we have been given. At the very least this meant for Yoder that Christians should embody unity in commitment to conversation with each other. It also meant that we should strive toward unity in discipleship, following Jesus Christ faithfully before and in encounter with the watching world.

Yoder's views on interchurch unity grew out of a dynamic interaction of a number of elements. First was Yoder's reading of Scripture that undergirded a Christ-centered, reconciling theological ethic and a trust that God inspires hermeneutic communities—local congregations or other visible Christian groups—who faithfully seek to discern God's will for specific times and places in light of Scripture (Acts 15). The Bible both calls Christians toward one another and serves as the common authority around which Christians from different traditions or who hold different theological views can gather. Second, his belief that the Spirit can speak to and through everyone in these discerning communities implied certain practices and attitudes for ecumenical conversation. Third was Yoder's reading of church history and his post-World War II observations of European state churches that led him to call for a "disavowal of Constantine" in cross-national mission relationships and to emphasize the transnational character of the church. Fourth, his doctoral study of Anabaptist disputations encouraged his awareness of and commitment to theological integrity and persistence in difficult intra-Christian relationships. Finally, a less well-known factor was the significant experience Yoder had with interchurch organizations and the related personal relationships he fostered with a wide range of Christians from different traditions. For example, he spent thirty years teaching at Notre Dame University, part-time for the first ten years, full-time after 1977, which drew him into direct conversations with Roman Catholics. The interaction of these elements gave rise to an ecumenical theology and practice that addressed the realities of interchurch life in the last half of the twentieth century with creativity and Christian integrity.

Interchurch Relationships

Interchurch unity was a life-long commitment of Yoder's. He did not just think about it; he fostered it. Both the restorationist and the Mennonite traditions have valued discipleship—clear integrity between what we say and do in relation to Jesus. For that reason, it is fitting to note some of Yoder's involvements in interchurch relations. I will highlight several significant involvements other than Yoder's well-known participation in the Reformed-Anabaptist conversations at Puidoux in the 1950s[3] and his many years of engagement in World Council of Churches and Faith and Order discussions. I will not address the influence on his interchurch thinking of his long association at Notre Dame and his academic involvements in professional societies.[4] These are areas for further research, but even without detailing them, it is clear that Yoder's interchurch theological ethics grew out of and continued to shape his own practice.

Interchurch Mission and Peace Work

Yoder began engaging significant Christian leaders from other traditions at an early age, writing "Reinhold Niebuhr and Christian Pacifism" in 1954 when he was twenty-seven. He produced an amazing amount of correspondence with those he met, beginning with his time in Europe. In addition to maintaining relationships with people he learned to know through the International Fellowship of Reconciliation, other peace groups, and the Puidoux conferences, Yoder carried on conversation with those he met as a World Council of Churches peace group theological adviser starting in 1968. He continued in this latter role for more than thirty years until his death in 1997.[5]

In addition, Yoder's relationships spanned the liberal-conservative theological divide. He lived in France among the French Mennonites, a still-traditional, parochial, and theologically conservative group in the 1950s. Yoder's interaction was not superficial. He married a French Mennonite woman, Anne Marie Guth, and served as an invited consultant to the churches, working respectfully with this variety of evangelical Mennonites and the conservative/fundamentalist groups to whom they related.

From 1954-57, Yoder worked part-time on the staff of the Mennonite Board of Missions from his base in Europe. From 1959—when he moved to Elkhart, Indiana—until 1965, he served full-time with the Mission Board, and he continued as a consultant from 1965-70, writing regular memos to staff. In his WCC role and his work as a missions administrator Yoder connected with such well-known mission theologians as Lesslie Newbigin, David J. Bosch, and W. A. Visser t'Hooft. Newbigin reported that Yoder wrote the most penetrating critique of his book *The Household of God* (1953) that Newbigin had received.[6] Bosch—who had been a student with Yoder in Basel, but lost contact with Yoder after Bosch returned to South Africa—happened to see a manuscript of Yoder's "From Exodus to Exile" and immediately asked permission to publish it in *Missionalia*, a journal that Bosch had recently founded. Yoder's paper helped make the case for opposition to apartheid, which Bosch sought to strengthen. This reconnection led to Bosch inviting Yoder, in spite of the controversial conscientious objector stance for which Mennonites were known in South Africa, to be one of twenty foreign guests to participate in the 1979 Southern Africa Christian Leadership Assembly, involving thousands of South Africans.[7]

Wilbert R. Shenk, a Mennonite missiologist who joined the Mennonite Board of Missions staff when Yoder began seminary teaching in 1965, noted that the mission board assignment had given Yoder a special platform for deepening his awareness of the dysfunctional divisions in the church and for supporting reconciling practices. This role gave him flexibility and an official location from which he developed contacts in the U.S. and abroad with a wide range of groups, both ecumenical and evangelical. And he exercised his influence on decision makers in other agencies. Yoder attended meetings of evangelical mission leaders at Winona Lake, Indiana and of ecumenical leaders in Geneva.[8] He began to develop more formal relations with the National Council of Churches and the National Association of Evangelicals.[9] "He refused to be pigeonholed," Shenk said. "Staff were also astonished at his ability to communicate no matter who he was with—rural village people in Africa or theological leaders in Europe."[10]

Yoder's mission-related work gave him numerous opportunities to cooperate across denominational lines. In 1954, while still living in Basel and serving as a part-time mission administrator, there was a terrible earthquake in Oran, Algeria. Yoder helped send a team of volunteers to engage in the reconstruction of houses for Algerians, in the process developing alliances with Church World Service and various French non-governmental organizations.[11] After assuming full-time work with the Mission Board in Elkhart, Indiana, in 1965, Yoder made particularly striking strategic contributions to the church situation in Nigeria. The fuller story, described in a recent article by David A. Shank, indicates the extreme dysfunction among Christian groups there, each imploring Western church groups to support separate church building and related projects.[12] Mennonites decided to work with some of the marginalized and divided indigenous churches, providing Bible teaching. According to Shenk, Yoder's leadership was remarkable in responding to these churches and designing a strategy for bringing together groups that functioned independently. Some of this leadership was practical, some theological. Edwin I. Weaver, a mission board worker in Nigeria, discouraged by the factionalism among Christians there, said that when he opened a missionary barrel and found Yoder's *Ecumenical Movement and the Faithful Church* on the top, he read it immediately. It spoke exactly to their situation.[13]

Yoder's mission board connections also led him to participate in conversations among various Mennonite and evangelical leaders regarding the theological viability of the church growth movement, encouraged by Donald McGavran and others. The substance of these discussions, available in *The Challenge of Church Growth,* demonstrates Yoder's incisive criticism.[14] He was especially concerned about the lack of attention to social ethics in church growth ecclesiology. But his manner during the conversations, Wilbert Shenk remembers, "was always courteous, always taking the other person seriously, seeking to be humble."[15] Shenk observed Yoder in his interchurch work trying, on the one hand, to encourage Mennonites to engage the world—not to set up boundaries that keep people "other"— and, on the other hand, "criticizing McGavran for being so open to others that some essential defining aspects of the church are lost."[16]

Evangelical-Ecumenical Conversations

Even less well known because the meetings were not publicized is Yoder's involvement with what came to be called the Malone conversations. These were a series of meetings that Yoder was involved in from 1961-1969 between North American mission leaders associated with the National Council of Churches and the National Association of Evangelicals.[17] Following the merger of the International Missionary Council (IMC) with the World Council of Churches (WCC) in 1961, after several years of discussion and negotiation, relations between ecumenical and evangelical mission-minded leaders deteriorated, each group criticizing the other. Evangelical leaders suspected that the "liberal" World Council of Churches was trying to extend its control over mission churches and also charged them with "universalism."[18] Leaders from the mainstream Protestant churches perceived evangelicals to be theologically intolerant and narrow. Shenk remembers that "there were important theological issues at stake, but the tone of the exchange was 'less than Christian.'"[19]

Two well-trusted bridge builders—R. Pierce Beaver at the University of Chicago and Everett Cattell, the Quaker president of Malone College in Kenton, Ohio, both of whom had been missionaries, in China and India respectively—and several "neutral" figures including John Yoder, considered how to deal with the poisoned atmosphere. They set up a gathering at Lake Forest, Illinois, that subsequently became an annual event at Malone College. The meetings deliberately brought together equal numbers of evangelical and ecumenical leaders who had been criticizing each other but who had not been talking face-to-face.

The meetings were kept off the record since some of the evangelical participants said that they would be in trouble with their constituents if it were known that they were talking with people from the National Council of Churches.[20] Structured by the presentation of papers that addressed agreed upon topics followed by mutual critique, the meetings "had an extraordinary leavening effect." A number of evangelical people who had been part of these events testified to Shenk that it was the most transforming event that had happened to them. He heard a well-known evangelical leader say more than once that "those meetings and that company we kept made me into a brother tolerant of other stripes of theology." [21]

"The various leaders were bearing false witness against each other," Shenk noted. "When they had to face and listen to each other they realized they were guilty of very bad behavior. Yoder was instrumental in the process. He demonstrated time and again the ability to listen carefully to someone's questions and to respond directly and thoughtfully to it, helping the main players speak more clearly. In many ways the process exemplified the genius and convictions of Yoder." For him, interchurch reconciliation was more than a theological proposition.

Believers Church Conferences

A final illustration of Yoder's substantial work in nurturing cross-denominational relationships was his almost thirty-year involvement with the Believers Church Conferences that brought together constellations of Baptists, Mennonites, Brethren, Quakers, restorationist groups, and several pentecostal groups. The idea originated as a "gleam in the minds of Johannnes Oosterbaan and his friend. J. Reling," the former a *Doopsgezind* (Mennonite) and the latter a Baptist, both from the Netherlands. Yoder wrote that Oosterbaan "was especially concerned that representatives of those member churches of the World Council which held officially to 'believers' baptism,' such as the Baptists, Disciples, and Church of the Brethren, were unwilling to consider that 'as a subject formally requiring aggressive ecumenical dialogue.'"[22] Oosterbaan attempted to set up a believers church conference in the Netherlands and invited Yoder to speak. When the conference fell through, he encouraged Yoder to urge Mennonites and Baptists in North America to "make common cause to further the ecumenical conversation."[23]

Through Yoder's suggestion James Leo Garrett Jr. and the faculty at Southern Baptist Theological Seminary in Louisville, Kentucky, picked up the idea and hosted a formative conference, "The Concept of the Believers Church," in June of 1967. Nearly 150 people attended. Yoder presented a paper, perceived by some as the most stimulating and exciting at the conference.[24] The participants at the conference appointed a "continuation committee." Yoder was not only a member of this ongoing planning group, but served as co-chair along with Brethren member Donald Durnbaugh for the next eleven conferences until 1996, the year before Yoder died.

Yoder's interchurch enthusiasm was evident from the beginning. Franklin Littell, involved in the planning for the initial conference, was concerned that of the ten members of the planning committee there were five Baptists, no Methodists, and no Disciples or "Christians." Yoder eagerly registered his "hope that neither the Peace Churches nor the Baptizers nor anybody else will define the ground of our dialogue so narrowly as to exclude Congregationalists, Methodists, and even Missouri Synod Lutherans and Roman Catholics who are moving along the path of classical Free Church concerns."[25] While in later discussion the planners decided to narrow the conference to believers churches (Free Churches would include Methodists and Congregationalists), in his administrative role Yoder continued to build relationships with individuals from the marginally represented groups. He took responsibility for organizing correspondence and helped arrange the appointment of Everett Ferguson of Abilene Christian College to the committee. Yoder also helped with "identifying a theological mode of operation."[26]

Yoder described the structure in the conference series as "radically Campbellite, depending for continuity and also for identity on the choice of topic made by the institutions inclined to invite us."[27] Such an informal approach was seen as "appropriate to an ecumenical vision which foresaw 'no central administration, no defined captive constituency, and no regular calendar.'" The Louisville group rejected an ecumenical vision "which seeks to relate the 'faith' or the 'order' or the administrative structures of entire 'denominations' or 'communions' and which makes decisions by instructed delegates, proportional representation, and majority votes."[28] Durnbaugh wrote that "these negations were designed to buttress the essentially congregational authority of church unity." Therefore conferences have only been held occasionally as sponsorship emerged, "as the Spirit has moved."[29]

As is evident from the archival correspondence, the between-conference consultation of Yoder and Durnbaugh with others was an important shaping factor in this set of evolving interchurch theological conversations. On several occasions Yoder presented papers as well. Once again it is possible to see his interchurch vision and practice feeding each other.

Yoder's views on interchurch relations, connected to his believers church perspective and tested in a variety of settings, were articulated in a number of articles and memos over the years. While his emphases varied depending on the audience he addressed, the overall contour of his interchurch theology, described in the remaining part of this essay, remained constant—a strong biblically-based call to Christian unity with integrity.

Ecumenical Integrity and Christian Unity

Christian Diversity

As others have done, Yoder delineated different kinds of theological and ethical diversity among Christians.[30] He affirmed diversity which arises when people are faithful in different situations with different challenges. Conversation among such Christian groups can lead to healthy reconsideration of provincial views and underline the need to root Christian witness "more centrally in the authority and character of Christ."[31] Yoder recommended limited pluralism in ethical styles as well. Representatives of different inherited styles of peace witness, he wrote, "should come into the decision and discussion process with the intentional desire of seeing the various styles interpenetrate, rather than with a sense of moral obligation to impose only one style on the other participants."[32]

The second type of diversity Yoder identified is that which Christians tolerate because more urgent issues are at hand and not all issues can be pursued at once. He noted that after one ecumenical meeting issues that participants had earlier fought about were withdrawn into a "penumbra of polite pluralism." "This is no reproach," he continued. "Ecumenical movements don't have to discuss all the issues all the time. Some issues to which a new generation turns may well be of more immediate importance, without claiming that the older ones have been resolved."[33]

Third, Yoder described diversity that results from unfaithfulness, false doctrine, and concrete disobedience.[34] Especially striking to Yoder, in post World War II Europe, was the tragic fact that Christians from one nation had not only killed, but justified killing Christians from another. Later, with some experience in mission administration and ecumenical-evangelical tensions and in the midst of the tumult of the civil rights movement in the U.S. and the development of liberation movements worldwide, Yoder wrote that the real divisions in the churches are between "rich and poor, between liberal and conservative, between races, between east and west. These divisions go down through the middle of existing denominations and are the separations which really would demand reconciling initiative."[35] This kind of diversity "is no blessing; the goal of full agreement in Christ must, though concretely unattainable, be our working hypothesis."

The question of truth, or engaging our assumptions about truth, cannot be set aside. According to Yoder, the idea that all denominations or Christian propositions have equal partial validity refuses to take human sin seriously enough. Such an attitude does not signal a healthy tolerance or virtuous humility, but indifference to questions of truth and ethics.[36] If the principles one holds are true only for oneself, why work so hard to maintain them, he asked. And if they are true before God, then they are true for other Christians.[37] "Not all varieties of vision—or of ethics—can fit together within a tolerant pluralism. What we need is tools to identify and denounce error, while welcoming variety and celebrating complementarity."[38]

Yoder recognized that some theologians account for the wholeness and unity of complex phenomena (e.g., God) by juxtaposing partial views of them gained from different points of vantage and then combining them and making legitimate reconciliations. Yoder felt that such a position, while it profoundly recognizes the "limitations of all human wisdom and the destructive effort of pride," elevates the virtue of humility to such an extent that it is no longer possible to vigorously claim the task of normative theology and ethics. Overemphasis on humility leads to reticence to express value judgments and may not, he concludes, engender the most desirable form of Christian unity.[39]

"What is really being lost, when we abandon the vision of being one body, is the glory of God and the credibility of the gospel witness. What is wrong with a divided church is not reduced efficiency, but a reduced gospel."[40] For unity to be meaningful at all, the church must discern and reject heresy. "The question of truth is part of the concern for unity."[41]

Faithfulness and Apostasy

Although Yoder felt it was important to define apostasy and error clearly, he did not assume the primary mode of error among Christians is doctrinal. He specifically challenged, on New Testament grounds, the idea that doctrine is more essential than church order or ethics as a test of faith.[42] In his reading of the New Testament, unity in ethical commitment was as essential as unity in faith and worship for the early church. He noted that in his own Anabaptist tradition church leaders accepted some daring thinkers with doctrinal deviations because "of their convictions that discipleship mattered first."[43] While creeds may be fruitful in defining the nature of a difficulty in Christian faith, they are not the sole test of faith, nor is it appropriate to focus the bulk of one's energies on debating them.[44] He also pointed out that in our contemporary situation it becomes harder and harder to define heresy in terms of doctrine because we do not know whether we are speaking the same language as that of the communities who defined the doctrines. Ethics, on the other hand, is a more helpful focus because "we do have a common world in which we behave because we behave with each other."[45]

At the same time, Yoder recognized that ethics must also respond to changing historical situations. Christians should neither determine apostasy by legalistically applying moral rules nor attempt to adopt every New Testament idea or practice. Ethical decision-making and biblically based theological reflection are carried out by a local community of believers who seek together God's intention in specific new situations in light of Scripture. Given this mode of interpretation and decision making, the most serious identifiable apostasy for Yoder involved refusal to engage in a corporate process of celebration and discernment which is shaped and guided by Scripture. Yoder underlined this corporate character of Christian thought and life in relation to the ecumenical context when he wrote that, in this case, apostasy is not so much doctrinal or moral as a congregation's failure to receive admonition and counsel from sister churches.[46]

The corporate process which Yoder advocated regards Scripture as the primary authority and standard that participants accept in the common search for truth and right. Yoder recognized that different individuals, particularly those who come from different Christian traditions, may bring different principles of interpretation and sources of theological authority to bear on the same Scripture. Yoder intended to guard against arbitrary interpretation by "constant recourse to the entire testimony of the New Testament, rejecting the concentration upon any one 'canon within the canon,' and rejecting as well the choice of any one postcanonical development." This kind of appeal to Scripture over the heads of all particular traditions "is the most ecumenical position possible."[47] Yoder did not intend by his heavy emphasis on Scripture to disavow other sources of revelation. Rather, "the question is how to keep them subordinate to the centrality of the guidance of Jesus."[48]

For Yoder, a community process of interpretation involved establishing what the meaning of the biblical material was in its historical, cultural, and theological context and then discerning how this material related to subsequent historical developments and theological and ethical understandings. Yoder could not affirm a serial or cumulative pluralism which describes and accepts all developments within Christian history because it denies the possibility of heresy or apostasy. At the same time, he rejected the position that a simple restitution of the New Testament pattern is the only appropriate choice. He suggested rather that there is valid and invalid development and that the ongoing task is to test whether or not the development is the work of the Holy Spirit.[49]

For Yoder, the process of discernment was not wooden application of New Testament practices to radically divergent historical contexts. Even in his early work Yoder emphasized that the Bible not only calls Christians to faithfulness but also provides a mandate to change. If Christians were simply to duplicate all New Testament patterns and commands, he pointed out, there would be no need to "test the spirits" (1 John 3:24-4:3), a phrase which refers to a norming process within the New Testament itself. In fact, according to Acts, "the Spirit continually forced innovations on the church, which the organization itself was not ready to undertake."[50] It is important to remember, he wrote in "Is There Historical Development of Theological Thought?" that no congregation is fully within one tradition. Nor should every Christian or congregation be exactly like another, since they are responsive to different times, places, and questions.[51]

Though not all new practices or ideas need to be found in and affirmed by Scripture, Yoder warned that we should be suspect of developments that are clearly *counter* to Scripture. He believed that reference to the "New Testament example and precept is not only a useful ecumenical criterion for asking about the appropriateness of proposed changes; it is especially significant as a guide in distinguishing between central and peripheral matters."[52] When the New Testament example *is* modified, it should be made by a studied, prayerful decision of a congregation, it should be clear what principle is involved, and the group should be convinced that the involved principle is served more faithfully by the change.[53]

Yoder moved beyond these general guidelines to identify specific examples of church traditions which in his judgment have gone astray. He pointed to the church's betrayal of the feminist elements of the gospel, the process of the veneration of saints moving into a new paganism, and the hoarding of wealth as forms of apostasy.[54] His most extensive comments had to do with the change in Christian views on the morality of violence. Yoder identified the movement from an early pacifism to just war theory—a change which occurred when Christians in the Constantinian era first acquired substantial public power—as a development which is counter to the New Testament emphasis and therefore likely signals serious apostasy.

Yoder took an additional step when he redefined "sectarian" in contrast to Ernst Troeltsch and H. Richard Niebuhr, who defined sectarian from the point of view of those standing within the major Christian streams. If the New Testament understands the unity of the church as a universal bond of faith, he wrote, "we can understand that the real sectarianism, in the biblical sense of unchristian divisiveness, was the formation of churches bound to the state and identified with the nation." Anabaptists, Brethren, Quakers, and Moravians, who were largely free from such ties, who were missionary in focus, who were more biblical than creedal, and who are often referred to as "sectarian," were the real proponents of ecumenical Christianity.[55]

Reconciling Conversation

In spite of his strong views on specific forms of apostasy, Yoder did not believe that Christians should separate themselves from Christians with whom they disagree. Rather, he called for reconciling conversation. This approach meant he needed to address Christian methods for dealing with disagreements. In relation to this, he distinguished two levels of corporate responsibility. One is to the specific local congregation of believers of which one is a member. The second is to Christian groups beyond that congregation.

In both cases, Yoder affirmed that unity is a positive Christian duty. The basis for unity is first of all theological. Ephesians 2-3 and Romans 9-11 both indicate that the gathering together of different kinds of people in one body is itself a central element of the gospel.[56] Yoder therefore reminded Christians that "the Church is bigger than our own back yard" and encouraged them to express unity in common service, witness, and worship, and to become acquainted with each other's concerns and needs by relating to Christians in other locations, offering reciprocal admonition, and creating limited organizational unions.[57] But Yoder made a basic distinction between expectations for unity on a congregational level and expectations for unity on a supra-congregational level. On the congregational level Yoder called for unity in discipleship and discipline, whereas on an interchurch level he called for commitment to ongoing conversation—noting, however, that wherever possible we should also strive for interchurch unity in discipleship.

Yoder emphasized that the primary focus for the experience and expression of unity should be the local congregation: "the group which meets with frequency and [with] continuity of membership and discipline."[58] His understanding of congregational unity was directly tied to what he saw as a New Testament emphasis on corporate responsibility among followers of Christ. For Yoder, baptism upon confession of faith was not a radically individual act, but "the foundation of the most sweeping communal responsibility for the life of all members."[59] Such responsibility is more than harmonious collaboration in common projects or worship. In his writing on "binding and loosing," he frequently cited Matthew 18, noting that Jesus calls his followers to have responsibility to the ones with whom they disagree about essential items of faith and practice. If such responsibility is ignored, the entire life of the congregation suffers. Yoder interpreted Paul in 1 Corinthians 5 and 6 as saying that "there is a kind of moral solidarity linking all the members of the body, so that if individuals persist in disobedience within the fellowship, their guilt is no longer merely the moral responsibility of those individuals alone, but becomes a kind of collective blame shared by the whole body."[60] He also referred to Galatians 6:1, which also assumes responsibility for erring members: "You who are endowed with the Spirit must set him right again very gently. Look to yourself, each one of you: you may be tempted too. Help one another to carry these heavy loads."[61]

The most common temptation in our time, Yoder suggested, is to assume that respect for others means not challenging another's personal decisions or actions. This assumption often ends in sweeping relativism. To be consistent with a commitment to follow Jesus' example of nonresistant love, a Christian should take care not to *coerce* others in their decision making, but "within the respect for the freedom of the other party to make his decisions one is responsible to put issues to him."[62] The biblical interpretation of difference, as Yoder read it, is that "the more important the difference is, the more binding is our obligation to work at it."[63]

Although Yoder affirmed the "rule of Christ" and the appropriateness of church discipline in order to maintain unity in discipleship in local congregations, he did not expect the same degree of accountability or unity in supra-congregational groups. His rationale for this approach was not simply pragmatic, but biblical and theological. He pointed, for example, to the pattern the Apostle Paul established in his ministry and to an understanding of baptism as incorporation into the church.[64]

Yoder noted that, in spite of Paul's disagreements with the Judaizers in Jerusalem, he went the second mile to maintain fellowship with them, "thus assuming a kind of continuing unity with those with whom he was not in agreement about an essential item."[65] That Paul worked so diligently to preserve these relations should teach Christians that they "are not authorized to break off relations of fellowship on a level other than that of congregational discipline, except when the initiative is not ours."[66] That is, if another party refuses to recognize one's integrity and reconciling intent, or if they refuse to question extra-scriptural authorities or to follow the claims laid upon them by the church, then it may be necessary to "accept, reluctantly, and only for a time, the break."[67] "Thus the fact that in a given interchurch situation other churches are unfaithful is no reason for not conversing with them; that reason exists only if they refuse to listen."[68] Limiting fellowship to churches with which one agrees is divisive, he concluded, "because it basically questions the validity of the faith of those whom it excludes."[69] Unity of fellowship in conversation does not mean that a person or congregation approves of the present belief and behavior of another group of Christians, but that they care enough about their relationship in Christ to seriously challenge them regarding what the gospel claims and implies.[70]

In addition to having a strong congregational polity, Yoder was skeptical about larger union efforts, especially institutional unions, because they necessarily focus on common denominators. He explicitly rejected a lowest common denominator approach for ecumenical unions because it tends to estrange local leadership and it "isolates itself from the broadening and deepening effects of conversation across the whole spectrum of Christian convictions."[71] Yoder's hesitancy to embrace institutional unity also stemmed from his experience as a minority church observer and participant within the World Council of Churches. For example, on the issue of church unity Yoder noted that if most Christians assume that the problems that divide Christians are located primarily between denominations, then the efforts made to express existing unity and to process diversity will be constructed on that model. In such a situation it is unavoidable that those who, like Yoder, define church primarily as a local, visible fellowship will always be "meeting in a context defined on someone else's terms."[72] For Yoder to have accepted the institutional model of unity as central would have involved some substantial compromise of his ecclesiology.

Although Yoder argued for the local gathering as the appropriate place to experience the deepest levels of Christian unity, he did not limit such encounter to the local context. From asserting the priority of the local congregation, which he wrote must be affirmed biblically, "it is a great and illegitimate step to move to the *exclusivity* of the local congregation."[73]

According to Yoder, denominations or other supra-congregational bodies are justified as instruments of fellowship, service, or witness when

1. doing the job alone would be wasteful or impossible;
2. the larger body assumes that the authority of the local congregation as "church" takes precedence over its own authority; and
3. when the larger group is open to new needs including its own extinction if it is no longer needed.[74]

Such organizations may be of short-term duration or they may be permanent. They may also be defined by joint tasks, and some may explicitly seek to deal with disagreements among groups of believers. Yoder pointed out that what congregations do together depends on the degree of agreement among them[75]: "Less unity is needed to converse than to commune; less unity is needed to evangelize together than to baptize together; less to advocate morality than to apply discipline; less to attack liberalism together than to agree together on what is sound doctrine. The essential for obedience in this realm is to go neither farther nor less far than existing agreement permits."[76]

Yoder recommended therefore that churches and individuals commit themselves to at least a minimal form of unity—unity in conversation. In addition, each person who confesses Christ is responsible to converse with other confessors particularly "at those points where, in life and doctrine, our given unity is hidden by disagreement."[77] Christians are released from this obligation only when they have reached agreement or when the "interlocutor refuses further to converse."[78]

Yoder's belief is that unity in Christ will be given as Christians express faith "which dares take the Brother seriously to the point of grappling with him in true conversation, in faith which will love and serve him" even if that means subordinating national, cultural, or other scriptural loyalties, "in faith which will be ethically responsible for him to the point of demanding of him the same full obedience" one demands of oneself. "To accept less, to believe less, than that *this* is the unity . . . would be to deny the Lord."[79]

In an ecumenical context, therefore, unity is neither present consensus nor compromise, but a relational unity, a process of "being led forward beyond where we were before into the discovery of a position which will not say that any of us were right in the past but will renew our unity because it deepens the definition of our mission."[80] This conception of unity is not preoccupied with institutional union schemes that tend to focus on common denominators, but seeks to lift up rather than minimize differences. Efforts to make every denomination conform, "thereby weakening the variety of options in the ecumenical conversations," Yoder writes, "is a counter-productive way to try to foster conversation and unity."[81]

Conviction and Humility

In a postmodern context where the question of "truth" is bracketed or redefined in terms of internal systemic coherence, Yoder's call to make room in interchurch relationships for strong assertions of particular denominational, congregational, or individual convictions can appear narrow and even arrogant. Yoder felt free to be vigorous in his epistemological and normative claims not simply when he believed he was right, but only as long as the structure of his relationship with his Christian conversation partners left them free to reject his views if they wished. For Yoder, the concern to protect the freedom of his "adversary" in conversation did not stem simply from a modern Western ideal of the freedom of the individual or from recognition of cultural relativity, but from the center of his theology itself. The God he saw revealed through the crucified Christ calls, confronts, and persuades—but does not coerce anyone, including the enemies of God, to love God or to act justly. Such a pattern of invitational love is characteristic not only of God-human relationships but is appropriate for relationships between humans as well. True unity in conversation depends less on the degree of humility dialogue partners communicate to each other than it does on the genuine freedom of both parties not to be coerced into agreement.

Yoder's theological commitment to congregational discernment and discipline as well as to broader unity of fellowship in conversation also provided a counterbalance to error and pride. He believed that if his specific views and judgments were wrong, their weaknesses would be revealed as they were tested through strong argument with others in the congregation and wider church. He assumed that arguing with conviction for a constructive, normative vision of reality or for specific ethical principles would be more valuable to another's "free" search for theological and ethical coherence than a position which qualified itself so thoroughly that it would not forcefully challenge others to explore it. He further argued that it is a deeper mark of humility consistently and intentionally to submit one's strong personal views to others and then to modify one's views when others offer good reasons to do so than it is to repeat the obvious statement that one's views are limited.[82]

Yoder sought to balance the twin concerns of judgment and love in his vision for interchurch relations. That combination is extremely difficult to maintain in practice. A prophetic voice is frequently judgmental and self-righteous; a pastoral one may be non-normative to a fault. Upholding an ethical standard like nonresistant or nonviolent love in interchurch settings for many years, as Yoder did, raised this tension forcefully. How could he hold to such a moral standard without self-righteously communicating that Christians who reluctantly accepted "justified" violence were not only "apostate" but second-class Christians?

Yoder attempted to avoid what might be called judgmental rigidity in ethics by employing different types of "patience" in relation to those whose judgments were different from his own. He identified a "string of different kinds of 'patience' which qualify the application of any ethical standard."[83] Although Yoder's exploration of these types of patience specifically addresses ethical absolutes, they could also apply to expectations regarding essential theological convictions. I have summarized below some of the nineteen kinds of patience that have particular relevance for interchurch relations.

1. Pedagogical patience takes account of the fact that human learning takes place in sequences and stages.
2. Corrective patience is needed when there are proper corrective uses of arguments that are not ultimately valid.
3. Pastoral patience takes account of the dynamics of the will, trauma and healing, trust and commitment.
4. Ecumenical patience is the result of our accepting willingly and not just grudgingly that we are conversing with people who have been educated otherwise than ourselves and have a different frame of integrity and accountability.
5. Multicultural or cosmopolitan patience is needed whenever there is cultural or linguistic diversity.
6. Meeting any interlocutor on his/her own terms (e.g., a pacifist who chooses to discuss war on just war terms with nonpacifists) requires patience that is a "spirituality and a lifestyle."
7. Corporate patience is dictated by respect for the roles of others in institutions.
8. Collegial patience is needed by the outvoted theologian or minority—coming to terms with a dominant view without being convinced by it.
9. The patience of repentance requires us to recognize that even if we believe our position is the correct one, we must recognize that it has often been represented inadequately or even unfaithfully.
10. The modest patience of sobriety in finitude is our recognition that we may be wrong and that "the certainty in which we have to act one day at a time must never claim finality."
11. There is the honest patience of ignorance.
12. There is the apocalyptic patience of waiting in hope.
13. There is the audience-sensitive patience of not making a point that a particular audience is not willing or able to hear.

Such considerations, Yoder suggested, could apply to "any kind of decent person taking a position by conviction on any important subject." But, he reflected, such patience might be "heightened if one held, as I do, to the view that the dignity of the enemy is such that one should especially love one's enemy and not do violence to his or her dignity. They would be especially weighty if one were convinced, as I am, that membership in a believing community is voluntary rather than imposed by a parental covenant. They would be especially appropriate if one believed, as I do, that decision making in the church should be free from manipulation by the power of the civil order. They would be especially appropriate if one believed, as I do, that authority in the faith community is decentralized and consensual rather than pontifical."[84] For Yoder a profound, peaceable patience is ultimately rooted in Jesus' call to participate in God's coming kingdom and Jesus' own example of prophetic, suffering love.

Sociological Exclusivism

One of the serious challenges to Yoder's strong emphasis on the visible, local church as the primary place where God's good news through Christ is embodied is the problem of sociological exclusivism. The dynamics of group-identity formation and maintenance, symbol-making, and boundary-keeping can be obstacles to building interchurch relationships. While particularism and insularity are dangers that sociologically distinct Christian groups must face, it is also the case that such groups serve as the context for worship, community life, and mission that "shape individuals and communities into conformity to the mind of Christ."[85] Local churches serve as a context for the development of virtues that are of value in interchurch relationships. As George Lindbeck put it paradoxically, "an open society needs doctrinally committed religious communities to inculcate the moral and creedal absolutes that are necessary in order to maintain openness."[86] In social contexts where many people's primary loyalties are to nation, ethnic group, or individual success, for example, perhaps a certain amount of "sociological sectarianism" is required if the church wants to maintain "highly deviant convictions in an inhospitable environment."[87] Particular Christian communities may need to function as "plausibility structures" that can nurture loyalty to an ecumenical community which transcends nation, race, and gender and can respond with careful respect to those who are not part of that community.[88]

Yoder's interchurch theological ethic guards against Christian withdrawal into local sociological ghettos in two primary ways. One is commitment to the unity of fellowship in conversation with the wider church.

Another is the church's outward movement into the world. Yoder believed that any reformulation of Christian faith "which would not necessarily eventuate in a missionary imperative," given the biblical witness and the call to love God and others, is not genuine Christian faith. Part of the transformation that has occurred in the process of outward focused mission and community service efforts since the nineteenth century was the breaking down of the provincial perspectives that had marked individuals, congregations, and wider church alliances.

In pointing Christians again toward the "politics of Jesus," Yoder highlighted biblical sources that directed Christians to respond with care to "strangers" and without retaliation to "enemies" in surrounding societies. Some of the most difficult sociological barriers to transcend are those connected with social, national, and economic power and influence, including those same barriers between churches. The attempt to build up strong sociological communities—ones that can embody openness to the Other (especially enemies), uphold the dignity of those who are different, and foster hope for human reconciliation—may indeed risk failure, such as falling into preoccupation with internal matters or becoming increasingly isolated from the larger church, but it is a risk that seems both imperative and warranted.

Unity with Integrity

In summary, Yoder's understanding of interchurch relations can be characterized by an emphasis on *ecumenical integrity* and on *unity of fellowship in conversation.* His theological ethics encourage such commitments as the following:

- While unity of discipleship and discipline on a congregational level is primary for Christians, it is not an adequate understanding of unity. Christians are called to *love one another in response to the reconciling love of God through Jesus Christ.* We cannot embody God's reconciling purposes on earth as insular communions. Building interchurch relationships is an important witness to the gospel.[89]
- We should *gather around Scripture* as a common source of authority.
- We can *trust in the guidance of God within and among hermeneutical communities* to inspire new insights regarding the

meaning of the gospel for our particular settings, to identify places where we must confess and be transformed, and to see where we must reach out to the world around us.

- In the search for unity we must *be willing to engage points of disagreement* among us, not just identify our convergences. We must speak from the deepest places of our traditions, not ignoring them because they might cause conflict.[90]
- We should *place more emphasis on actions together than on doctrinal dialogue.* We should conceive of our interchurch relationships as a dialogue of lives. Intra-Christian unity should be formulated in personal more than formal or structural terms.
- We should *give priority to local interchurch cooperation and conversation.* Nurturing local cooperation and relationships is the first and immediate step toward visible reconciliation and may make it possible for more people to invest with more enthusiasm in more extensive forms of cooperation.[91]
- Formal interchurch dialogues and conferences also have their relative place. In such situations, we should *adopt conversational practices that reflect our call to be ministers of reconciliation on earth.*[92] For example, we should seek structures, ideas, and attitudes, such as the following, that support conversational process and recognize that God's Spirit may speak through any participant:
- Consider who is included in the exchange. Are those on the margins of ecumenical activity included in the conversation? Are they truly welcome as friends in Christ?
- Be attentive to power dynamics. How do size, access to money, national status, and gender affect participation in theological dialogue? Commitment to reconciling practices in interchurch relationships must address the factors that impact those who are poorer, from minority Christian traditions, or whose social or national status undermines their voice.
- Protect the freedom of conversation partners to think or act differently from one's own or the majority view. This is a theologically grounded imperative that is the foundation of genuine love.

- Establish ground rules for and nurture virtues that undergird peaceable conversation, dialogue that bears the fruits of the Spirit. The virtues of humility, respect, and patience are compatible with incisive analysis and criticism.
- Expect persistence and fidelity in initiating and sustaining interchurch relationships, even when relationships become rocky. Those who seek to follow Jesus' way of reconciling love do not withdraw from conversational fellowship.[93]

The main contours of Yoder's interchurch theology and ethical practices remain relevant for many Christians today, in spite of changes in the ecumenical landscape in the past fifty years. His concern for *ecumenical integrity* speaks to those of us who readily lift up the things we hold in common with Christian brothers and sisters but who are too polite to grapple with the hard issues on which we differ from one another. Yoder's call to *ecumenical unity* speaks to those of us who remain enclosed in our comfortable ecclesial communities, not initiating or building up interchurch relationships. In relation to members of the various branches of the Stone-Campbellite tradition, I imagine that Yoder might present somewhat different points for conversation.

Perhaps Yoder's conclusion to *The Politics of Jesus* is a fitting word not only for Christian political and social efficacy, but also in relation to the kind of denominationalism that wrongly divides the church. The power of God for those who believe, the kind of power that is able to create a new social community, a power that rejects violence and seeks just and reconciling love, is also a power that can renew the household of God far beyond our expectations. As Yoder testified, echoing both Scripture and the Christian disciples over time who chose the way of the cross and resurrection, "Our Lamb has conquered; him let us follow."

Endnotes

[1] Lee C. Camp's essay in this volume, which was previously published as "Restoration and Unity in the work of John Howard Yoder," *Restoration Quarterly* 44, no. 1 (2002): 1-14, has already begun such thoughtful and creative work.

[2] In the Mennonite community, you are more likely to hear the word "interchurch" than "ecumenical" in referring to our efforts to connect with other Christian traditions.

Mennonites historically were uneasy about the term "ecumenical." Insofar as the term referred to a desire for institutional unity and an emphasis on theological convergence that appeared to lead toward loss of voice for minority traditions, Mennonites were wary of ecumenical commitment. Of special concern was the way in which loss of voice could potentially diminish the testimony that pacifism and peacemaking are integral to the gospel. Even after the approval of the merger of two large Mennonite conferences in 2001, after which we appointed a small, mostly volunteer group to oversee ecumenical issues, this history was reflected in the name chosen for this group: the Interchurch Relations Committee. I will use both terms—interchurch and ecumenical—interchangeably, but there is an ecclesial reason for the prominent use of "interchurch."

[3] See Earl Zimmerman's excellent account in chapters 3-5 of *Practicing the Politics of Jesus: The Origins and Significance of John Howard Yoder's Social Ethics* (Telford, PA: Cascadia, 2007). Zimmerman does not adequately represent, however, Yoder's substantial involvements with evangelicals during his sojourn in Europe and his genuine appreciation for their strengths.

[4] For more information on the "Puidoux theological conferences," the first extended conversations since the Reformation between the historic peace churches and the state-supported churches in central Europe, see Stanley Hauerwas, et al., eds. *The Wisdom of the Cross: Essays in Honor of John Howard Yoder* (Grand Rapids: Eerdmans, 1999), 15. As a young doctoral student Yoder participated in these meetings and gave a paper on a Free Church understanding of the relationship of the church and state. While in Europe Yoder was also part of a group that worked on a document, "Peace Is the Will of God," seeking to make more concrete the World Council of Churches' 1948 statement that "war is contrary to the will of God." He continued life-long service as a participant-observer in WCC discussions related to war and peace. At the University of Notre Dame, Yoder was chair of the program in nonviolence, regularly engaging students and faculty, including groups of ROTC students, in conversation about the ethics of war and peace. As a colleague in the field of Christian ethics, Yoder also served for many years on the war and peace subgroup of the Society for Christian Ethics and was elected President of the Society for one annual term, 1987.

[5] See the 241 boxes of Yoder letters, papers, and related correspondence that are preserved at the Mennonite Archives in Goshen, Indiana. Yoder wrote the Mennonite response to the World Council of Churches' *Baptism, Eucharist, Ministry* document, World Council of Churches' Faith and Order Paper, no. 111 (Geneva: WCC Publications, 1982), and a significant paper that sought to advance believers church conversations with infant baptism churches: "Adjusting to the Changing Shape of the Debate on Infant Baptism," in *Oecumennisme* (Amsterdam: Algemene Doopsgezinde Society, 1989), 201-214. Yoder was also on a first-name basis with John Stott, a well-known British evangelical theologian, and engaged in serious dialogue with Stott on the latter's views of the "powers and principalities." Wilbert R. Shenk, E-mail to author Gayle Gerber Koontz, May 5, 2009.

[6] Newbigin said this at a meeting in Nepal to Wilbert R. Shenk, who became the main administrator of the Mennonite Board of Missions immediately following Yoder's full-time involvement there. Reported by Shenk in presentations in the course "John H. Yoder's Theological Legacy," Associated Mennonite Biblical Seminary, Elkhart, Indiana, November 16, 2006 and October 9, 2008.

[7] Mark Thiessen Nation, who was a student at the Associated Mennonite Biblical Seminaries when Yoder returned from the trip, reported to me that when Yoder talked about the trip in class he was almost in tears at points, he was so moved by the commitment of South African Christians.

[8] The Winona Lake conferences held annually were sponsored by the Evangelical Foreign Missions Association (affiliate of the National Association of

Evangelicals) and the Interdenominational Foreign Mission Association (EFMA and IFMA).

[9] Because the National Association of Evangelicals did not permit member churches to also hold membership in the National Council of Churches, Yoder recommended that Mennonites join neither but relate to both. This remains the Mennonite Church USA position today.

[10] Shenk, presentation, October 9, 2008.

[11] This response led to Mennonite Board of Missions (MBM) involvement in Algeria within the year. The last MBM worker left in 1976.

[12] David A. Shank, "John Howard Yoder, Strategist for Mission with African-Initiated Churches," *Mission Focus: Annual Review* 15 (2007). Available online at the Associated Mennonite Biblical Seminary website: http://www.ambs.edu/.

[13] Shenk, presentation, October 9, 2008. Yoder, *The Ecumenical Movement and the Faithful Church* (Scottdale, PA: Mennonite Publishing House, 1958).

[14] Yoder, "Church Growth Issues in Theological Perspective," in *The Challenge of Church Growth: A Symposium,* ed. Wilbert R. Shenk (Elkhart, IN: Institute of Mennonite Studies, 1973), 25-47. Yoder also participated in a "Consultation on the Homogenous Unit: McGavran's Theory," held in 1978 in Pasadena, California.

[15] Shenk, presentation, October 9, 2008.

[16] Ibid.

[17] Joe Pfeiffer, "John H. Yoder and the Malone College Consultations, 1961-1967," student paper in the course "John Yoder's Theological Legacy," Associated Mennonite Biblical Seminary, fall 2008. There was no consultation in 1968. An additional meeting followed the one in 1969, but Yoder was no longer involved.

[18] Ibid., 3.

[19] Shenk, presentation, October 9, 2008.

[20] Unfortunately, someone reported briefly in *Christianity Today* in the late sixties on one of the meetings. The "covenant" regarding publicity having been broken and some of the substantive agenda having been dealt with, the meetings petered out.

[21] Shenk, presentation, October 9, 2008.

[22] This last quoted phrase is from Yoder, introduction to *Baptism & Church: A Believers Church Vision*, ed. Merle D. Strege (Grand Rapids: Sagamore Books, 1986), 3-4. Although the conferences never materialized in Europe, concerns voiced by the Dutch Mennonites and Yoder at the WCC level did have an impact. In the 1960s several Protestant groups were engaged in Church Union Negotiations in Ghana. WCC staff serving as consultants urged that the Ghana Mennonite Church's concerns for believers baptism be recognized. Roelf Kuitse, Dutch Mennonite missionary assigned to the Islam in Africa Project, serving Ghana, was asked to draft a statement to the Church Union Negotiations committee presenting this alternative view of baptism. This document was accepted and incorporated into the Plan of Union. Although this plan did not materialize, the responsiveness of the dominant ecumenical leaders was a direct fruit of the Dutch Mennonite-Yoder representations at the global level. Wilbert R. Shenk, E-mail to author, May 7, 2009.

[23] Donald F. Durnbaugh, "The Origins and Development of the Believers Church Conferences," paper presented at the Eighth Conference on the Concept of the Believers Church, Bethany Theological Seminary, Oakbrook, Illinois, September 2-5, 1987, 5. Durnbaugh underlines the point that the founding idea "was the desire to participate more fully in ecumenical consensus-building" so "a more effective witness could be made to fellow Christians" (6).

[24] Several letters attest to this. Yoder personal papers, IX-15 Box 1 (Large), Folder 8, Mennonite Archives, Goshen, Indiana. See Yoder, "A People in the World: Theological

Interpretation," in *The Concept of the Believers' Church: Addresses from the 1967 Louisville Conference,* ed. James Leo Garrett Jr., (Scottdale, PA: Herald Press, 1969), 250-283.

[25] Letter to Garrett, August 2, 1967, Yoder personal papers, Mennonite Archives, IX-15 Box 1 (Large) Folder 10.

[26] Letter to Clyde L. Manschreck, November 14, 1967, Yoder personal papers, Mennonite Archives, IX-15 Box 1 (Large) Folder 10.

[27] Yoder, "The Believers' Church Conferences in Historical Perspective," *Mennonite Quarterly Review* 45, no. 1 (January 1991): 17.

[28] This later quote was from the Findings Committee Report in James Leo Garrett Jr., ed., *Concept of the Believers' Church*, 319.

[29] Durnbaugh, "The Origins and Development of the Believers Church Conferences," 8.

[30] Yoder, review of Gordon Kaufman, *The Context of Decision*, in *Mennonite Quarterly Review* 37 (April 1963): 138.

[31] Yoder, "The Contemporary Evangelical Revival and the Peace Churches," in *Mission and the Peace Witness: The Gospel and Christian Discipleship,* ed. Robert L. Ramseyer (Scottdale, PA: Herald Press, 1979), 90.

[32] Yoder, "The Limits of Obedience to Caesar," paper prepared for the General Conference Mennonite Church Commission on Home Ministries Study Conference, June 1978, Associated Mennonite Biblical Seminary Library, unpublished papers, 15.

[33] Yoder, "The Authority of Tradition," in *The Priestly Kingdom: Social Ethics as Gospel* (Notre Dame: University of Notre Dame Press, 1984), 65.

[34] Yoder sets his comments here in relation to the problems of Christian moral laxness, unthinking accommodation to cultural patterns contrary to Christ, and the tendency toward rationalization of almost any actions.

[35] Yoder, "The Free Church Ecumenical Style," in *The Royal Priesthood: Essays Ecclesiological and Ecumenical* (Grand Rapids: Eerdmans, 1994), 234.

[36] Yoder with David A. Shank, "Biblicism and the Church," *Concern Pamphlet #2* (Scottdale, PA: By Concern, 721 Walnut Avenue, 1955), 56-57. This essay was recently reprinted in Virgil Vogt, ed., *The Roots of Concern: Writings on Anabaptist Renewal 1952-1957* (Eugene, OR: Cascade Books, 2009), 29-43. References here are to the original.

[37] Yoder, *Ecumenical Movement and the Faithful Church*, 18.

[38] Yoder, "Authority of Tradition," in *Priestly Kingdom*, 76.

[39] Yoder, "How H. Richard Niebuhr Reasoned: A Critique of *Christ and Culture*," in *Authentic Transformation: A New Vision of Christ and Culture*, ed. Glen H. Stassen, Diane M. Yeager, and John Howard Yoder (Nashville: Abingdon, 1994), especially 41, 66, and 80-82.

[40] Yoder, "The Experiential Etiology of Evangelical Dualism," *Missiology: An International Review* 11 (October 1983): 455-56.

[41] Yoder, "Christian Unity within a Divided North American Protestantism," Memorandum on Mennonite Board of Missions and Charities stationery, March 1, 1967, Associated Mennonite Biblical Seminary Library, unpublished papers, 6.

[42] Yoder, "The Contemporary Evangelical Revival," 101.

[43] Yoder, *Ecumenical Movement and the Faithful Church*, 40 (reference here is to the original pamphlet, not its reprinting in this volume).

[44] Yoder, *Preface to Theology: Christology and Theological Method,* published posthumously (Grand Rapids: Brazos Press, 2002), 222-223.

[45] Ibid., 394.

[46] Yoder, "Is There Historical Development of Theological Thought?" in *The Witness of the Holy Spirit: Proceedings of the Eighth Mennonite World Conference* (Napanee, IN: Evangel Press, ca 1967), 388. References here and following are to the original essay, not its reprinting in this volume.

47 Yoder, "Free Church Ecumenical Style," in *Royal Priesthood*, 238.

48 Yoder, "Radical Reformation Ethics in Ecumenical Perspective," in *Priestly Kingdom*, 120.

49 Yoder, "The Authority of the Canon," *To Hear the Word* (Eugene, OR: Wipf & Stock, 2001), 105, employs the image of a pruned vine for understanding valid growth and diversity. A pruned vine includes several branches that are genuinely and authentically derived from and dependent on the root and are subject to being judged by it. Yoder notes that Luke does not need to think just like Paul. Yoder appeals to this image also in "The Authority of Tradition," in *Priestly Kingdom*, 69.

50 Cf. Yoder and Shank, "Biblicism and the Church," 51.

51 Yoder, "Is There Historical Development of Theological Thought?" 386.

52 Yoder, *The Fullness of Christ: Paul's Vision of Universal Ministry* (Elgin, IL: Brethren Press, 1987), 87.

53 Yoder and Shank, "Biblicism and the Church," 39.

54 Yoder, "Authority of Tradition," in *Priestly Kingdom*, 73. Since Yoder is primarily committed to a congregational process of discernment, he continues to raise these issues for further exploration and criticism both in his own Mennonite context and in wider ecumenical conversation.

55 Yoder, "Peace without Eschatology?" in *Royal Priesthood*, 156.

56 Yoder, "Christian Unity within a Divided North American Protestantism," 2.

57 Yoder, "What Are Our Concerns?" in *Concern Pamphlet #4* (Scottdale, PA: By Concern, 721 Walnut Avenue, 1957), 29. This essay is reprinted in *The Roots of Concern*, 164-176. References here and following are to the original.

58 Yoder, "Free Church Ecumenical Style," in *Royal Priesthood*, 235. Yoder refers to the centrality of the congregation in Concern Pamphlet #2, 58-59. He also wrote that Christians need to see this visible fellowship as primary and the larger structures as derivative so that "the separateness of Christians that is a scandal to the world is not first the separateness of these agencies" ("Another 'Free Church' Perspective on Baptism and Ecumenism," in *Royal Priesthood*, 274).

59 Yoder, "Binding and Loosing," in *Royal Priesthood*, 340. Yoder notes that this sense of responsibility for members is often absent in contemporary congregations. He suggests that moral oversight of one's neighbor has for many North American Christians been turned over to such agencies as the F.B.I. or the draft board (335).

60 Ibid., 336.

61 Translation from the *New English Bible*.

62 Yoder, "Conflict from the Perspective of Anabaptist History and Theology," 4, paper presented at the Mennonite Graduate Student Fellowship, Cornell University, Ithaca, NY, December 28, 1969, Associated Mennonite Biblical Seminary Library, unpublished papers.

63 Yoder, "Contemporary Evangelical Revival and the Peace Churches," 100.

64 For Yoder, baptism signals reception into a specific congregation of disciples. Yoder emphasizes that members are accountable to one another for their spiritual lives, which engages them together in theological interpretation, ethical discernment, and action. Such accountability is an integral part of the meaning of baptism.

65 Yoder, "War and Peace and the Evangelical Challenge," 12, paper presented at the National Association of Evangelicals, Denver, Colorado, April 19, 1966, Associated Mennonite Biblical Seminary Library, unpublished papers.

66 Yoder and Shank, "Biblicism and the Church," 54-55.

67 Yoder, *Ecumenical Movement and the Faithful Church*, 37.

[68] Yoder, "What Are Our Concerns?" 32. While Anabaptists and the heirs of Anabaptism have frequently been characterized as believing that division from the broader Catholic and Protestant church is a sign of faithfulness, Yoder argues that this view was not true of the earliest evangelical Anabaptists. They kept trying to dialogue with the state churches, he says, until the larger church would no longer tolerate their questions and claims on the basis of Scripture. Anabaptists did not walk away from the debates, but others walked away from the Anabaptists. According to Wilbert R. Shenk, this idea, one of the conclusions of Yoder's doctoral work, was *the ecumenical principle* that became operative for Yoder. Faithfulness required continuing engagement with other Christian streams—erstwhile "opponents." This was counter-intuitive for Mennonites who felt that Catholic and Reformed Christians had wronged the Anabaptists. Those who suffered for their beliefs had reason to walk away. Shenk, presentation, November 16, 2006 and October 9, 2008.

[69] Yoder and Shank, "Biblicism and the Church," 56. Yoder specifically notes that while there are some bases for exclusion from fellowship, denominational difference is not one of them. Ibid., 54.

[70] Yoder, *Ecumenical Movement and the Faithful Church*, 36.

[71] Yoder, "The Nature of the Unity We Seek," in *Royal Priesthood*, 230.

[72] Yoder, "Another 'Free Church' Perspective on Baptist Ecumenism," in *Royal Priesthood*, 267.

[73] Yoder, "A Non-Baptist View of Southern Baptists," *Review and Expositor* (Spring 1970): 223.

[74] Yoder, "What Are Our Concerns?" 24.

[75] See James M. Lapp, "Principles and Guidelines for Interchurch Relations," a statement drafted on behalf of the Interchurch Relations Committee of Mennonite General Conference, August 1971, and based on Yoder's position papers from 1962-70. Yoder also notes that while ecumenical openness is desirable, not every minister, missionary, or congregation should be expected to be wide open in every direction. Local situations may not allow that. In some situations unity might be "limited to the willingness to recognize that other brethren in the same denominational framework may with good conscience and integrity invest their efforts in a quite different direction from oneself and still be wholeheartedly accepted" as part of the denominational community. Yoder, "Christian Unity within a Divided North American Protestantism," 13.

[76] Yoder, *Ecumenical Movement and the Faithful Church*, 38.

[77] In conversation with Roman Catholics, for example, Yoder would seek to combine openness to Catholic views and his assertion of Christ as the primary authority by clearly challenging the Catholic axiom of the authority of the church "while being still quite interested in listening to that history, in learning from it, and in sympathizing deeply with what it was trying to say." Yoder, *Preface to Theology*, 223.

[78] Yoder, "The Nature of the Unity We Seek," in *Royal Priesthood*, 223.

[79] Ibid., 230.

[80] Yoder, "Radical Reformation Ethics in Ecumenical Perspective," *Journal of Ecumenical Studies* 15 (Fall 1978): 660.

[81] Yoder, "The Unique Role of the Historic Peace Churches," *Brethren Life and Thought* 14 (Summer 1969): 140. Yoder is more interested in "catholicity" than a unity which assumes it will be instantiated in any one institutional form. Cf. "Catholicity in Search of Location," in *Royal Priesthood*, 302.

[82] I have described Yoder's view here on the basis of various personal conversations and encounters during 1981-82.

[83] Yoder originally articulated some of these in "'Two (or a Dozen) Ways Moral 'Absolutes' Are Qualified," memorandum, September 7, 1982, Yoder personal files, Elkhart, Indiana. He revised and expanded this memorandum, which was eventually published as "'Patience' as Method in Moral Reasoning: Is an Ethic of Discipleship 'Absolute'?" in *Wisdom of the Cross*, ed. Stanley Hauerwas, Chris K. Huebner, Harry J. Huebner, and Mark Thiessen Nation (Grand Rapids: Eerdmans, 1999), 24-42. Much of the material is quoted and some paraphrased from the published essay, 25-34.

[84] Yoder, "'Patience' as Method in Moral Reasoning," in *Wisdom of the Cross*, 35.

[85] George A. Lindbeck, *The Nature of Doctrine: Religion and Theology in a Postliberal Age* (Philadelphia: Westminster Press, 1984), 68.

[86] Ibid., 77.

[87] Ibid. Also see George Lindbeck, "The Sectarian Future of the Church," in *The God Experience*, ed. Joseph P. Whelan (New York: Newman Press, 1971), 226-243.

[88] Ibid.

[89] Yoder, "As You Go: The Old Mission in a New Day" (Scottdale, PA: Herald Press, 1961), 12, notes that Paul did not do what modern missionaries do, that is, enter countries or areas where people do not profess faith in the true God. Rather Paul nurtured the faith of the scattered worshipers.

[90] Yoder's tone was less conciliatory than mine. He wrote that theological ethics needs to deal with arguments "cold-bloodedly, critically, and without respect to persons." Yoder, *Karl Barth and the Problem of War* (Nashville: Abingdon Press, 1970), 18. He measured care for Christian brothers and sisters and humility before God not in terms of the mildness of his views or his defense of them but in terms of their clarity, accuracy, and appeal to the criterion of revelation—Jesus Christ.

[91] This emphasis was part of a Mennonite Church document on interchurch relations that Yoder influenced. See Lapp, "Principles and Guidelines for Interchurch Relations." It is also a low budget way of proceeding and has the potential to enhance the missional character of local congregations—helping them perceive and join what God may be doing in their geographical and civil communities.

[92] I have formulated the following list in my own words, but I think it fairly reflects the concerns that emerge in Yoder's writings.

[93] In his writing on "binding and loosing," in relation to the unity of congregational discipleship and discipline, Yoder does leave room for excommunication, though the weight of his writing was on reconciling intent and ways to resolve conflict and offense. However, when Yoder affirmed "excluding from fellowship those who obstinately refuse to conform to truth whose validity they cannot deny," he referred to such actions only in the context of local congregational life and only after careful process to see if the matter is one of truly unrepentant disobedience. Yoder and Shank, "Biblicism and the Church," 57. He did not provide justification for such withdrawal from interchurch unity of fellowship in conversation.

Chapter Four

THE LIBERAL READING OF YODER
The Problem of Yoder Reception and the Need for a
Comprehensive Christian Witness

CRAIG A. CARTER

The influence of John Howard Yoder now extends far beyond his own
Mennonite tradition. There is no need for this chapter to document
the steadily increasing number of publications that indicate the significant influence his thought is now exerting on both Roman Catholics and
Protestants and, within Protestantism, on both Evangelicals and Liberals.
But as Yoder's influence grows the problem of how to receive his work
becomes more complex and more contested. This paper is too brief to
reflect this complexity; there may be as many as five or six different interpretations of Yoder on offer at the moment. Due to limitations of space, I
do not deal here with the best known approach to Yoder interpretation, the
postliberal interpretation of Stanley Hauerwas, nor with the new book by
Nathan Kerr, which seeks to "rescue" Yoder from Hauerwas and presents
a radically Barthian, apocalyptic Yoder.[1] My concern here is the growing
number of scholars and activists who have pressed Yoder into the service
of their liberal theological agendas. It is a concern because it makes use of
Yoder's thought in such a way as to imply that his theology has nothing to
offer beyond the realm of the immanent and the human. Such theology is not
properly theology at all, but merely a dressed-up form of humanistic social
science or secular politics. Ironically, some Mennonite scholars have been
at the forefront of this trend, cheering on the liberal use of Yoder, having

consciously or unconsciously made their own personal decision to interpret the Mennonite tradition as a subset of liberal Protestantism, rather than as having more in common with either Evangelical Protestantism or the Roman Catholic tradition.

This approach, which I have called in my title, "The Liberal Reading of Yoder," is of concern on two levels. On the one hand, it is a concern strictly on the level of historical theology. The liberal reading of Yoder is debatable and needs to be challenged on the basis of the evidence so that scholarly opinion can come to a reasoned judgment in the matter. On the other hand, it is a concern on the level of how we ought to go about doing theology and ethics in our contemporary situation and what kind of resources Yoder offers to this on-going work of the church. Let me be more specific about these concerns.

There are two main pillars of Yoder interpretation for which I have argued in the past and which are, I think, central to this debate. First, there is a high degree of continuity in his thought over the course of his career, which implies that his later work on the importance of the Jeremianic turn and the exile for the shape of Christian ecclesiology and mission can and should be interpreted in the light of his earlier thought and not as a radical departure from it.[2] Second, his thought is rooted in the theology of Karl Barth, especially in Barth's confession of deeply traditional versions of the doctrines of Revelation, Trinity, and Incarnation. Sometimes the roots are explicit, while other times they are implicit; but Yoder can be interpreted as presupposing and extending the Christocentric theology of Barth in the realm of ethics and ecclesiology.[3] Despite the fact that these two lines of interpretation are ones I have advanced and continue to defend, I must acknowledge that they are not being accepted by a good number of Yoder's interpreters today, as we shall see below.

Many who are inclined to be sympathetic to classical orthodoxy tend not to be sympathetic to Yoder, and this may well be due to the way in which those who advocate an immanent, ethical-political reading of the Christian gospel often attempt to assimilate Yoder to their essentially modern project. Those of us who continue to insist on interpreting Yoder in a way that is not hostile to the "Great Tradition" of historic Christianity are fighting an uphill battle and, in the end, it may even prove to be a lost cause. Yet, it seems to me that those who stand within the "Great Tradition" of catholic and evangelical orthodoxy stand to experience a considerable loss if Yoder's ecumenical reception results in the assimilation of the politics of Jesus to the modern, liberal tradition in which we find such movements as the social gospel and liberation theology.

My purpose in this chapter is to examine and critique the liberal reading of Yoder and to offer some thoughts on how Yoder can be received by the ecumenical church. I argue that the liberal reading fails as a contribution to ecumenical theology and that my interpretation, while not without problems of its own, at least renders it possible to read Yoder as a theologian of the Christian church, rather than as a sectarian despiser of the majority tradition of Christian orthodoxy down through the centuries. For those for whom sectarianism is no vice, my interpretation undoubtedly will seem like a perverse attempt to "tame" Yoder. But, for those who cherish the church catholic throughout the centuries, I hope that my reading will enable Yoder's work to enrich Christian reflection on ethical and political issues across the ecumenical spectrum. Before turning to the liberal reading of Yoder, I summarize briefly my own reading.

My Reading of Yoder's Pacifism

Yoder did not view his "pacifism of the messianic community" as interchangeable with liberal pacifism. In the third edition of his *Nevertheless: Varieties of Christian Pacifism*, Yoder lays out sixteen major and twelve minor types of pacifism before coming to his own preferred view in chapter nineteen. Here he writes, "To say that this is the pacifism of the *messianic* community is to affirm its dependence upon the confession that Jesus is Christ and that Jesus Christ is Lord. To say that Jesus is the Messiah is to say that in him are fulfilled the expectations of God's people regarding the coming one in whom God's will would perfectly be done. Therefore, in the person and work of Jesus, in his teachings and his passion, this kind of pacifism finds its rootage, and in his resurrection it finds its enablement." Yoder goes on to write, "It follows that the character of such a messianic-community position can be known only in relation to Jesus Christ."[4]

Now this is an epistemological point: we cannot know this kind of pacifism from any other source, such as experience, nature, or world religions because it is bound up with the historical particularity of God's self-revelation in Jesus Christ. But it is also a Christological point. Yoder goes on to say, "Note well that although all the positions reviewed above are held by Christians, this is the only position for which the person of Jesus is indispensable. It is the only one of these positions which would lose its substance if Jesus were not Christ and would lose its foundation if Jesus were not Lord."[5] Note that he says that the *substance* of the pacifism of the messianic community is known only through Jesus Christ. Jesus is not merely an inspiration to take up a pacifist position that was previously known but perhaps not embraced out of lethargy or fear. It is not that we all know what pacifism is already and Jesus merely provides compelling leadership to get us moving in the right direction; what Yoder is saying here is that we would not even know what pacifism is without the Incarnation, including the sinless life, radical teachings, miracles, saving death, bodily resurrection, ascension, present session, and future return of Jesus Christ. It is Jesus Christ who gives content and meaning to Christian pacifism with the result that our pacifist action is taken up by the Spirit of God and made into a true witness to the gospel.

I interpret this passage as being in harmony with his statement in *The Politics of Jesus* to the effect that, from the perspective of dogmatic theology, his view of Jesus is "more radically Nicene and Chalcedonian than other views."[6] He explains that demonstrating this point is not his task in this book because his focus is exegetical, rather than dogmatic. But he gives a strong hint that a dogmatic defense of the politics of Jesus is possible, which is to say that one does not need to reject the tradition of classical trinitarian and Christological orthodoxy in order to embrace the politics of Jesus.

In *The Politics of Jesus*, Yoder is at pains to distance himself from what he calls "the mainstream ethical consensus" and "the theology of the natural" by which we develop an ethic of "vocation" or "station" or "the situation" or "natural law." Yoder says that the problem in all of these cases is that it is "by studying the realities around us, not by hearing a proclamation from God, that we discern the right."[7] When Yoder speaks of "a proclamation from God" here, we should not imagine some sort of private inspiration received by an individual, or a consensus developed through congregational discussion, or a discovery made by employing the tools of social scientific analysis, but rather what Paul in 1 Corinthians calls "the gospel," that is, the proclamation of the saving events centering on the life, death, and resurrection of Jesus Christ. The gospel is the central proclamation of the church and the inalterable source, foundation, and warrant for the kind of pacifism Yoder is advocating.

The Liberal Reading of Yoder

In what I am calling the liberal reading of Yoder, however, these emphases are largely reversed or ignored. Instead of pacifism being known only through the gospel, pacifism is known in advance of hearing the gospel. Pacifism is understood as a message of nonviolence found in many religions, such as in Hinduism and Buddhism for example, and in many cultures and periods of human history. Nonviolence becomes a principle which is known rationally and functions as a tool for the ideological critique of the entire Christian tradition, including the Scriptures and the Creeds. The kind of natural theology that Yoder rejected seeks to root itself in black, womanist, and feminist experience with the result that Jesus becomes a symbol of our commitment to inclusion, tolerance, and peace. This reduction of the gospel to natural theology results in catastrophic damage to important doctrines, including the nature of God, the atonement, and the authority of Scripture. In each case, nonviolence functions as an ideological critique of traditional Christian orthodoxy and a premise for theological revisionism. A good example of a theologian who risks turning nonviolence into natural theology is J. Denny Weaver.

J. Denny Weaver

Weaver, in his book *The Nonviolent Atonement*, develops a new atonement theory called "narrative *Christus Victor*" in an attempt to avoid problems inherent in existing atonement theories, especially in the satisfaction and penal substitutionary theories. He writes, "This book presents the results of the efforts to develop an understanding of atonement that made sense in its own right as a statement about the universal significance of Jesus Christ but also answered questions raised by the contextual theologies. The working assumption in development of this model is that the rejection of violence, whether the direct violence of the sword or the systemic violence of racism or sexism, should be visible in expressions of Christology and atonement."[8]

Here we see a correlationist approach in which what makes sense as an expression of the universal significance of Jesus Christ is correlated with questions raised by contextual theologies. The social analysis that produces constructions such as "racism" and "sexism" is taken as a given and the job of the theologian is assumed to be bringing systematic theology into line with these social scientific constructions. Weaver goes on to define violence very broadly as "harm or damage." He says that this broad definition includes killing, of course, but it also includes physical harm, injury to bodily integrity, and "a range of acts and conditions that include damage to a person's dignity or self-esteem." Slavery, contemporary racism, and "social practices that proscribe set roles for women and limit their opportunities" are all considered by Weaver to be violence. Even the criminal justice system, insofar as it inflicts punishment and is not purely restorative, is violent. Interestingly however, and not entirely consistently, when it comes to defining nonviolence, Weaver allows that nonviolent resistance is not violence.[9]

Weaver argues that nonviolence is intrinsic to "the story of Jesus" and therefore "should be a constitutive, shaping element of Christian theology, rather than emerging as an issue to deal with after one has established the theological foundation or the framework on some other basis." Perhaps sensing the implications of his view of the centrality of nonviolence as a principle, he states that "this does not reduce Jesus or the gospel to nonviolence."[10] While I agree that recognizing the teaching of Jesus on nonviolence in the Scriptures *need not* necessarily reduce Jesus or the gospel to nonviolence, I am not so sure that this outcome is avoided in Weaver's own theology. Weaver is clear that the question of nonviolence is a matter that goes beyond Christology to the issue of God's nature.[11]

Let us note the logical steps in Weaver's argument. First, he has taken the words of Jesus in the Sermon on the Mount about enemy love and used them to justify a broad definition of nonviolence, the content of which is filled out by modern ideologies and social scientific tools of cultural analysis. Second, this theory of nonviolence is used as a criterion to reject certain atonement theories, specifically satisfaction and penal substitutionary theories that work by means of violence. Third, in the process of this revision of atonement theories, the issue of God's character arises. Is God a God of wrath? Does God judge sin and sinners? Must not God be nonviolent if Jesus reveals God and Jesus is nonviolent? All violence is assumed to be immoral, and punishment is considered to be violence. Fourth, in response to these questions, the depiction of God as wrathful and determined to punish sin is based on a false view of God as immoral and violent. God therefore must be reconceived altogether and much of the traditional doctrine of God must be revised. Fifth, this also has implications for the doctrine of the authority of Scripture, since God in the Old Testament (and in the New Testament!) is depicted as a God of wrath and judgment. Specifically, the wars of the extermination of the Canaanites by Israel under Joshua must be judged to be immoral and so the God of the Old Testament narrative cannot be the God of Jesus. This argument results in a thorough-going revision of biblical authority, God, sin, atonement, and the Christian life.

In some ways, however, Weaver's revisionist proposals are rather conservative and tame compared to some of the other theological trajectories that have started from his premise, such as the "death of God" theologies. At least Weaver in this book does not give up the Christian teaching on the divinity of Christ or reject the Christian God altogether. Weaver is conservative in that he attempts to develop an atonement theory in which the resurrection still has a normative and central place. This is crucial to his contention that his theology does not make Jesus dispensable. Gandhi cannot stand in for Jesus because Jesus was raised from the dead and Gandhi was not. The person of Jesus remains as necessary for Weaver as for Yoder, at least so far as Weaver is concerned.

Unfortunately, there is a serious internal inconsistency in Weaver's theory that practically guarantees that those who find his views persuasive will not be able to resist going further in the process of abstraction thereby losing the particularity of Jesus Christ as a unique revelation of God. Weaver criticizes other atonement theories for their employment of divine violence. He writes, "Unavoidably, therefore, the satisfaction theory implicates God in the sanction of violence." He expands on this statement: "Stated crassly, in satisfaction atonement God orchestrates the scenario in which Jesus is sent to earth for the purpose of dying to satisfy the offended honor of God. . . . When analyzed from a nonviolent perspective, it is apparent that satisfaction atonement depends on violent imagery—death is needed to satisfy God—with the attendant implication that the sanction on this violence is intrinsic to the character of God. God is the one who arranges for that death to satisfy God. This is intrinsically an image of a violent God or a God who sanctions violence."[12]

Leaving aside the question of whether or not this is a fair depiction of the actual satisfaction theory as it has been held in the Christian tradition, I want to focus on Weaver's point that God is violent because God sanctions violence insofar as God "arranges for" Jesus' death. The obvious implication here is that if God were nonviolent, God would find a different way than allowing Jesus to be killed. But a problem immediately arises: in Weaver's narrative *Christus Victor* theory, God accomplishes the atonement through Jesus' death on the cross by which he defeats the powers and then raises Jesus from the dead to demonstrate Jesus' Lordship. Obviously, there can be no resurrection without a death. So if the resurrection is the key to Weaver's atonement theory, how convincing is it to say that Weaver's theory, unlike all the others, does not "need" the death of Christ?

Weaver recognizes that he has a problem here and he admits that narrative *Christus Victor* contains violence, but he argues that "it is not God's violence, nor violence sanctioned or needed or used by God. The violence in narrative *Christus Victor* comes from the side of the forces of evil that killed Jesus."[13] But what can Weaver possibly mean by saying that God does not "need" Jesus' death in order to accomplish the atonement? Suppose Jesus had lived to a ripe old age and died of natural causes. Would the atonement still have taken place? If we say yes, the death and resurrection of Christ was optional in God's plan—a contingency rooted in the free will of human beings. If we say no, we are back to God somehow "needing" Christ's death. So it appears, on Weaver's premises, that the answer must be yes, the "atonement" is thinkable apart from the death and resurrection of Christ.

Yet if it is meaningful to state that God could have saved us without the death of Christ, then how important can the atonement really be? Why not dispense with the whole concept of atonement altogether? Those in the Socinian and Unitarian-Universalist traditions are happy to do just that. Weaver does not want us to go this far. So he must somehow convince us that his theory really *does* require the death and resurrection of Jesus Christ. But he has backed himself into a corner and cannot do it, lest his critique of other theories rebound on his own.

Weaver contrasts his view with other atonement views, saying, "*Christus Victor* does contain violence, but it is not God's violence . . . . The violence in narrative *Christus Victor* comes from the side of the forces of evil that killed Jesus.[14] The problem here is that *any* theory of atonement could say as much. Anselm and Calvin portray the death of Christ as being caused by the human and demonic forces of evil, as does the New Testament itself.[15] But Anselm, Calvin, and the New Testament (Acts 2:23) all agree that this horrendous evil was foreseen by God and yet God sent Jesus anyway—knowing in advance that Jesus would die—because this was the only way for God to redeem his good creation. It seems to me that

Weaver must either deny that God had foreknowledge or say something very similar to what Anselm, Calvin, and the New Testament say. How it is not "divinely sanctioned violence" for the Father to send the Son knowing in advance that the Son would die in narrative *Christus Victor*? Will those who follow Weaver and build on his thought see this as a meaningful distinction? There is already evidence that the answer is no.

Philip E. Stoltzfus

In an essay presented at a Yoder conference held in Toronto in 2007,[16] Philip E. Stoltzfus argues that Yoder should have been bolder in following Gordon Kaufman in his program of imaginative theological construction. The reason he thinks so is that he sees Yoder as locked into the dilemma of believing in a nonviolent Jesus and a violent God. Stoltzfus refers to an article by Ray Gingerich in which Gingerich accuses Yoder of inconsistency in continuing to hold to an explanation for holy war in the Old Testament that presupposes that God can justly punish sinners without thereby becoming violent and immoral.[17] Yoder's explanation of how the Father of Jesus Christ could be one and the same as the Old Testament God who ordered the extermination of the Canaanites is a failure, according to Gingerich and Stoltzfus. Yoder understands the institution of holy war in pre-monarchial Israel as one in which Israel is meant to be pacifist because God fights for Israel and defeats the enemy in a way epitomized by the Red Sea event and the battle of Jericho. Yoder argues that later in Israel's history, as a result of disobedience, Israel institutionalized warfare under the kings and in so doing was disobedient. God's plan, from which the monarchy was merely a distraction, was actually to preserve Israel miraculously as God's witness among the nations. Hence Yoder saw the exile as God's will for his people.

The problem with this line of thought for Gingerich is that it supposes that divine judgment is moral, a belief which Gingerich, like Stoltzfus and Weaver, rejects. Stoltzfus agrees with Gingerich that Yoder never came to grips with the violent God of the Old Testament, but unlike Gingerich, Soltzfus has a solution. Stoltzfus proposes that if Yoder had taken more seriously the idea that God is a "concept" or "model" invented by human beings and that the task of theology, as theologians such as Gordon Kaufman and Sally McFague have contended, is to create models of God by an act of creative imagination that can speak to our contemporary situation, then Yoder could have overcome this contradiction. In other words, if Yoder had allowed nonviolence to become his "principle of principles" in constructing a new model of God for the twenty-first century, he could have had a nonviolent Jesus *and* a nonviolent God.

Now, faced with the apparent contradiction in Yoder's thought identified by Gingerich and the residual "violence" involved in narrative *Christus Victor*, what will a younger generation of theologians influenced by Weaver do? It seems to me that Stoltzfus has already identified the wave of the future. Stoltzfus notes three reasons Gingerich gives as to why he thinks Yoder never addressed the contradiction between a violent God and a non-violent Jesus and he sees in them an agenda for where Mennonite theology needs to go next. First, Yoder was a product of the Mennonite community and, perhaps more important, he had immense loyalty to it. He creatively expanded the theological paradigm of his mentors but never broke out of it. Yoder could not break free of the conservatism of Mennonite church life and embrace the theological revisionism dominant in the secular academy. Though Yoder laid the foundation for the next step, he was unable to take it for personal, familial, and cultural reasons. Second, Yoder was, to the end of his life, a tempered Barthian and a "biblical realist." This framework did not allow sufficient freedom to view Scripture more dialogically as the product of a fallible and faltering people of God, that is, as a collection of writings produced and preserved by communities in which power politics was at times more determinative than faithful prophecy and servanthood. In other words, Yoder was trapped by a high view of biblical authority. Third, Yoder seems to have had an innate urge to sacralize the Hebrew worldview or, more specifically, to view certain events in ancient Israel's history as *Urgeschichte*, beyond the pale of historical analysis.[18]

Where Gingerich and Weaver stop in their analysis, Stoltzfus begins. For Stoltzfus, it is out with Barth, in with Kaufman; out with biblical realism, in with philosophical naturalism; out with the traditional doctrine of God, in with late modern experiential models of God. After Weaver's narrative *Christus Victor* theory, which rejects other atonement theories because in them God needs the death of Jesus but still wishes to retain the death and resurrection of Jesus as necessary and central to its doctrine of the atonement, where can we expect theology to go next? The next natural step is to do away with the concept of atonement altogether and to construct a model of God out of modern identity politics—a model that allows us to view Jesus as one of many symbols of nonviolence and one of many ways to a nonviolent God, a model that has been purged of Christian particularity, the centrality of the Incarnation, and the idea that the salvation of the world came exclusively through the death and resurrection of Jesus Christ.

An Ecumenical Reading of Yoder

In *The Politics of the Cross*,[19] I interpret Yoder as a Barthian, biblical realist who stands in the Great Tradition of classical Christian orthodoxy and whose defense of the politics of Jesus presupposes both a high Christology and a high view of biblical authority. The most important implication of this interpretation is that Yoder is an ecumenical theologian who must be taken seriously by the whole Christian church.

I still hold to this interpretation of Yoder, but reading the literature on Yoder over the past eight years has prompted me to wonder what it is about Yoder's thought that makes it at once so attractive, yet also in need of serious revision, to those who are attracted by the modern project of revising Christian faith to make it compatible with a modern, secular, scientific, liberal, individualist worldview. The typical modern revisionist views all of Christian thought from the Apostles to the Enlightenment as so much "fundamentalism" and laments the persistence of such thinking into the postmodern era. The main task of many university departments of religion and liberal seminaries today is to search through the rubble of this "fundamentalist, pre-modern theology" in search of fragments that can be rescued and somehow fit into the modern worldview as "proof" that the project is not the rejection of Christianity outright. The attempt to claim the mantle of Yoder for an essentially modern project strikes me as slightly absurd, but no more so than the attempt to co-opt other well-known Christian figures, whose prominence as spokesmen for their traditions makes them important symbols of continuity for a project that is essentially discontinuous with the tradition of the church.

In the last section, I want to examine six strategies that can be pursued and to evaluate each one as to its effectiveness in promoting an interpretation of Yoder that does not make him say the opposite of what he actually said in the service of modern revisionism.

Strategy #1

Emphasize Yoder's high view of Scripture and rule out any interpretation of his thought that requires a low view of biblical authority

This strategy emphasizes Yoder's biblical realism and the high view of biblical authority that the biblical realist movement shares with the church throughout history. While Catholics and Protestants may differ over the role of tradition in the interpretation of Scripture and the formulation of dogma, they agree that the Bible is the inspired Word of God and must be interpreted, rather than denied, replaced, or ignored. The strength of this approach is that it strikes at the heart of the modern project of locating truth in the self-positing, thinking subject, rather than in God and in divine revelation. The weakness is that modern revisionists have two centuries of experience stretching the biblical text into strange shapes in order to evade the charge of denying it outright, and so the debate over whether, for example, the wars of Israel were actually commanded by Yahweh is likely to be interminable. Revisionists are adept at obtaining by obfuscation what they are unable to win by clear argument. Will this strategy suffice alone? I strongly doubt it will prevent the use of Yoder for revisionist purposes in isolation from other strategies. This weakness is shared by much conservative Evangelical theology.

Strategy #2

Insist on Yoder's distinction between divine judgment and human violence and reject the reduction of the former to the latter on theological grounds

This second strategy develops the fundamental insight that God is God and not human. The infinite gulf between God and humanity means that it is dangerous simply to apply human concepts to God. All theological language is analogical, and every comparison between God and humanity involves more dissimilarity than similarity. This strategy involves making fine distinctions between divine judgment, human force, and violence.

Judgment is properly and primarily applied to God alone, although there is a pale imitation of it among humans. The paleness of such imitation is the result of original sin. We may try to judge righteously, but we often fail completely and never get it perfectly right. God, on the other hand, is presented in Scripture as "the righteous Judge," (e.g., Ps 96), who judges in a perfectly equitable, just, and fair manner at all times. God is holy, so he hates sin, and righteous, so he must punish sin. Therefore, "the wrath of God is being revealed from heaven against all the godlessness and wickedness of men who suppress the truth by their wickedness" (Rom 1:18 NIV). Nothing in the teaching of Jesus or the New Testament as a whole contradicts this essentially Jewish, Old Testament teaching about the nature of God. The whole concept of human government in the Judeo-Christian tradition is built, as Oliver O'Donovan points out, on the function of right judgment.[20]

Force is the use of disciplinary, police, or military means to make laws effective and stop evil. It can also be used to shape character. Force is different from violence in that it is constrained by law, limited in scope, and rationally deployed. Force consists of various grades up to and including lethal force. But force always operates within rationally determined limits. If it exceeds those limits it turns into violence, which is a constant threat in a fallen world. The difference between God's wrath and human force is that God's wrath is always an exact reflection of his righteous judgment, whereas human force is, at best, an approximation and, at worst, a demonic mockery of God's righteous judgment. An example of disciplinary force would be parental punishment of children. An example of police force would be policemen arresting murderers or thieves. An example of military force would be just war, but not total war, crusades, or nuclear holocaust.

Violence can be defined as the human use of force when it is unconstrained by law, unlimited in scope, and irrational. Force may turn into violence at any moment; it lives on the boundary between law and lawlessness. Parental discipline can become violent if parents are not self-controlled. In certain situations, large scale use of force almost inevitably morphs into violence as, for example, in a large scale war in which irrational powers such as nationalism or racism come into play and commandeer the whole enterprise. This is one of the most troubling problems with the deployment of just war theory in the real world.

Since God is the author of judgment, not violence, the apparent discrepancy between a nonviolent Jesus and a "violent" God disappears as a misunderstanding of what divine judgment is. Liberals collapse all three categories into one and reject them all. Yoder would reject all violence and most force, but not judgment. There is no need to reject divine judgment in order to reject violence. This approach is crucial, in my view, for guarding Yoder and the wider Christian tradition from misinterpretation.

Strategy #3
Distinguish between Yoder's Christologically-based view of discipleship and a natural theology of nonviolence of which Christ becomes a mere symbol

This third strategy distinguishes between the basis of Christian pacifism and the basis of liberal pacifism and argues that they are different in substance and not merely in how they are known. This approach builds on Yoder's own thinking in *Nevertheless* and involves the differentiating of the motives, goals, priorities, and shape of the Christian life from those of the "noble pagan," "secular humanist," or "liberal individualist." For one thing, Christian patience with error is not the same as liberal tolerance, which tends to view all human ethical choices as equally valid simply because they are free. This is to replace morality with values and to eviscerate the Christian understanding of creation and God's law as the basis of true morality.

Christians have as their highest priority the evangelization of the world during this time between the times, the era between Jesus' first and second comings. As part of their witness to the reality of God, the sinfulness of the human race, the need for forgiveness of sin, and the provision of reconciliation through the cross of Jesus Christ, Christians are bound to bear witness to the fact that for one human being to take the life of another simply for the convenience of the stronger person is intrinsically evil. It is an example of what Christ came to save us from. We cannot preach the gospel if we turn sin into choice and remove guilt from choices that violate God's law. My point here is that Christians have theological and evangelical reasons why they cannot interpret nonviolence in such a way that it becomes a cover for the will to power of the strong. It is not only a matter of justice; it is a matter of faithfulness to our Lord in the life of discipleship.

Strategy #4

Stress the differing God-ordained roles of the church and the state in the current time between the first and second comings of Jesus and the necessity of the church to be nonviolent because of its commission to preach the gospel of salvation and the necessity of the state to use force to restrain evil even though the risk of falling into violence is always a danger

This strategy involves stressing something about which Yoder was ambiguous. Yoder argued that God, in some way, "orders" the state and makes use of its employment of the sword so as to preserve at least a rough kind of order in fallen human society. Yet he rejected the idea that we need a "theory" of the state and avoided any talk of the state being used by God to establish or enforce Christianity. Yoder argued stringently against the over-interpretation of Romans 13 in *The Politics of Jesus*, which holds that, because the state has a divinely sanctioned or permitted role in preserving public order for the common good, Christians should play a part in the state. For Yoder, the state is a pagan institution that will always be there in one form or another and which Christians must not trust too much.

This careful, nuanced approach to the state is a long way from modern messianic concepts of the state as provider of the necessities of life and bringer of justice as equality that characterize much of modern thought. However, Yoder's view of the modest role of the state stands in some tension with his tendency to push the boundaries of what can be accomplished in the political realm in the name of justice and peace. Since he sought to avoid the isolationism of his conservative Mennonite forebears and wished to engage the world, he was drawn toward a stance of calling the state to nonviolence.

This could be seen as opening the door to pressing Yoder into the service of liberal pacifism and its lamentable naivety about the effects of sin and its sunny utopianism. It must be admitted that this tendency builds on a regrettable ambiguity in Yoder's thought and is not a misuse of it in the way that certain other uses of his theology are. Here we must be clear that if we wish to maintain a pacifist stance, we must accept that sometimes (often?) the world will pronounce us "irrelevant" and rule us out of a place at the table. This is the price that must be paid for a consistent pacifist ethic and it should not be assumed that it can be finessed in every case by convincing non-Christians to join us in our pacifist stance.

Strategy #5

Accept Karl Barth's "practical pacifism" in place of "absolute pacifism" so as to leave the door open a crack for the possibility of God commanding Christians to exercise lethal force in extreme situations (that is, the Grenzfall or borderline situation)

This fifth strategy involves accepting something that Yoder did not accept. In his book on Barth's ethics of war, Yoder discussed the notion of the *Grenzfall* in chapter nine.[21] Barth utilized this notion in order to preserve God's freedom to command exceptions to general rules in exceptional circumstances. However, as Yoder points out, the definition of an exception is actually left to human reasoning processes rather than being a literal command from God. [22] Yoder agrees that the *Grenzfall* helpfully reminds us of our limitations as finite human beings to know in advance what God's command must be in any new situation. But he adds that it is equally impossible to know in advance that God might actually command someone to kill. In other words, the theological value of the *Grenzfall* in protecting the freedom of God and reminding us of our own finitude in no way translates into our certitude that war will turn out to be morally right in some cases. Yoder concludes that "the analysis of the concept of the Grenzfall itself has given us no new information on the war question."[23] Insofar as it functions to inform us that sometimes war is justifiable, Yoder argues, it has become a form of natural theology and therefore inconsistent with Barth's overall theology.[24]

It seems clear to me that Yoder is correct in his analysis of Barth's use of the *Grenzfall*. The only way to approve of what Barth is doing is to approve of natural theology and to hold that it is possible to know from an analysis of the situation that war is sometimes just. Yoder is therefore right to think that Barth would be more consistent simply to eliminate the *Grenzfall* from his ethics altogether and simply say no to war altogether.

Strategy #6

Accept Yoder's case for pacifism as a convincing case for the proper place of pacifist groups within the Christian church as a witness to the future, escha-tological kingdom of peace, while also accepting that the involvement of other Christians in just war constitutes a necessary witness to the current fallen world in which an imperfect peace is kept by the sword imperfectly as a witness to the doctrine of the fall and the need for redemption

This strategy involves making a major modification of Yoder's thought, one which he certainly would not have approved. It involves saying that Yoder was wrong to insist that pacifism is required of all disciples, which implies that those who try, in good conscience, to follow the just war theory necessarily are wrong and disobedient. If we make this modifica-tion to Yoder's thought, we can incorporate a vocational pacifism into a church that also allows for participation in just war for those not called to vocational pacifism. To make such a modification is basically to save Yoder from liberal Protestantism by making him a Catholic. However, this is tan-tamount to denying that Anabaptism is a viable third way.

Roman Catholics and Protestants, because of their different histories, inevitably hear Yoder's call to radical discipleship and pacifism differently.

For Catholics, it is possible to respond to Yoder's call to pacifism without leaving their tradition, since the Catholic tradition has always included both pacifist and non-pacifist Christians in the same church. The monastic orders, the secular clergy, and the hierarchy have always been pacifist, even though the vast majority of the faithful have been permitted to use limited force in police and just war actions. It has been thought that a complete Christian witness requires both a pacifist and a just war component. On the one hand, the faithful were allowed to engage in limited just war as a testimony to the tragic reality of original sin and that, in this time between the first and second comings of Jesus Christ, the kingdom of God has not yet come in its fullness. On the other hand, the witness of the religious orders and clergy was necessary to point toward the Christian hope for the eschatological kingdom and to emphasize that the kingdom has already begun in the person of the King—the Lord Jesus Christ. When the pacifist part of the witness is missing, the truth of the first coming is compromised and the reality of the Spirit's work in the church today is denied; when the just war part of the witness is missing, the truth of the second coming is compromised and the door is left open to utopian disasters rooted in the denial of original sin and the pretentiousness of thinking we can establish the eschatological kingdom here and now. So for a Catholic to read Yoder and become a convinced pacifist does not entail changing the Catholic tradition; it merely means adopting a pacifist vocation.

For Protestants it is considerably different. At the time of the sixteenth-century Reformation, the magisterial reformers sought protection against their papist enemies from the princes of northern Europe. At this time, the nation states of modern Europe were beginning to form and so church and state became deeply intertwined in Germany, England, and elsewhere, as Protestant state churches came into being. The new state churches had no counter-balancing international identity as Catholics had in the institution of the Papacy, which led to a situation in which Protestants, eager to please their protectors, became zealous in their rejection of anyone who would not fight in defense of the new Protestant governments. This meant that the Anabaptists were in trouble. In the Thirty-Nine Articles of the Church of England, for example, Anabaptists were singled out for condemnation for refusing to bear the sword under the authority of the magistrate.[25] In addition, Protestantism rejected and destroyed monasticism as monkish works righteousness. So, instead of the Anabaptists becoming a pacifist wing of Protestantism and fulfilling a similar role as monasticism in the pre-Reformation church, they were mercilessly persecuted by Catholics and Protestants alike.

Against this historical backdrop, when a Protestant encounters Yoder's politics of Jesus, the reaction is quite different from the Catholic's reaction. There are two choices for the Protestant. One may convert to a Mennonite church and regard Protestantism as sub-Christian, or one may embrace pacifism in a Protestant way by concluding that all true Christians must be pacifists and preaching pacifism for everyone. The magisterial Protestant logic is one state, one church, and one theology. Even in a context of the formal separation of church and state, Protestants are so used to being in charge that they assume their theology should be the theology of the state. But this "pacifism for everyone" stance leads directly to liberal pacifism and engenders the revision of the whole of Christian theology according to the principle of nonviolence. So the project of theological revisionism in which Weaver and company are engaged seems to be a straight-forwardly Protestant endeavor.

Although conservative Protestants continue to reject pacifism as heretical and the historic peace churches as sectarian, liberal Protestants are open to the idea of pacifism or nonviolence because they have already come to reject original sin and a literal second coming. Since liberal Protestants are open to modern ideas of progress, pacifism seems to them appropriate for anyone wishing to work for peace and justice in the world. Liberal Protestantism is inherently Constantinian, it seems to me, and this explains why Protestants find it difficult to receive Yoder without becoming liberal pacifists. This constitutes the single most important problem in Yoder reception today. It seems to me that, in order to receive Yoder without becoming liberals, Protestants must, in important ways, become catholic.

Conclusion

How are interpreters of Yoder likely to respond to these six possible strategies for ensuring that the liberal reading of Yoder does not prevail? It seems to me that the first three are unlikely to arouse much opposition from serious readers of Yoder. Each one has a textual basis in the Yoder corpus and does not contradict anything he wrote. Scholars are free to disagree with Yoder on these points if they think he is wrong, but they are obligated not to misrepresent him by suggesting that Yoder would have agreed with their revisionist views.

We could almost say the same about the fourth strategy in that Yoder definitely allowed that the state bears the sword legitimately in a way the church cannot. The question is whether Yoder can be interpreted as arguing for minimizing state violence by advocating nonviolent conflict resolution methods and nonviolent resistance tactics wherever possible, or whether he advocated calling the state to unilateral disarmament and total pacifism. The former seems more likely to me. But complicating the picture is the ambiguous position of those who press Yoder into the service of their agenda. Liberal social activists can sound very pacifist most of the time and yet swerve into militarism at the last moment, as many in the American progressive tradition did with regard to World War I. So one is never quite sure whether "total exceptionless pacifism" or "near pacifism" or "pragmatic (as long as it works) pacifism" is being advocated. I think it highly doubtful that Yoder envisioned a totally pacifist state in our fallen world, but those who press Yoder into advocating "near pacifism" or "pragmatic pacifism" have some Yoder texts on their side. This, however, opens Yoder to charges of encouraging forms of violence and disaster that a more "realistic" geopolitical strategy could have avoided. It would be better, I think, if the church was less dogmatic about what the state should do in specific situations, especially when the expected outcome of certain recommended actions might well be martyrdom.

This leaves the fifth and sixth strategies. If we choose to employ such strategies, we had better be forthright in admitting that we are going beyond interpreting Yoder to correcting his position. Barth's position could be described as "practical pacifism" but, alternatively, it could be described as strict just war theory. Yoder's critique of Barth makes that plain. To embrace Barth over Yoder at this point may not entail immediate practical differences, but it does entail major ethical and theological differences. As for the sixth strategy, this is even more the case, although it is only the logical extension of the fifth strategy. To admit that Reinhold Niebuhr was basically right in affirming vocational but not absolute pacifism would be a bitter pill for Yoder to swallow and no one should delude himself into thinking that Yoder would approve. But the question that remains is whether or not the first four strategies are sufficient to guard against a liberal interpretation of Yoder.

I want to raise one final question in conclusion and that is to wonder out loud what it means if the middle does not hold. What if Yoder scholarship splits into two streams, one that declares his orthodoxy inconsistent with his pacifism and therefore seeks to revise his theology in a liberal direction, and another that comes to believe that his high view of Scripture, his acceptance of the legitimacy of divine judgment, and his high Christology simply do not justify an absolute pacifism? In that case, we would have some scholars rejecting Yoder's pacifism and others rejecting his orthodoxy. I am convinced that Yoder himself held the two together. But will his legacy be a school of theology that continues to hold to an orthodox pacifism, or will it degenerate into two schools of interpretation that ultimately have little in common with each other and become subsets of liberal and Evangelical theologies, instead of challenging both liberal and Evangelical Protestantism to follow Jesus in the way of peace while believing in Jesus as the divine Saviour of the world?

Endnotes

[1] Nathan R. Kerr, *Christ, History and Apocalyptic: The Politics of Christian Mission* (Eugene, OR: Cascade Books, 2009).

[2] The continuity of Yoder's thought is contested by Paul Martens who argues that there is a loss of Christian particularity and focus on Christology and Ecclesiology in the later Yoder in "Universal History and a Not-Particularly-Christian Particularity: Jeremiah and John Howard Yoder's Social Gospel," in *Power and Practices: Engaging the Work of John Howard Yoder*, 131-146, ed. Jeremy M. Bergen and Anthony G. Siegrist (Scottdale, PA: Herald Press, 2009).

[3] This is contested by some who deny that Barth's influence was as pervasive as I imply. For example, see Philip Stoltzfus, "Nonviolent Jesus, Violent God? A Critique of John Howard Yoder's Approach to Theological Construction," in *Power and Practices*, 29-46.

[4] Yoder, *Nevertheless: Varieties of Christian Pacifism*, 3rd ed. (Scottdale, PA: Herald Press, 1994), 133-34, original emphasis.

[5] Yoder, *Nevertheless*, 134.

[6] Yoder, *The Politics of Jesus: Vicit Agnus Noster*, 2d ed. (Grand Rapids: Eerdmans, 1994), 102.

[7] Ibid., 9.

[8] J. Denny Weaver, *The Nonviolent Atonement* (Grand Rapids: Eerdmans, 2001), 7.

[9] Ibid., 8, 9.

[10] Weaver, "The Nonviolent Atonement: Human Violence, Discipleship and God," in *Stricken by God? Nonviolent Identification and the Victory of Christ*, ed. Brad Jersak and Michael Hardin (Abbotsford, BC: Fresh Wind Press, 2007), 316.

[11] Ibid., 317.

12 Ibid., 338.

13 Ibid., 337.

14 Ibid.

15 See Calvin's comments on Acts 3:13-14 in John Calvin, "Commentary on the Gospel According to Acts of the Epistles," trans. Christopher Fetherstone, ed. Henry Beveridge (Grand Rapids: Baker Book House, 2005), 1:146. Calvin emphasizes the guilt of those who killed Christ. St. Anselm is adamant that "God did not compel Christ to die . . . but Christ himself freely underwent death, not by yielding up his life as an act of obedience, but on account of his obedience in maintaining justice, because he so steadfastly persevered in it that he brought death on himself." St. Anselm, "Why God Became Man," in *A Scholastic Miscellany: Anselm to Ockham, Library of Christian Classics*, Volume X, ed. and trans. Eugene Fairweather (Philadelphia: Westminster Press, 1956), 113. In the New Testament, there are a number of passages to which one could point. See especially Acts 2:23 and 3:13-14.

16 Stoltzfus, "Nonviolent Jesus, Violent God?" in *Power and Practices*.

17 Ray C. Gingerich, "Theological Foundations for an Ethics of Nonviolence: Was Yoder's God a Warrior?" *Mennonite Quarterly Review* 77, no. 3 (July 2003).

18 Ibid., 426.

19 Craig A. Carter, *The Politics of the Cross: The Theology and Social Ethics of John Howard Yoder* (Grand Rapids: Brazos Press, 2001).

20 Oliver O'Donovan, *The Ways of Judgment* (Grand Rapids: Eerdmans, 2005), esp. ch. 1.

21 Yoder, *Karl Barth and the Problem of War and Other Essays on Barth*, ed. Mark Thiessen Nation (Eugene, OR: Cascade Books, 2003).

22 Ibid., 51.

23 Ibid., 53.

24 Ibid., 62.

25 "The Thirty-Nine Articles of the Church of England," in *Confessions and Catechisms of the Reformation*, ed. Mark A. Noll (Grand Rapids: Baker Book House, 1991), 211-27. Numbers 37-39 were directed against the Anabaptists and 37 says, "It is lawful for Christian men, at the commandment of the magistrate, to wear weapons and serve in the wars" (226).

Chapter Five

YODER AND STONE-CAMPBELLITES
Sorting the Grammar of Radical Orthodoxy and Radical Discipleship

JOE R. JONES

It is a great pleasure for me to participate in the coming together of sometime estranged friends from the Stone-Campbell Movement to discuss the work of John Howard Yoder, one of the most trenchant theologians of the twentieth century. While intending an irenic spirit, in his writings Yoder "took no prisoners": his analysis of issues bristled with such clarity that his patient readers were compelled *to think hard* about what he wrote and where they stood in relation to it. Yoder may not have answered every question we readers might have brought to the text, but he did speak directly and repeatedly to a decisive set of beliefs and practices that are at the heart of what it means to be a *disciple of Jesus and a member of his ecclesial body.*

In this presentation I do not promise any original contribution to the ongoing work of Yoder scholars.[1] But I do hope to consider the example of Yoder to help us think about what I regard as the Achilles Heel of the Stone-Campbell Movement. In short, I intend to explore the Movement's hesitation—in all three of its branches—to wrestle with trinitarian orthodoxy and its connection to a more radical understanding of the Christian life and the church in relation to whatever world it might find itself. It is, of course, not the case that other church traditions that claimed trinitarian orthodoxy did in fact obviously succeed in being the community of radical disciples. Yet, neither is it so—given the theological baggage we toted around—that many Stone-Campbellites were able consistently to be a people of radical discipleship.

The nub of the problem, it seems to me, is that the Stone-Campbell Movement's intent to recover the New Testament church and bypass the orthodox-creating creeds of Nicaea and Chalcedon left the movement utterly exposed to the political world in which it was being born—namely, the rise of American-style democracy and its need for civil religious rationale and support. As a peculiar and self-consciously American movement openly embracing its free-church non-established status, the Stone-Campbell Movement (hereinafter referred to as SCM) simply could not resist being co-opted by the needs of American sectionalism and nationalism and their politics. It might be helpful to see this continual and differentiated co-opting as a facsimile of what Yoder has called the "Constantinianization" of the church.[2] And Yoder is exactly right: a Constantinian church finds radical discipleship *practically* impossible.

My aim is not to provide all the historical documentation of just how it was that all three branches of the SCM—in their differing ways—were simply overwhelmed by American politics, principalities, and powers. Rather, my aim is fourfold: 1) to provide some diagnostic comments about orthodoxy and orthopraxis within the SCM, especially in its first century; 2) to propose an understanding of "radical orthodoxy" as trinitarian in character and radical in relation to any and every world in which it might exist; 3) to explore some central convictions of Yoder regarding Christology and ecclesiology pertaining to radical orthodoxy and radical discipleship; and 4) to engage Yoder and the SCM by constructing a brief *theological imaginary* of trinitarian orthodoxy and radical discipleship.[3] Hence, by examining how certain trinitarian theological convictions and practices conceptually interpenetrate, I hope it is clearer how radical discipleship might be kept more keenly on the minds and hearts of the movement's pastors, teachers, and laity.[4]

Orthodoxy and Orthopraxis in the Stone-Campbell Movement

I have argued elsewhere that any Christian ecclesial tradition simply cannot avoid questions of orthodoxy (right belief) and of orthopraxis (right practice).[5] Such questions are *practically unavoidable* in so far as any ecclesial body cannot persist without identifying in its *actual discourses* those beliefs and practices considered essential to its own self-identity as an ongoing Christian tradition. *Essential* here means those actual *identity markers* the tradition repeatedly returns to and acknowledges as minimally constitutive of its own self-understanding and in the absence of which it would become confused about its own identity and persons outside the tradition would be confused about what it would mean to become an active member. How to decide these matters is, of course, difficult and contentious, and in good Calvinist practice I contend that, however questions of orthodoxy and orthopraxis might be answered, they are always *reformable*.

Surely members of the SCM are keenly aware that in our tradition there was from the start a competing worldly creed: "nobody can tell me what I ought to believe; it is my own private decision." I would, however, propose that the SCM from the beginning intended to make the confession of "Jesus Christ is my/our Lord and Savior" as the minimal heart of church belief. Yet all three branches choked at developing any binding or guiding understanding of what it meant to say "Lord" and "Savior" about Jesus and see therein any strong implication about the reality of "the Father" and even less about "the Holy Spirit."[6] It is sufficient for my purposes to note that the anti-creedal disposition of all three branches repeatedly obscured from themselves what right beliefs and practices they did have and thereby prevented the communal identification and clarification of theological convictions that might have been beneficial to our ecclesial faithfulness. Further, according to the way in which I am using the term "orthodoxy," it should not be assumed that all orthodoxies get expressed as "creeds," though ecclesially they are cousins.

So, in the first century of their lives, what might it have meant in the SCM branches to have even talked about "right belief" and/or "right practice"? In a way that might offend many in all three traditions—to which I apologize now—I would suggest something close to the following is what counted as orthodox within the earlier and common years of the movement.

1. Orthodoxy was the right belief that the New Testament alone was sufficient for identifying those beliefs and practices that are essential to the church and the Christian life.
2. Orthodoxy was the right belief that Jesus Christ is my/our Lord and Savior.

3. Orthodoxy was the right belief that "where the Scriptures speak we speak and where the Scriptures are silent we are silent."[7]

4. Orthodoxy was the right belief that the church is comprised of baptized believers only, whereby baptism is by immersion for the remission of sins.

5. Orthodoxy was the right belief that issues of church governance could be settled by reference to the singularly clear pattern of governance of the church in the New Testament.

6. Orthodoxy was the right belief that creeds are human artifices stultifying to Christian understanding and commitment.

7. Orthodoxy was the right belief that the church of the New Testament is more nearly a *movement* among local congregations than what can be called *denominations*, with their defining creeds.

8. Orthodoxy was the right belief that only a *movement* of Christian congregations could achieve genuine Christian unity.

9. Orthodoxy was the right belief that the United States of America, as a democratic republic, was a God-ordained nation important in God's providential governance of the world, however true it might also be that many Americans lived perversely in sin.

10. Orthopraxis was the right practice of observing the Lord's Supper whenever the faithful gather for worship, independent of ordained priests, apostolic or otherwise.

11. Orthopraxis was the right practice of baptizing by immersion only adult or near-adult persons who have confessed that Jesus Christ is their Lord and Savior.

Each of us could extend or contract this list according to our own experience and historical judgment.[8] The point of my list is that, in spite of our resistance to orthodox confessions or creedal statements, the SCM was literally and continually awash in orthodoxies, but few were willing to name and defend the orthodoxies as orthodoxies. Of course, the twentieth century saw the SCM breaking apart as de facto issues of orthodoxy and orthopraxis began rendering the branches unintelligible and opaque to each other. So the question never should have been whether there are orthodoxies or not, but *which orthodoxy and which orthopraxis?* And, *why that orthodoxy and that orthopraxis and not another?*[9]

We are now in a position to recognize that none of the branches ever developed any consensus about trinitarian orthodoxy nor about any orthopraxis of discipleship such as, for example, refusing to return evil for evil, turning the other cheek when injured, being a slave to Christ, loving the stranger and the enemy, forgiving those who wrongly use and abuse you, refusing to use violence against another, and the making of peace. Surely these practices that Jesus taught in the New Testament might have been foundational of any orthodoxy and orthopraxis in a movement publicly putting the emphasis on being *disciples of Christ.*

Toward a Trinitarian Radical Orthodoxy

What might it mean to talk of "radical orthodoxy"? A contemporary movement calls itself "Radical Orthodoxy," with such prominent and interesting theologians as John Milbank, Catherine Pickstock, and Graham Ward.[10] While I admire the aim of this movement to critique the way modern political liberalism, secularism, and capitalist culture co-opted much of Protestant Liberal Christianity, in this essay I am not interested in exploring and critiquing its arresting proposals. I simply mention this movement because it has promoted a verbal expression—*radical orthodoxy*—important to me in my early years of teaching in those notoriously conflictual times of the late 1960s and the early 70s. My use of "radical orthodoxy" intends no explicit or extended continuity with this current movement.

I wrote my dissertation on Karl Barth, and it was Barth who was pulling me away from my previous Tillichian and Reinhold Niebuhrian inclinations in theology and political ethics. With war raging in Vietnam and in the streets, amidst racism shattering society and churches and political assassinations devastating to political hope, almost every traditional societal pillar was coming under attack: education, religion, economics, politics, and government. It was common for protesters and revolutionaries, inside and outside the church, to blame and dismiss traditional orthodox Christian beliefs as wooden, heavy, and incapacitated to deal with the modern world. In particular, this question loomed heavy and threatening: how could so many American church traditions have ever supported racism and going-to-war in such seemingly unjust ways?

I found it helpful during this turmoil to inform students that it was one of the great curiosities—indeed scandals—of church history that traditions self-identified as orthodox had repeatedly gone to war so easily in the name of king and nation, had repeatedly absorbed the ethos and politics of the particular nation or culture in which it was located, and had repeatedly identified the purposes of God with the political aspirations and causes of its nation, class, or ethnic group.[11] In spite of the accusation that the church's orthodoxy repeatedly succumbed to the ruling principalities and powers and that such orthodoxy was the root of the church's dreadful subservience to the powers, I averred in return that the problem was more nearly that *the church was not radically orthodox enough*. Were the church truly and radically orthodox, I argued, then it would consistently be clear to the church that it serves God first and that God's reality and will is known in the compelling contours of the life, death, and resurrection of Jesus Christ, very God and very human. Only by bearing this in mind could the church refuse to identify God's will with the arrangements of power and politics in any particular human government and culture. Hence, it was precisely a Chalcedonian Christology and clear trinitarian beliefs— not succumbing to a presumably natural theology that any rational person should properly believe—that would be the radical orthodoxy and radical orthopraxis that had the power and authority to critique the variety of human political loyalties, governments, and social arrangements.

It was this sort of theologizing by Barth that had also empowered and authorized his critique of and nonviolent resistance to the Nazi overpowering of the German church traditions. Once we state firmly that God as revealed in Jesus of Nazareth is sovereign and *not* Hitler, we can all play out the logic or grammar of this tenacious, radically orthodox belief. This sort of Barth-like radical orthodoxy should be a theological prophylactic to the church's inclination to serve the reigning lords in whatever political and cultural arrangement it might find itself. Yet it was only in my later encounter with Yoder that the orthopraxis of nonviolence emerged as important to that theological prophylactic.[12]

The orthodox creeds of Nicaea (325 CE) and Chalcedon (451 CE) intended to clarify the reality of Jesus' life, death, and resurrection and the reality of the God of Israel, the Creator of the world.[13] If Jesus is where God's sovereignty, will, and purpose are truly and decisively manifest— having become incarnate—then this is the understanding of divinity that critiques all other appeals to divine sanction. Trinitarian belief is not about how three-in-one are magically important; it is about clarifying the divinity of Jesus, how he might be understood as the Lord of all things, and how that Lord is at work in the world. The ruling belief of a genuinely radical orthodoxy is that God is incarnate in Jesus the Jew from Nazareth at a particular time and geography, that this Jesus' life and teaching, his death and resurrection convey an identifiable pattern of beliefs and practices. People who confess this and who thereby follow Jesus are a peculiar people who live differently and serve a Lord different from the various lords and powers found in human societies.

In making this case about the church and radical orthodoxy, I also formulated my first version of the nature and mission of the church, later formulated as:

> The church is that liberative and redemptive
> community of persons
> called into being
> by the gospel of Jesus Christ
> through the Holy Spirit
> to witness in word and deed
> to the living triune God
> for the benefit of the world
> to the glory of God.

Hence, in those uproarious and uprooting times, if the church were truly radically orthodox it would have had a more radical sense for what it might have meant to be disciples of Jesus prepared to love in odd ways and suffer for such loving. Such discipleship—as radical orthopraxis and radical orthodoxy—is neither complacent about the reigning political lords nor incessantly seeking ways to overthrow those lords, whether by violence or nonviolence, in order to become the *dominant* power in the world. As might now be apparent, it was Yoder who helped me clarify and develop these concerns further. Even so, my definition emphatically affirms that the church exists to witness in word and deed *for the benefit of the world*. It is the world, with all of its sinful violence and conflict, that God loves and is intent on redeeming! Hence, the abiding issue is how to be *for* the world without being for the world on the terms determined acceptable by and subservient to the world.

Considering Yoder's Contributions

Salutary Traits of Yoder's Work

You may be reading this because in some way or another you have found the work of John Howard Yoder particularly challenging and illuminating and perhaps provocatively disturbing. Some of you have also spent more effort than I trying to interpret Yoder to an increasingly larger ecclesial and political audience. I applaud those efforts: Yoder is a gift to the Christian church and every encounter we might have with his works should be an encounter that is spiritually athletic and theologically stringent. Allow me now to identify some of the salutary traits of Yoder's work as I see them.

First, Yoder is continually striving for clarity in his writings: it is more important to him most of the time to be searchingly clear about the subject matter under discussion than to be consoling and encouraging. Of course, the primary clarity he seeks has to do with Jesus of Nazareth and the biblical testimony to him. A great bulk of his writings are about or pivot about who this Jesus is—what sort of life he lived and what sort of teachings he conveyed and embodied in his life and in his death on the cross, and what it would mean to regard him as Lord and Savior of one's life and to be a member of a people who live their lives as his body and his disciples. It is from this centering on Jesus that issues about pacifism, politics, and ecclesiology emerge. If he is wrong about Jesus, then in his own mind he is wrong about pacifism, politics, and ecclesiology. It is not that Yoder thinks what he writes is authoritative because of his own authority as scholar; rather it is Jesus and the New Testament witness to him that is authoritative, and Yoder is the earnest student-scholar intending to understand the nature and content of that authority.

Second, there is amazing complexity as well as simplicity in Yoder as he explores what is involved in being a follower of Jesus. He does surprise us from time to time, refusing to say what we think he should have said or saying what we thought he would never have said.[14] Let me give a couple of examples of his refusal to elaborate, as it might also clarify some of my use of Yoder.

I think Yoder is profoundly trinitarian in his theological understanding, though only in a few instances does he discuss some of the theological issues at stake at Nicaea and Chalcedon.[15] But he never wavers in his belief that Jesus is the revelation of the God of Israel and that his life, death, and resurrection incarnates God's presence in the world. Jesus is the Lamb of

God revealing the "grain of the cosmos."[16] In the same connection Yoder claims that Jesus is the beginning of a new aeon, a new creation, and that eschatology is decisive for Jesus' preaching and way of life. But I am not aware that Yoder gives any extended attention to such traditional eschatological themes as the status of death and life-beyond-death and salvation eschatologically understood. Though he does not systematically address these topics, it would be wrong to conclude that he did not think them worthy of a disciple's concern. I have wondered whether Yoder ever gave a funeral homily or even commented on death and churchly grieving and hope. Other issues such as justification and grace, the work of the Holy Spirit, the relationship of God to those who do not confess Christ—which is not the same question as their relation to God—and whether God suffers are left unexplored.[17]

I make these comments about Yoder in order to suggest that Yoder does not write in order to satisfy all our theological concerns and questions. I say this also in order that we not prematurely conclude that if Yoder did not explicitly and fully explore a particular issue or question then it must not have been important to him and therefore need not be important to us.

Radical Orthodoxy and Radical Discipleship in Yoder

I turn now to identify those aspects of Yoder's theologizing that warrant my identifying him in terms of radical orthodoxy and radical discipleship.[18] First, Yoder's pivotal concerns are Christological and ecclesiological: Jesus of Nazareth, a Jew, is the very revelation and incarnation of the God of Israel; and in his life, death, and resurrection, Jesus teaches, exemplifies, and conveys a way of life that summons persons to follow him by becoming gathered into a community of belief and practice that is an alternative way of life to the ways of life that seem so evident in the human social and political worlds. It is in the work of Jesus that God is bringing forth a new creation—a new aeon—and thereby revealing the meaning and goal of human history. It is this eschatological claim about Jesus and his work—and therefore about his reality and being—that is at the center of that *ekklesia* of folk summoned into a new way of life.

We should note that these basic claims about Jesus, God, and the new ecclesial community and its way of life are never proposed from any other perspective than as *confessional*.[19] Yoder is, of course, interpreting the New

Testament and in that way interpreting Jesus and stands ready to discuss whether he has interpreted the New Testament and Jesus correctly. On a variety of grounds it can be debated whether Yoder has adequately interpreted the New Testament in its testimony to Jesus. But he does not discuss whether anyone should believe these big claims about Jesus by way of arguments independent of Scripture that would corroborate that Jesus is indeed truly God, for example. There is no retreat to an independent metaphysics or social ethics to confirm that Jesus is Lord. In these respects Yoder is akin to Barth.

Second, if the above is an accurate representation of Yoder, for the purposes of discussing Yoder in the context of the SCM branches, what might we construct as *orthodox* for Yoder? I propose the following theses for our consideration:

1. That Jesus, the Jew from Nazareth, is the very revelation of the reality and will of the God of Israel, the Creator of the world, and as such, Jesus is divine.

2. That Jesus' life, death, and resurrection reveal a new way of being the people of God, though such a way is a congruent development within the life of Israel.

3. That Jesus proclaimed that the kingdom of God is bringing in a new social/political/ethical way of life that centers on love of neighbor, stranger, and enemy, on the refusal to return evil for evil, and on the refusal to use violence and to seek to rule the world through domination and coercion.

4. That Jesus called into being a new community of persons to be his disciples, to follow his path of servanthood, and to practice the new politics among themselves and in relation to the world, and that by so doing this new community will be an alternative community in relation to the other communities/cultures/nations/peoples that presume to give order to their worlds.

5. That this new community—the new ecclesia—will struggle to maintain its identity as a community of disciples of Jesus in a variety of ways in relation to the world, intending to be for the world without being so on the world's own terms.

6. That this new ecclesia, as the body of Christ in the world, confesses that God is in control of history and that such history has purpose and goal, and thereby the church gives up the belief or assumption common among various peoples that they are in charge of the world and it is their task to order the world and to do so by a 'justifiable use of violence.'

As should be obvious, this delineation of Yoder's orthodoxy is also a delineation of orthopraxis: these beliefs must be believed and these practices must be lived.

What is not included in Yoder's orthodoxy? While Yoder insists that Jesus is divine and acknowledges that this belief is the occasion for trinitarian thinking—that is, trinitarian thinking only arises because of the apostolic claims about Jesus' divinity—Yoder does not seem willing to make trinitarian beliefs essential to the beliefs of the church. Optional, yes, but not essential. Yoder does not include the belief in an inerrant New Testament—though certainly an authoritative New Testament—and thereby he keeps the focus of the church on Jesus and his commandments and promises rather than on each and every sentence in the New Testament as having equal authority. Yoder does not include the belief that the reality of the church is dependent on the presence of "apostolic successors" as an unbroken line of leaders ordained by God.

In what sense, then, might it be illuminating to understand Yoder as embracing *radical orthodoxy* and *radical discipleship*? What is it in Yoder's work that would justify applying radical orthodoxy to him in differentiation from just the traditional orthodoxies of the church? I suggest that the radical orthodoxy of Yoder consists in his tying two elements inseparably together: 1) the belief in a divine Jesus who summons into being a new community of voluntary disciples defined by their confession of his Lordship, and 2) the community's practices of forgiveness; of loving neighbors, strangers, and enemies; of making peace and refusing to use violence for presumably justified ends; and of refusing to seek coercive domination of the world. The church's Lord is Jesus, the church's way of life is discipleship to Jesus, and the church, as an alternative community, lives differently from the ways of the world. This sort of *radical orthodoxy is inseparable from radical discipleship*, and without the practices of radical discipleship, the church becomes dominated and formed by the principalities and powers of the worlds in which it lives.[20]

A Theological Imaginary Engaging Yoder and the Stone-Campbell Movement

A Grammar of Radical Orthodoxy as Trinitarian

As I mentioned in my earlier brief discussion of "radical orthodoxy," I am gripped by the conviction that the church must be clear about its identity if it is not to be repeatedly overwhelmed by and conformed to the worlds in which it exists. I am gripped even more by the conviction that *the church's most basic identity is irrevocably tethered to the identity of God*, or as I have put it, by the radical grammar of the word "God" in the church's life. Precisely because there are many uses historically of "God"—and therefore many gods seductively hiding under the word "God"—the church cannot maintain a faithful identity in its life through the centuries without an ongoing and relentless conversation about the identity of God. It is in answering this question that the church must confront issues of orthodoxy, and it is in answering this question that the historic traditions of the church laboriously—and often languidly—developed and embraced trinitarian language.

I want now to engage Yoder—and therewith also the SCM—in the question of why trinitarian language is intelligible but only optional. *Why isn't trinitarian language essential to answering the questions of the identity of God and the identity of the church?*

It is beyond question that for Yoder it is essential to Christian understanding that Jesus is Lord and therefore Jesus is divine. And Yoder has acknowledged that the great trinitarian theologizing in the early church was a search for the proper and adequate Christian understanding of God. It is obvious that in the New Testament the names "Father," "Son," and "Spirit/Holy Spirit" are used as though they are *distinct*—e.g., the Father did not die on the cross—and yet fundamentally *one*. But do we have a grammar here that would fit well within the polytheistic possibilities of Greco-Roman philosophical and religious life? Supposing now you are an elder in a congregation in Asia Minor engaged in teaching the faith to new converts or would-be-converts and one of them asks, "How it is that Jesus is divine and our Savior but this affirmation is not polytheistic?" What do you say? Trinitarian conversation and the creeds of Nicaea and Chalcedon are attempts by the church to put some exclusionary brackets on some ways of construing God the Father and Jesus of Nazareth. Nicaea confirmed that the Father and Jesus are one basic divine reality. Chalcedon confirmed that Jesus is both divine and human, and any attempt to deny either is to undermine the capacity to call Jesus Lord and Savior. These decisions are basic grammar for the church, even though there is much more to be said.

Now when some other ecclesial tradition, like the SCM, says we need neither Nicaea nor Chalcedon—we just need the real, human Jesus—the question looms as to how this real, human Jesus is our Savior. In what way is Jesus Savior and what does he save us from? Aside from the important sense in which Jesus summons persons to a new way of life, it must be admitted that Yoder tarries not over further questions about the meaning of salvation. He refuses to stress anything like an *experience* of being converted by Jesus, though there are such experiences and they were bread and butter for much of the SCM. And Yoder is certainly wary of developing atonement theories and he hesitates to clarify any imaginary of ultimate salvation.[21]

Suppose now some tradition goes on to say that it is *inappropriate* for the church to attempt to answer these questions in some definitive way and that it must be left up to each individual to answer the questions for herself. The identity of God is left up to the individual to determine for herself, as though the church—as a community of engaging theological conversation—is incapacitated to distinguish between its own common teachings and the predictable struggles individuals might have in understanding, accepting, and appropriating those teachings? Isn't that a recipe for unremitting conflict, confusion, illusion, and despair?

Suppose one then says, as does Yoder, that *God is in control of history and the world process.* What sort of *control* are we talking about, such that earnest would-be-believers might know how to conform to and pray to God? As for Yoder, I think he answers this by referring to the life, death, and resurrection of Jesus: God has power sufficient to bring God's kingdom to culminating presence in the world and yet God rules in the way Jesus rules as the Lamb of God slain for the redemption of the world. Yoder avers that trinitarian language arises from these concerns and intends to render these questions intelligible to the church, but he makes no further attempt to explore and construct such trinitarian understanding as though it is crucial to the church's understanding of God and therefore also the church's understanding of itself.

I believe that the creedal conversations and rule-making of Nicaea and Chalcedon are theologically crucial to the life of the church, even though I admit some of the church's use of the creeds has been confusing. In these creedal conversations, the church assumed that the identity of the Father—as the God of Israel and Creator of the world—was clear and noncontroversial. Using some metaphysical concepts at hand, the Father was assumed to be immutable, impassible, infinite, all-powerful, and simple. The theological problem was getting Jesus—the Jewish human being who suffered and was crucified—understood in relation to the divinity of the Father. However, at various points in the church's life it was able to *reformulate the question* to become*: how does the divinity of Jesus, given his life, death, and resurrection, affect and modify our understanding of the divinity of the Father?*

I think Yoder saw the radical character of this way of putting the question of the identity and divinity of God, perhaps under the influence of Barth. But he abstained—or thought irrelevant to his concerns—from making further inroads on trinitarian conversation. My concern is that in the absence of such further work, it is virtually unintelligible why anyone should suppose Jesus is Lord and humans are summoned to be his body in the world. Put another way, to say "Jesus is Lord" is to say more than "Jesus is the Lord of *my life*"; it is also to say "Jesus is Lord of the whole creation, whether anyone believes it or not." Jesus' Lordship does not depend on our believing, even though it is important that the disciples believe he is Lord. Isn't this why the church cannot confess the Lordship of Jesus without moving into trinitarian language about the reality of God and what God has done on behalf of human salvation?

Further, had Yoder pushed more firmly into trinitarian elaboration, he would have had to confront issues concerning the status of the Holy Spirit. Yet in this regard, Yoder is akin to the SCM with its almost complete neglect of the Holy Spirit. Such neglect poses sharply the question of how the language of the divinity of Jesus as Lord and Savior can be sustained and intelligible to the church without a trinitarian understanding of the unity and the complexity *within* the divine life. Furthermore, *it is trinitarian grammar that empowers the church to understand the life, death, and resurrection of Jesus as not only a historical series of events but also as salvific events internal to the complex Life of God on behalf of the salvation of the world.*

I invite you to look further at my Grammar book to see the virtues, as well as the truthfulness, of a trinitarian understanding of God. It capacitates the church's discourses to think of God as dynamically both one and com-plex in which there is real otherness, movement, and relationship within God's Life and in God's free and loving interaction with the world for the redemption of the world. The incarnational narrative about Jesus in the New Testament will surely fall into disarray in the absence of a robust trini-tarian understanding of God. Hence, the radical orthodoxy I propose is one in which the divinity of Jesus reshapes and deepens the church's own life.[22]

A Grammar of Radical Discipleship and Ecclesial Identity
I have claimed that it is helpful to understand that issues of radical ortho-doxy and radical discipleship are the deep grammar of the church's con-strual of the *identity of God and the identity of the church*. I remind you that I am also concerned with the perennial problem of the church's relation to the worlds in which it invariably exists and how the church is empowered to maintain a self-understanding that clarifies its ongoing and unavoidable being-in-the-world. What sort of identity must the church have if it is to be *for* the world without being *of* the world or being the vassal of the world? It is herein that I think Yoder's claims about radical discipleship will be help-ful for us to examine further.

Radical discipleship is, of course, discipleship to Jesus as Lord and Savior. It is Jesus' life, death, and resurrection that summon the church into existence as the community of persons who live a distinctive way of life. While I think there is more to say about that distinctive way of life than Yoder emphasizes, nevertheless he is right to place discipleship to Jesus as central in the church's life. To drop out or minimize this discipleship and locate the identity of the church by some other conceptual means is for Yoder to cease being the church of Jesus Christ. *The church exists, wherever it exists, only in the form of discipleship.*

How then does Yoder give definiteness to this alternative community's life of discipleship? That way of life includes confessing sins and repent-ing; accepting sins as forgiven by God and learning thereby how to forgive others; seeking the good of the neighbor, the stranger, and the enemy and refusing to take the life of another; refusing to use violence against another; refusing to seek retaliation for wrongs done to oneself or to another; refus-ing to put limits on forgiveness; making peace with others; refusing to rule others as the Gentiles rule by lording over them; and more. Since these practices are clearly identified throughout the New Testament as practices summoned by Jesus, it would be absurd to say Jesus did not really mean to so summons and form the church as his body.

But! But what?

To understand this ever recurring *but* in the historical lives of the churches, let us focus on the disarming title of one of Yoder's most important books: *The Politics of Jesus*. Why the use of this word *politics*? Yoder tells us that he is aiming to question and counter a typical way in which many liberal Protestant theologians/ethicists have argued that the ethics of Jesus, which we have identified above, are irrelevant to the political realities of the world. They claim that the ethics or politics of Jesus are a useful *norm* but are not a useable *guide* to the church's concrete witness to and life in the world. If Christians really care about the world and its infelicitous conflicts and wars—so a non-Yoderian might argue—then the church must have a social ethics or a politics amenable to the politics of the world. Yoder counters this by claiming that Jesus provides an actual politics—a social ethics—that in fact bears upon and interacts with the world's politics. The way of Jesus is also the way of the cross and may include cross-bearing suffering as a consequence of discipleship to Jesus. Hence, the church properly, as the body of Christ in the world, lives an alternative way of life to the ways of life the world promotes and demands. To live in conformity to Jesus' way of life is the basic calling of the church.

Yet, have not even the various church traditions thought they were living differently from the world, even if they lived often in some *partial conformity* to the world's politics? How then is such done? Perhaps it might be argued that at the heart of the church are the practices of neighbor love—agapic love—in which the Christian and the church seek the good of the neighbor, even the stranger and the enemy as in the category of the *neighbor*. Might it happen, then, that the church so seeks the good of its many neighbors that it takes up—or is willing to endorse and support the taking up of—the sword to protect the neighbor in peril? Ah, there is the rub: the willingness to use violence against another in order to protect oneself or another from violence. For Yoder, that simple allowance of violence in the name of the world's various political orders is the source of *how* the church itself loses its own identity and becomes the vassal of the larger political world in which it exists. When the church sanctions the use of violence in the environing politics of the world, then, according to Yoder, it has forfeited its summons to radical discipleship and will thereby lose its distinctive way of life and perhaps its deepest theological identity.

Critics of Yoder are right to see that Yoder tethers the church's identity to radical discipleship to Jesus as that is also tethered to agapic love and agapic love to nonviolence. And yet they criticize Yoder for tethering all these together to comprise the identity of the church. They want a church that can also engage the interests of the world's politics on the world's own terms. But how is that done? It is done by appealing to some other set of principles that will endorse the use of restrained and justified violence in the political orders of the world in order to control violence and disorder. What principles? Consider how *natural law* can come into play or principles of *political realism.* The church comes to grips with two orders: its own internal order of love, forgiveness, and nonviolence, and the order of the world's various dependencies on violence in the name of peace and protection from harm.

Lest his critics or his followers think Yoder has erected pacifism into an independent principle that is in general persuasive to thoughtful folk, Yoder writes another book, *Nevertheless: Varieties of Religious Pacifism,* aiming to distinguish the church's radical discipleship as Messianic Pacifism from a host of other pacifisms with different rationales. Hence, it is not any sort of political pacifism that Yoder is endorsing; it is the pacifism of radical discipleship to Jesus.[23] It is extremely important to note, however, that Yoder is arguing that nonviolence is essential to the church and its radical discipleship, but he is *not* arguing that the politics of the states and nations could be better organized were they to adopt policies of nonviolence. Yet it is certainly clear that Yoder is harsh with Christians who would recommend state violence by reference to the New Testament or the teachings of Jesus. The politics of Jesus are not the politics of the state; the state—in its more or less liberal democratic rationale and form—is of necessity committed to the principled use of violence in order to control random violence and disorder, and whatever role the church might have in stately politics, it would only be to ameliorate specific practices of state violence.[24]

To put in clear focus the dilemma of church theology in relation to the use of violence by the nation-state, Yoder argues that Jesus Christ is at the heart of the church, radical discipleship is the form of the church, and such discipleship involves the refusal by the church and the disciple to use violence against another human for whatever urgent or long-term reasons.

A church that practices this sort of radical discipleship is a church that will never be in danger of having its identity given to it or overwhelmed by the world in which it lives. God, Jesus, church identity, discipleship, and nonviolence are tethered together as radical orthodoxy and radical orthopraxis.

Hence, the real worry about the Constantinianization of the church is not primarily about the church being *established* and under the domain of the state; rather it is about the church losing its radical discipleship to the various ways in which the state or cultural powers prevail upon the disciples to conform to the state's or the society's endorsement and authority and to relinquish the nonviolent character of discipleship.

Conclusion

So how did we Stone-Campbellites become so formed by our worldly circumstances that we—presuming to restore simple New Testament Christianity—stumbled along submitting ourselves variously to American individualism, Southern and Northern warring sentiments and animosities, trusting an inerrant Bible that reduced Jesus to every "jot and tittle" of the text, and casually supporting racism and violence toward women for decades? How did it come about that we fell into reducing discipleship to Jesus to discipleship to American democracy or to our local idiosyncrasies or to our devotion to free market capitalism or to our willingness to go to war to defend American "freedom" or to our passion for liberal politics or to a multi-culturalism that relativizes even Jesus? Might our branches have stayed together and been on target if we had cleaved to a radical orthodoxy *and* radical discipleship? Is it not even now the case that each of the branches has its own way of characterizing the other branches as folk who have forsaken the original dynamism of the SCM?

Speaking boldly—as if for the first time?—are there even the theological resources, commitments, and appetites remaining in our various branches to engage robustly the sort of radical orthodoxy and radical discipleship that Yoder seems to envisage and that I have pushed even further? Or in what respects would any who stand within the SCM tradition find good theological reasons for questioning or even rejecting the basic outlines of Yoder's vision?

I have my own demurs from Yoder, but I like the stringency of his understanding of church and discipleship. Yet I do not think a simple affirmation of the divinity of Jesus is sufficient without a richer exploration of what Jesus' divinity means for our identification of who God is, and I do not see how the identification of God can finally avoid or walk away from trinitarian articulation. I have tried elsewhere to outline a trinitarian orthodoxy that is compatible with much of Yoder, but also more than Yoder. I am skeptical there can be a real "reformation" of the church in the absence of a profound principle of identity and critique that reminds the church in all of its life that it has a Lord—Jesus Christ—who summons it to radical discipleship as a radical alternative community to whatever world in which the church lives. In the absence of that reforming principle of identity and critique, the struggling body of the church will inevitably but variably submit to and rejoice in being the chaplain—or perhaps even a cranky prophet—of the various politics and economics of its world's dominant principalities and powers.

For my own branch of the SCM, the Christian Church (Disciples of Christ), it is hardly imaginable what it would mean to be radical disciples of Jesus in Yoder's sense. But then, whatever could it mean to call ourselves Disciples of Christ? Yet I also must admit that my own Christian pilgrimage is deeply rooted in that loose-jointed heritage, even though it is also the case that most of my lifetime of theological work and writings are hardly legible, much less acceptable, to my tradition's present discourses and practices in their utter disarray. That surely makes me sad, but Paul repeatedly reminds me that we have *these treasures in earthen vessels* that are always in need of reform.

I conclude these reflections on Yoder and Stone-Campbellites with the question of whether there is even that solicitous and convicting *theological imaginary* among us of a proper radical orthodoxy centered on trinitarian discourses arising from the divinity of Jesus and a proper radical discipleship that comprises the church as a genuinely alternative community—a community neither simply *at-war-with* nor *in-bed-with* the various nations and communities of the world, but also *for-the-world* as those creaturely arrangements of power and goods that need radical redemption.

Endnotes

¹ I was a Johnny-come-lately to Yoder. I began seminary instruction in philosophical and systematic theology in 1965. I did not purchase Yoder's *The Politics of Jesus* until 1985, and it was only in the late 1980s and the early 90s that Mark Thiessen Nation, then a bright and engaging student of mine at Christian Theological Seminary, insisted that I read Yoder since he thought Yoder and I shared a host of theological convictions. I owe Mark much gratitude for pushing me into having Yoder as a conversation partner, which also opened the door to re-engaging a graduate school colleague of mine from Yale days, Stanley Hauerwas.

² A theme much articulated by Yoder and much discussed by others. See Yoder, *The Priestly Kingdom: Social Ethics as Gospel* (Notre Dame: University of Notre Dame Press, 1984), esp. 135-147.

³ The expression *imaginary* comes to me by way of its use by Sheldon S. Wolin and Charles Taylor, and I have found it a rich way of talking about the deep interrelation between discourses and practices as construals of the social worlds in the church as well as in other social relationships. See Wolin, *Democracy Incorporated: Managed Democracy and the Specter of Inverted Totalitarianism* (Princeton: Princeton University Press, 2008), 17-40, for "political imaginary" and Taylor's *Modern Social Imaginaries* (Durham, NC: Duke University Press, 2004), 23-30, for "social imaginary," a concept that he also used extensively in his recent work, *A Secular Age* (Cambridge, MA: Harvard University Press, 2007).

⁴ I have enjoyed two previous opportunities to work with SCM theologians. See my contribution, "On Being the Church of Jesus Christ," in a special issue of *Leaven* on "The Church's One Foundation," 15, no. 1 (First Quarter, 2007), 6-11. See also "Spiritual Formation and Christian Discourse: The Shaping Power of Christian Discourse," in *Spiritual Formation and the Future of Stone-Campbell Churches* (Bloomington, IN: Ketch Publications, 2008), 1-20; also reprinted in *Encounter* 69, no. 2 (2008), 29-44.

⁵ Put succinctly, pertaining to the church's witness, I distinguish between 1) questions of orthodoxy and orthopraxis: what must *always* be said and done; 2) questions of heresy and heretical praxis: what must *never* be said or done; and 3) questions of permissible and nonschismatic disagreement and diversity. See Joe R. Jones, *A Grammar of Christian Faith: Systematic Explorations in Christian Life and Doctrine*, 2 volumes (Lanham, MD: Rowman & Littlefield, 2002), 40-43. Hereinafter this work will be referred to as GCF.

⁶ In ways I seek to justify in GCF, 158-66 ("Patriarchy and 'Father' Language"), for particular purposes I will use *Father* as an appropriate—but not the only—way of referring to the First Person of the Trinity.

⁷ This belief often became the practice that if a belief could be found in the "plain sense" of the New Testament, then it was "right to believe it." How else might we explain the Movement's continual obfuscating of differences within the New Testament, especially on large issues such as slavery and the status of women?

⁸ Folk from the Churches of Christ might also identify a cappella worship as orthopraxis supported by the orthodox right belief that worship without musical instruments is commanded by God.

⁹ The SCM never reached real agreement about *how* it is that Jesus *saves us*, but neither Nicaea nor Chalcedon elaborated on salvation.

¹⁰ See John Milbank, *Theology and Social Theory: Beyond Secular Reason* (Cambridge, MA: Blackwell Publishers, 1990); *Being Reconciled: Ontology and Pardon* (London: Routledge, 2003); *The Future of Love: Essays in Political Theology* (Eugene, OR: Cascade Books, Wipf & Stock Publishers, 2009). For a useful introduction to and exploration of Radical Orthodoxy, see James K. A. Smith, *Introducing Radical Orthodoxy: Mapping a Postsecular Theology* (Grand Rapids: Baker Academic, 2004). I think the movement falters in

openly espousing a more Platonic or Neo-Platonic frame of metaphysics. Such a meta-physics, in spite of the admirable attempts by these theologians, can never adequately develop much sense for the agency of God.

[11] For a less tendentious historical account of orthodox political theologies, see Oliver O'Donovan, *The Desire of the Nations: Rediscovering the Roots of Political Theology* (Cambridge, UK: Cambridge University Press, 1996); *The Ways of Judgment* (Grand Rapids: Eerdmans , 2005); with Joan Lockwood O'Donovan, *Bonds of Imperfection: Christian Politics, Past and Present* (Grand Rapids: Eerdmans, 2004); and Oliver O'Donovan and Joan Lockwood O'Donovan, eds., *From Irenaeus to Grotius: A Sourcebook of Christian Political Thought 110-1625* (Grand Rapids: Eerdmans, 1999). On the other hand, see Joerg Rieger, *Christ and Empire: From Paul to Postcolonial Times* (Minneapolis: Fortress Press, 2007); and Kwok Pui-lan, Don H. Compiers, and Joerg Rieger, eds., *Empire and the Christian Tradition: New Readings in Classical Theologians* (Minneapolis: Fortress Press, 2007).

[12] Concerning The Barmen Declaration of 1934, see *Creeds of the Church*, ed. John H. Leith, 3d ed. (Louisville: John Knox Press, 1982), 517-522. Among many books on Barth and the subjects in this essay is the spirited book by Timothy J. Gorringe, *Karl Barth: Against Hegemony* (Oxford: Oxford University Press, 1999). See also *Karl Barth and Radical Politics*, ed. and trans. by George Hunsinger (Philadelphia: Westminster Press, 1976). Yoder was a careful student of Barth's theology, writing an early essay on Barth and war in 1954, which was published in an expanded version as *Karl Barth and the Problem of War* (Nashville: Abingdon Press, 1970) and republished along with some other Yoder essays on Barth as *Karl Barth and the Problem of War and Other Essays on Barth*, ed. with a foreword by Mark Thiessen Nation (Eugene, OR: Cascade Books, Wipf & Stock Publishers, 2003).

[13] For the texts of the Nicene and Chalcedonian creeds, see Leith, *Creeds of the Church*, 28-36.

[14] While it is unquestionable that Yoder and Stanley Hauerwas were good friends, with Hauerwas being one of the compelling champions of Yoder's work, it at least brings a smile to see the title of Yoder's 1997 book, *For the Nations: Essays Evangelical and Public* (Grand Rapids: Eerdmans, 1997) in contrast to Hauerwas' *Against the Nations: War and Survival in a Liberal Society* (Minneapolis: Winston Press, 1985). Perhaps the difference is more tone than substance, with Hauerwas battling liberal theology and ethics in the high precincts and cathedrals of Protestant theological education. But, as mentioned above, I have long favored an understanding of the nature and mission of the church closer to Yoder's phrasing—"for the benefit of the world"; see GCF, 25-29, 609-617. Cf. Yoder, "See How They Go with Their Face to the Sun," in *For the Nations*, ch. 3, for a surprising and powerful meditation on Jeremiah, Judaism, and the ecclesial power to endure foreign residency without hostility or obsequiousness.

[15] Sometime in the early 1990s Mark Thiessen Nation indicated to me the existence of mimeographed notes of Yoder's lectures in systematic theology at the Associated Mennonite Biblical Seminaries in Elkhart, Indiana, delivered over several years from the mid-1960s to about 1980. I bought the lecture notes, gave them a quick scan, and placed them in a Yoder file. It was heartening to see these lectures newly edited and introduced by Stanley Hauerwas and Alex Sider, published in 2002 as *Preface to Theology: Christology and Theological Method* (Brazos Press). In preparation for writing this essay, I read this later text with some care. I am impressed with Yoder's fair and probing discussion of issues at stake in Nicaea and Chalcedon. While he never quite recommended trinitarian constructions, he did not dismiss them either, clearly recognizing that the creedal controversies were addressing the genuinely serious question of how to explain the divinity of Jesus.

[16] As in the title, *The Politics of Jesus: Vicit Agnus Noster* (*Behold the Lamb! Our Victorious Lamb*), 2d rev. ed. (Grand Rapids: Eerdmans, 1994), esp. 246-47.

[17] Yes, I know Yoder discusses Paul on "justification by grace through faith" in *Politics of Jesus*, 212-227. Without nitpicking what he says about Paul, it is important to understand Paul's language of "justification" and "reconciliation" as involving a *family of uses* that do not yield a precise definition that covers all the uses. But I am concerned that Yoder and a host of recent Pauline scholars neglect a fundamental Pauline conviction, namely, *that something happened in Christ Jesus that affects the universal human situation before God and is prior to any person's acceptance of Jesus as Lord.* That is the priority of God's grace, which it appears to me Yoder systematically underplays. Perhaps this is the Barth-side of me, but it affects how issues of salvation can be analyzed and understood. See GCF, 503-509 and 513-19.

[18] In this section I understand myself as doing no more than identifying convictions and arguments that are so common in Yoder and among Yoderian scholars that I am foregoing the tedious need to footnote all the major points.

[19] As I recall, in the early 1990s one of the reasons Mark Thiessen Nation thought I would enjoy reading more of Yoder was because of my radically confessional understanding of theology. At that time Mark was keen on issues arising in philosophical and theological circles concerning "anti-foundationalism" and was convinced Yoder also was anti-foundationalist. See my discussions of some of these issues in GCF, 17-19, 24-25, 70-79, 101-109, and 141-47.

[20] In the language of the New Testament and the church, the uses of the word "world" are varied but interrelated. I have tried to sort out some of the differences and their interrelation in GCF, 47-52, under the heading of "The Dialectic between Church and World." In short, I distinguish among the following uses of *world*: 1) the world as the cosmos of creatures created by God; 2) the world as any human culture/society with its given structures and relations of order; and 3) the world as any human culture/society infected and skewed by sin. *The church is in the world in all three senses and the world is in the church in all three senses.* Hence, there arises a profound and ineradicable dialectic between church and the world.

[21] See GCF, 503-509, for some brief diagnostic comments on the various meanings of "salvation" language.

[22] See GCF, 149-232, for a full discussion of the case for trinitarian grammar, while at the same time adjusting the way some parts of the traditions have talked about God.

[23] Revised and expanded edition (Scottdale, PA: Herald Press, 1992).

[24] It is generally conceded in all philosophical discussions of the politics of the nation-states these days that Hobbes is foundational: citizens concede a monopoly on violence to the state in order that the state will protect them from harm internally within the state and externally from harm by other states and powers. Yet the Yoderian/Mennonite advocacy of nonviolence has never quite clarified how the church might reckon with the "police" function of the state in which the issue is not whether to go to war but how might the church construe, accept, and participate in and limit this more modest use of force and coercion. These issues are thoughtfully explored in a recent book edited by a Yoder student and containing essays from some Mennonite and Roman Catholic thinkers: *Just Policing, Not War: An Alternative Response to World Violence*, ed. Gerald W. Schlabach (Collegeville, MN: Liturgical Press, 2007). The book advances the thesis that, in light of the "fact" that modern war is beyond any serious ethical justification, neither just war theories nor complete nonviolence can seriously come to grips with the need to control violence in the world and to engage in active peacemaking.

Chapter Six

John Howard Yoder's Reading of the Old Testament and the Stone-Campbell Tradition

Paul J. Kissling

The Problem of the Old Testament for the Stone-Campbell Tradition

Gary Hall in reviewing the place of the Old Testament in the Stone-Campbell tradition has noted: "The Stone-Campbell Restoration Movement has had a love-hate relationship with the Old Testament. Many do not see it as having any authority or relevance for the church. On the one hand, it is part of the Bible and the Bible is the inspired word of God. So the Old Testament must remain in the canon. On the other hand, many find much in the Old Testament that is helpful and useful but do not know quite how to interpret it."[1]

John Howard Yoder's Free Church ecclesiology shares many features in common with the Stone-Campbell tradition. Among many salient points which could be mentioned in this regard are his rootedness in Scripture, his reading of church history as in significant measure a deviation from apostolic norms, and his concern over authoritarian models of leadership. In this essay I would like to explore whether Yoder's Old Testament narration, with suitable amendments, might be of help to the Stone-Campbell tradition in its love-hate relationship with the first 78% of the Bible, specifically as that narration prepares for a reading of the New Testament church and the early church which followed it in what Yoder and the Stone-Campbell tradition would regard as its most faithful expressions.[2]

How Yoder Helps with This Problem

Yoder's reading of the Old Testament leads naturally into his reading of Jesus and the early church and of the history of the early church. For Yoder the Old Testament's narrative strategically positions Israel in a more or less permanent state of diaspora as minority outsiders in a sometimes hostile empire. Far from being merely the result of Israel's disobedience and the Lord's consequent judgment, diaspora existence is the normative shape of God's people which is bequeathed to the followers of Jesus. The revelation of the normativity of diaspora existence only takes place after a long and fractured story of the relationship of God with humanity and specifically with Israel. Israel's experiments with an immoveable temple, a monarchy, and perhaps even only one specific land, ultimately demonstrate for Yoder the futility of such structures and the need for God's people, whether Israel or the church, to embrace a life without them. That life is centered on interpreting and living out the Scriptures in a structure led by groups of elders (the synagogue) and embracing a minority existence with a communal way of life that serves as a sign to the world. While a complete description of Yoder's approach to the Old Testament cannot be attempted here,[3] two issues of particular importance will be addressed.

Yoder's Reading of the Monarchy

First is Yoder's reading of the monarchy. Much Old Testament scholarship has been conducted within the environment of a Constantinian form of Christianity in which the idea and ideal of the Christian nation has been in the ascendency. A significant part of the biblical justification for the wedding of religious commitments to nationalistic aspirations is the monarchy of Israel. Valorizing the Davidic monarchy from the earliest days of biblical criticism, the academic study of the Old Testament has succumbed to the temptation which the Torah warned Israel about: seeking a king like the other nations. Yoder quite rightly sees that the Old Testament's macronarrative is, in the end, anti-monarchical. The monarchy is a sort of concession to Israel, and the first of its kings, Saul, is a kind of parable of what to expect. Even David, evidently the man after God's own heart, cannot avoid the trappings of royal power. When compared to the norms of the only law that directly addresses the kingship (Deut. 17:14-20) the monarchy is a disaster which results in division, violence, oppression, idolatry, and ultimately divine judgment. The Torah envisioned a people among whom there was to be a strict separation of powers with judges (Deut. 16:18-20), the people as a whole (17:1-7), priests (17:8-13), and prophets (18:14-21) sharing decision making. In that context a king is allowed for only as a concession and only under the strictest of conditions which would severely limit his power (17:14-20).[4] That Israel never sees the re-establishment of the monarchy is as it should be. The attempt to re-establish it by violence as in the cases of the Maccabees and the Zealots is an unfaithful aberration and a refusal to learn the lessons that God was teaching his people through the failure of the monarchy. Instead, God's people should accept their lot as people not intended to be in charge of society and strive to be a sign of the in-breaking of God's kingdom. Like most Christian traditions, the Stone-Campbell tradition has tended to valorize the monarchy and its founder David. Yoder is helpful in pointing out the perspective of the Old Testament's macro-narrative on the monarchy. Whatever nostalgic glory the reigns of David and Solomon, Hezekiah and Josiah might inspire, the final word of the Old Testament on the monarchy is that it was an unfaithful departure from the Torah and the Lord who gave the Torah.

Yoder's Reading of Old Testament Warfare

A second area in which Yoder's reading of the Old Testament narrative can be helpful to the Stone-Campbell tradition is in his treatment of war, particularly the so-called conquest with its call to wipe out the Canaanites (Deut. 7). The alleged difference between the God of war in the Old Testament and the God of love in the New Testament is one of the primary justifications for the "practical marcionism" so prevalent among restorationist traditions and others. In "If Abraham Is Our Father,"[5]Yoder surveys several traditional explanations for war in the Old Testament offered by those who agree that the New Testament demands nonresistance. Yoder regards the first four of these as inadequate.

Inadequate Approaches Rejected by Yoder
First, in the new dispensation approach, the Old Testament is not relevant for the Christian either because of the evolution of religion or because of a view of God's sovereignty "within whose privileges it must always belong to change His orders, to establish a new basis upon which men are to live, without being accountable to anyone for seeming inconsistency or contradiction."[6] Yoder quite rightly rejects this view. In many ways the Stone-Campbell

tradition has fallen prey to this explanation. Alexander Campbell's view of the New Testament as a sort of constitution for the church allows for an entirely different constitution for Israel. Second, others address the issue by suggesting that commands to destroy the Canaanites are a concession to the disobedience of Israel at the time. Using the divorce text in the Sermon on the Mount with its reference to Deuteronomy 24 as its basis, this view asserts that war was allowed for Israel as a concession to the hardness of their hearts. Just as Deuteronomy's concession of divorce is no longer valid for the followers of Jesus, neither is the command to exterminate the Canaanites. A third view, which Yoder rejects, he terms the pedagogical concession. Israel was not yet ready for moral maturity. According to this view, God was making an adjustment to an innocent, primitive moral maturity. Perhaps insight into the destructiveness of violence and the redemptiveness of love is a very refined kind of cultural understanding accessible only to cultures with a certain degree of advancement. Fourth, Yoder rejects the explanation which resorts to a division of levels or realms. The imperatives of nonresistance only apply to the Christian individual in his primary relationships in the church—not to the civil order. The Old Testament is addressing the civil order where violence is appropriate within certain bounds; the New Testament is addressing the individual in her or his non-civil life, and there violence must be rejected.

Yoder's Approach

Yoder's preferred approach involves careful attention to the concrete historical, anthropological meaning of the Old Testament's warfare commands. This explanation avoids reading backward into the Old Testament from the perspective of the New, and thus distorting our understanding. Yoder uses the command to sacrifice Isaac as an example. Something we quite rightly regard as inherently immoral because of "Modern Western personalism," especially in regard to "the deep sentimental attachment of the father to the son,"[7] is misunderstood if we do not take account of the historical circumstances under which the command was given. In Israel's religious environment the command to sacrifice a child was, according to Yoder, common. When Abraham was asked to sacrifice Isaac, the intended audience did not ask about the morality of child sacrifice. The story is about whether Abraham will trust and obey the Lord's command.

Yoder then analogously explains the holy war of ancient Israel. The question was not about the morality of war *per se*. The question was whether Israel would trust Yahweh even in times of war. Such wars were conducted as religious rituals, were based on *ad hoc* charismatic events, and were not the result of military planning. Yahweh fought the holy wars, not Israel. Yoder then traces the progress of revelation into the Diaspora period to show that "the holy war of Israel is the concrete experience of not needing other crutches for one's identity and community as a people than trust in Jahweh as king, who makes it unnecessary to have earthly kings like the other nations."[8]

He notes that Chronicles and the later prophets "do not derive from the tradition [of holy war] the conclusion, 'Israel slaughtered the Amalekites and therefore we should put to death all the enemies of God.' The point made by the prophets is rather, 'Jahweh has always taken care of us in the past; should we not be able to trust His providence for the immediate future?' Its impact in those later prophetic proclamations was to work against the development of a military caste, military alliances, and political designs based on the availability of military power."[9]

Yoder makes several points about Israel's entrance into the land and the battles which that entrance elicited. They might be fleshed out in the following way. First, the battles depicted there are better termed Yahweh's wars rather than holy war, as that term has been used throughout history to claim the holiness of military campaigns. Holy war in the Bible is fought by the Holy One. As Yahweh's wars, Yahweh is responsible to fight for Israel and Israel is responsible to trust him for victory. Israel is essentially a witness to the battle which Yahweh fights for her. War is won by miracle, not by human strategizing through the accumulation of weaponry and the training of a standing army. Israel's participation in Yahweh's wars, when she is not merely a passive witness, is based on a direct and specific revelation of God in the situation and that participation cannot be used as a standing justification for war without such specific revelation. Yahweh uses nations as tools of his judgment. This is as equally true of his judgment on the inhabitants of Canaan in the time of Joshua by Israel and his use of Assyria later on as a tool of judgment against Israel (Isa. 10:5, 6).

Yoder thus helps those of us in the Stone-Campbell tradition to see that the narrative trajectory of the Old Testament leads us to reject violence and trust in the Lord to secure our future. The teaching of Jesus against violence is an extension of what is happening in the latter portions of the Old Testament and is in continuity with it. We need not posit radical discontinuity between the testaments regarding the nature of God and the way he has called us to live peaceably as his people in the world.

How Yoder's Approach Helps More Generally

In addition to Yoder's help on such matters as the Old Testament's ideology of the monarchy and Yahweh's wars, Yoder's approach more generally has the potential for overcoming the Stone-Campbell tradition's love-hate relationship with the Old Testament.

The Narrative Trajectory

For those in the Stone-Campbell tradition who have retained a high view of Scripture, the Old Testament presents a particular challenge. Since church practice can only be based on New Testament precedent, the Old Testament is often unconsciously relegated to the role of mere historical precursor to the fulfillment found in Jesus and the early church. But as recent work in Biblical Theology has convincingly demonstrated,[10] the Bible has a story or macro-narrative which begins in Creation and ends in New Creation. It reads as a sort of drama. Regarding the Old Testament as primarily of historical interest results in disregarding the Bible's macro-narrative and splintering Scripture. As I have argued elsewhere,[11] Alexander Campbell's schema (institutionalized in Robert Milligan's *Scheme of Redemption*) of starlight, moonlight, and sunlight for the Abrahamic, Mosaic, and New Covenants respectively represents muddled thinking about that narrative trajectory. Yoder's approach suggests that the Old Testament has an implied narrative structure and trajectory which stretches forward to the ministry of Jesus and the early church and ultimately to the eschaton in a quite natural fashion.

The Progress in Revelation

While progressive revelation is a part of the Stone-Campbell tradition's interpretation of the Old Testament (there is "progress" from starlight to moonlight to sunlight), Yoder's approach provides a way to recognize this without disenfranchising the importance of the Old Testament's witness. For him, showing the way forward from the first Joshua to the second Joshua (Jesus) is of vital importance.[12] Yoder speaks of an "evolution" in the Old Testament "from Joshua to Jeremiah, and in postcanonical Judaism the further evolution through Jochanan ben Zakkai to Judah 'the Prince.'"[13]

While "evolution" would not be my preferred word to describe this phenomenon, Yoder intends a sort of natural progression in which the end result toward which the Old Testament is pointing is already established.

A Better Balance between Continuity and Discontinuity

In assessing the use of the Old Testament in the Stone-Campbell tradition, I have previously noted the exaggerated way in which the tradition posits radical discontinuity between the Abrahamic, Mosaic, and new covenants.[14] The New Testament does not regard the Abrahamic covenant as radically different from the New Covenant. The Old Testament itself plainly recognizes that the Mosaic covenant is outmoded and in need of replacement (Jer. 31:31-34). It is nevertheless also a covenant founded on grace even though it is conditional. To compare the Abrahamic and Mosaic covenants to starlight and moonlight in contrast to the new covenant's sunlight is just not theologically tenable. Yoder's approach does a much better job of stressing the continuity between these covenants without in any way denying that the Old Testament is not written to Christians and that we should not confuse ourselves hermeneutically in imagining that we are in some simplistic sense directly addressed by Israel's Scriptures. Yoder sees a sort of progress through the centuries which nevertheless leads naturally to the diasporan stance of the church in the New Testament.

Problems with Yoder's Approach

Yoder's approach to the Old Testament is not without its problems, particularly from the perspective of an Old Testament scholar. While I will spend some time on these, none of them is so fundamental to Yoder's project as to damage it beyond repair. In fact, a more nuanced reading of the Old Testament and contemporary research on the post-exilic literature in particular would only strengthen Yoder's project in regard to the Old Testament.

Jeremiah 29:7 as Proof-text and the Jeremiah Line

Yoder's Old Testament prooftexts for his diaspora-laden theory are Genesis 11, the Babel narrative which he reads not primarily as a judgment from God but as a blessing on humanity,[15] and Jeremiah 29:4-9. The latter text records a letter to the exiles of 597 B.C.E. warning them of the emptiness of hopes for an early return from exile. He counsels them to "build houses, and dwell in them; and plant gardens, and eat the fruit of them. Take wives, and beget sons and daughters; and take wives for your sons, and give your daughters to husbands, that they may bear sons and daughters; and multiply there, and do not be diminished. And seek the peace of the city [salvation of the culture] where I have caused you to be carried away captive, and pray to the LORD for it; for in its peace you shall have peace."[16]

For Yoder this text stands as the normative interpretation of the exile and a paradigm of the way God's people, both Jew and Christian, are to live in the world from the time of Jeremiah on. The return from exile is, therefore, never to be seen as much more than the attempt to reestablish something that has already been found wanting. In contrasting his approach with "standard scholarly accounts" of the theological course of history Yoder comments,

> The standard account sees the course of history moving back from Babylon to Jerusalem with Sheshbazzar and Zerubbabel, Ezra and Nehemiah, and the construction of the Second Temple. The Maccabees are part of that story, i.e., of the effort to reinstate Palestinian kingship as the normative posture, and they too failed. A more consistently Jeremianic account will need to retell that story of the *too-early returns to the land, attending both to the events and to their theological interpretation by prophets and by the several priestly historians and redactors.* According to one way of disentangling the sources, the books of Ezra and Nehemiah are not two faces of the same story, but alternatives. To take Jeremiah seriously, it would seem to me as a lay reader not versed in historic de- and re-construction, that both of them need to be seen as *inappropriate deviations* from the Jeremiah line, since each of them reconstituted a cult and a polity as a branch of the pagan imperial government. Of course the Maccabees were *even more a mistake* as was the Sadducean collaboration with the Roman Empire, in order to maintain the cult, the system which was in charge in Jesus' time [my emphasis].[17]

For Yoder Jeremiah 29:7 is the normative line for the future of the nation. The returns recorded in Ezra-Nehemiah are "too-early" and "inappropriate deviations from the Jeremiah line." But of course the Jeremianic line, insofar as it is based on the text of Jeremiah, is a fiction of Yoder's imagination.

Only three verses later we read, "For thus says the LORD: Only when Babylon's seventy years are completed will I visit you, and I will fulfill to you my promise and bring you back to this place" (NRSV). Jeremiah's point is that the return from exile will not be quick, and the exiles and those still in the land in 597 B.C.E. should not be deceived by those false prophets claiming otherwise. As Peter Ochs comments, "It is helpful for us to be reminded of Jeremiah's patience and openness to seek the welfare of the city, so long as we are reminded, as well, of his own desire and plan to return to, and seek the welfare of, the city of Jerusalem. Yoder has made a beautiful monument of one chapter of Jeremiah's ministry. But there are many chapters."[18]

If there is a turn or new line in the Old Testament, it comes not in Jeremiah 29, but in Daniel 9. There Daniel reflects upon Jeremiah's prophecy of a 70 year exile and prays for its immediate fulfillment. He is told in a vision that the final fulfillment of return will not be in the return in the time of Cyrus, but much later; not 70 but 70 sevens—In other words, long after the so-called return from exile.[19] The concept of long-term diaspora existence which Yoder champions does have a scriptural foundation of sorts, unfortunately Jeremiah 29:7 may not be the best text to describe it.

The Marginalization of the Partial Return (Anti-Ezra-ism)[20]

John Goldingay quotes Yoder narrating Ezra-Nehemiah as "thinking through ritual purity to renew a nation without political sovereignty but with the coercion of a centralized cult backed by the authorization of the Persian empire" and suggests in a footnote that "the context [of this quote] suggests that Yoder's anti-Ezra-ism is the left hand of his Christology."[21] Is Goldingay correct in characterizing Yoder's position as "anti-Ezra-ism"? And, if so, is there an alternative way of reading second temple literature such as Ezra-Nehemiah that would allow someone like Yoder to embrace the entirety of the Old Testament Scriptures while maintaining his core ethical commitments? The actual Yoder quote to which Goldingay refers does not prove Yoder's "anti-Ezra-ism," but it is obvious that he can and has been read that way by both Goldingay and others. Yoder speaks of three failures from Hebrew history that Jesus' ethic casts judgment upon that instruct us: 1) the failed model of kingship "like the nations" in the time of David and Solomon; 2) the failed model of Ezra and Nehemiah trying to use ritual purity to renew a nation that had no political sovereignty of its own but used Persian authorization to establish a centralized cult that had coercive force; and 3) the failed vision of the Maccabees of holy liberation.[22] To acknowledge that the renewal of the nation through ritual purity ultimately failed, if that is the best way to characterize what Ezra and Nehemiah are trying to do, is not necessarily an indictment of Ezra or an indication of "anti-Ezra-ism."

In order to understand Yoder's concerns one must understand his paradigm of the diaspora as Jewish (and Christian) mission. For Yoder the diaspora existence of Jewry and the original diaspora existence of Messianic Judaism (later known as Christianity) is the normative paradigm for faithful discipleship and faithful congregational life. Christians are not called to be in charge in the world; whenever they have been in charge it has discredited the mission of the church and diluted the impact of its witness. The synagogue, which developed first in the Diaspora, not the temple, is the normative model for the church. The challenge of becoming a light for the nations in exile is also the challenge of the church prior to Constantine, or at least prior to Justin Martyr.[23]

For Yoder the return under Ezra and Nehemiah is a move away from the normative paradigm of diaspora. This is because their cult (i.e., temple worship) and their polity (i.e., their "civil" government) were underwritten by—and therefore under the thumb of—the Persians. Yoder comments, "Most of the text of Ezra is about the politicking for imperial authorization to rebuild the temple. In 7:12 Ezra is called 'the scribe of the law of the God of heaven.' To Artaxerexes [sic] these words meant 'secretary for Jewish affairs.' It was the title for a cabinet role in the pagan empire."[24]

Certainly Yoder has a sort of "anti-Ezra-ism" if that be defined as regarding the returns recorded in Ezra as "too early" and the reestablishment of the cult as an inappropriate deviation from the normative mode of diaspora existence. It should not be assumed, however, that Yoder has nothing positive to say about Ezra-Nehemiah. Yoder refers to the Jeremianic turn or shift to comment on the lack of advocacy of armed revolt against the Persians in Ezra-Nehemiah: "What the books of Ezra and Nehemiah recount . . . [is that] all that happens stays well within the constraints of submission to the Gentile empire. Nothing like 'kingship' or 'statehood' is advocated by any party as desirable for the honour of God or the dignity of the people. Thus the reorientation of identity by the Jeremianic shift even comes back to give a new quality to the part of the story which returns to *Eretz* Israel."[25]

Recognizing the ambiguity of the situation on the ground in the time of Ezra and Nehemiah, Yoder argues that "it is clear by now (whether "now" be the first century of our era or the twentieth) that the adequate fulfillment of that promise was not in Ezra or Nehemiah, or in the Maccabees or Bar Kokhba. Most Christians do not say either that it was fulfilled without remainder in Jesus."[26] Here the issue is not Ezra-Nehemiah in and of itself, but those who would interpret the return recorded in Ezra-Nehemiah as the "adequate fulfillment of the promise" by reading the ongoing story in a land-centered way. For Yoder the adequate fulfillment of that promise would only happen by "messianic miracle" and not "politicking elders."[27] In an article in *Cross Currents*,[28] Yoder argues that "Ezra and Nehemiah reestablish the community precisely without national sovereignty"— something decidedly positive from Yoder's point of view. So Yoder can, on occasion, say positive things about the time of Ezra and Nehemiah, although one might notice that if these are the most positive things Yoder has to say about Ezra-Nehemiah, Goldingay's caricature stands.

Why Is Yoder Anti-Ezra?

Goldingay's comment would seem to suggest that Yoder's anti-Ezra-ism is directly tied to his pacifist Christology. But before that suggestion can be assessed I would like to explore several other options. Why is Yoder's reading "anti-Ezra"? Here are some possible reasons.

Yoder reads Ezra poorly

While Yoder's biblical exegesis is typically remarkably astute for a self-confessed "amateur," here his reading of Ezra-Nehemiah lacks his usual subtlety. Though the author of Ezra-Nehemiah and the characters portrayed therein are cautious about being overtly critical of the Persian government, in fact the book is secretly and subtly subversive of the Persians. Yoder's preferred chief source of interpretation for the "post-exilic"[29] literature is Daniel L. Smith-Christopher, a Quaker Old Testament scholar who studied with Yoder's "rabbi" Steven Schwarzchild. In Smith-Christopher's more recent work *A Biblical Theology of Exile*,[30] published several years after Yoder's untimely death, he argues for a more nuanced reading of Ezra-Nehemiah which recognizes its subtle critique of Persian hegemony. Smith-Christopher comments that the "post-exilic Jewish community is trapped by competing claims to authority made by the local non-Jewish officials and the Persian court."[31] The Persian correspondence recorded in Ezra-Nehemiah is interpreted in such a way as to "illustrate the ambiguity of the Jewish attitude toward the Persian ruler." He notes the subtle ways in which resistance is indicated, noting finally Ezra 9:7-8 and Nehemiah 9:36-37 in which the situation of the "post-exilic" community is described as "slavery." Ezra also complains that the land gives its increase to the kings who have power over the returnees' bodies and cattle to use as they please (Neh. 9:37). Smith-Christopher concludes, "The attitude of the editors of Ezra-Nehemiah toward their Persian overlords is neither gratitude nor warmth. Their attitude is both the realistic assessment of forced subservience, and in response, a faithful nonviolent resistance to any idea that Persian power or authority is greater than God's spiritual armament of the faithful. Thus the editors of Ezra-Nehemiah represent a subversive theology, a hidden transcript that reserves recognition of authority to God alone, while maintaining a necessarily polite demeanor to the imperial representatives."[32] Ezra-Nehemiah thus shares the "insider language" characteristic of apocalyptic literature where criticism of "overlords" is done in such a way that insiders understand it while outsiders do not. Or, to speak historically, Ezra and Nehemiah are careful to criticize the Persians when there is no one there to report them to the king, or the authors of Ezra-Nehemiah are careful to tuck such criticisms away into books which the Persian authorities are unlikely to read.

Yoder also fails to recognize (or silently dissents from) the new Exodus/ new Conquest typology in Ezra-Nehemiah which affirms that the return of some Jews from exile is a part of the fulfillment of God's promises through the pre-exilic and exilic prophets.[33] Some examples of this typology are the decision to return on the day after Passover (Ezra 8:31), the prayer for a "straight way" (Ezra 8:25) echoing the new Exodus terminology "make his way straight" in Isaiah 40:3, and the description of the intermarriage problem as though the women who the Jews were marrying were aboriginals from the original inhabitants of Canaan (Ezra 9:1).[34] While numerous texts (including Ezra-Nehemiah) make it obvious that the return led by Ezra is not the ultimate return promised, Yoder fails to acknowledge the legitimacy of even a partial fulfillment in the returns narrated in Ezra-Nehemiah. This is in conflict with the theology of the book of Ezra.

Furthermore, the work of Tamara Cohn Eskenazi on Ezra would seem to dovetail nicely with Yoder's concerns had he been aware of it.[35] She argues that "three dominant themes combine in Ezra-Nehemiah to deemphasize the heroic and affirm the prosaic."[36] Each of these echoes prominent Yoderian themes which Yoder would describe as arising out of the Diaspora.

Firstly, for Eskenazi, Ezra-Nehemiah shifts the focus from leaders to participating community. Ezra-Nehemiah "places the people as a whole, not merely famous individual leaders, at the center of its narrative as the significant actors in the book."[37] The rise of the laity is not merely a reflex of the Diaspora experience. It is found in the returned community as well.

Secondly, for Eskenazi, Ezra-Nehemiah "expands the concept of the house of God from temple to city. Such expansion broadens the arena of special sanctity to include all who dwell in the holy city (Neh 12:30)."[38] Holiness is thus no longer limited to the temple itself. This would seem to democratize holiness without ritualistic restrictions in a way that Yoder might identify as diasporan.

Thirdly, says Eskenazi, "Ezra-Nehemiah emphasizes the primacy of the written text over the oral as a source of authority. In doing so, Ezra-Nehemiah wrests power from charismatic figures and provides a more publicly accessible, and publicly negotiable, source of authority."[39] Once again the authority of the written word, which can be publicly negotiated, is one of the features of the Diaspora synagogue which Yoder values so much. Eskenazi attributes the beginning of this trend to the work of Ezra-Nehemiah.

A particular insight of Eskenazi is the contrast in Ezra-Nehemiah between portrayals of what might be called the "passive" leadership style of Ezra and the more activist style of Nehemiah.[40] She argues that Ezra-Nehemiah is subtly affirming Ezra's approach over Nehemiah's. Her description reminds one of models of leadership where authority is shared and not concentrated in a single individual leader which Yoder emphasizes. Eskenazi notes that Ezra does not initiate the identification of the problem of intermarriage (Ezra 9:1), nor does he suggest a solution (10:2-3), nor does he presume the right to lead the nation in addressing the issue (10:4). When the nation gathers to consider the matter under Ezra's leadership, the assembly suggests a more deliberate procedure (10:12-14) to which Ezra and most of the other leaders with him accede (10:15). Eskenazi's work, had Yoder known of it, would have cautioned him from rejecting the ideology of Ezra-Nehemiah out of hand.

Yoder Fails to Make Good Use of Inaugurated or Realized Eschatology

Yoder's "anti-Ezra-ism" is also caused by his failure to recognize the use of the concept of realized eschatology within the Old Testament itself. By using this terminology I am not suggesting that the realized part of Old Testament eschatology is somehow on a par with the realized part of New Testament eschatology. However, the new Exodus/new Conquest typology in Ezra-Nehemiah is designed to affirm the return from exile as a part, however small, of the fulfillment of God's promises through the pre-exilic and exilic prophets. While many texts clarify that the ultimate fulfillment is some time off in the future (e.g., Dan. 9), there is no point in ignoring or attempting to deny the theology of partial fulfillment. Ezra-Nehemiah in its wider canonical context has a form of the New Testament "already-but-not-yet" theology. Yoder is quite conversant with this concept but fails to consider it in the case of Ezra-Nehemiah.

Yoder Posits a Binary Opposition between Land and Diaspora

Alain Epp Weaver notes Boyarin's notion of the diasporized state and suggests a diaspora consciousness *in* the land as a viable and more appropriate way to think about landedness in the current Israeli-Palestinian conflict than Yoder's approach which places too much emphasis on diaspora without landedness.[41] According to Weaver, Yoder falls into the trap of either diaspora or landedness. But to be fair to Yoder he does hint at such a diasporized concept of the state, as noted above. Nevertheless his take on Ezra-Nehemiah could be greatly strengthened by more focus on this concept. Mark Brett, reflecting on his own work with Australian aboriginals, challenges the way Yoder's ideal of diaspora existence can be twisted into justification for depriving aboriginals of reparations for historical injustice in regard to the land.[42] Yoder cannot be faulted for the way his thought can be twisted, but the relative lack of emphasis on legitimate aspirations for landedness in Yoder's work should give us pause.

Can Yoder's Anti-Ezra-ism Be Fixed?

One could argue with Goldingay that the deficiencies detailed above flow from Yoder's Christology which forces him into the mistakes delineated. The question then becomes, "Can Yoder's pacifist Christology be sustained without his anti-Ezra-ism?" In other words, can anything be done? I would observe the following. In Yoder's discussions with pacifist Jewish Rabbi Steven S. Schwarzschild, the Maccabean experiment of trying to use violence to reestablish the Davidic monarchy is rejected by both; but as Schwarzschild often quipped, "Maccabees is in your [i.e., Christian] Bible, not in ours."[43] Yoder sees the work of Ezra and Nehemiah as one of a line of attempts to accomplish by human effort what can only occur by messianic miracle.[44] But to place Ezra and Nehemiah in the same line with Maccabees is problematic. Can Ezra and Nehemiah be blamed for what evolved from their work? Is there any indication in Ezra-Nehemiah of the advocacy of violence? Yoder's Christology can be sustained by an adjustment of his reading of diaspora and restoration to a position which has more balance. Both the return from exile by the minority and the continuance in Diaspora by the majority formed the nation for its future purposes in the outworking of God's sovereign plan. Yoder's "anti-Ezra-ism" does not have to be the "left hand of his Christology."

Yoder and Other Diaspora Old Testament Texts

Yoder's approach to the wars of conquest in Joshua has been dealt with earlier. A question that arises in connection to this is the violent "self-defense" of the Jews in Esther 9. Faced with an edict encouraging the annihilation of the Jews in the Persian Empire, Esther and Mordecai manage to convince the Persian king Ahasuerus to issue another edict allowing Jews to defend themselves against those who attack them. They defend themselves against 800 people in the capital and 75,000 throughout the empire. We thus have a Diaspora text which could be taken to justify violent self-defense. Yoder does not explicitly address this issue insofar as I have been able to discover.[45] Conversely, Yoder speaks positively of the lessons of Esther for Diaspora Jews.[46] How could Yoder respond to this question, even though he evidently did not? Yoder notes that the conquest narratives in Joshua are not used by later texts in the Old Testament to justify violence; instead they serve to remind Israel that Yahweh fights for them. The echoes of the book of Joshua in such "post-exilic" texts as Ezra-Nehemiah and Esther show that the new "Conquest" typology is at work in these texts. The use of this typology may imply a parallel between the situations faced by God's people in the post-exilic world and in the book of Joshua.

In the case of Esther, two particular echoes might be noticed. In 9:15-16 the Jewish people did not take the plunder just as Israel at Jericho was prohibited from doing.[47] For Jews in the time of Esther the war is thus seen as a type of "Yahweh war" or "holy war." A second echo is the fact that the "war" in Esther is a war of self-defense. This is also the case in the book of Joshua. With the exception of Jericho and Ai the so-called "Conquest" is actually two battles of self-defense. The first is in defense of Israel's new covenant partners, the Gibeonites, when the Southern coalition of kings attacked them (Josh 10:1-7). The second battle was initiated by the Northern coalition against Israel (Josh 11:1-5). The attack upon the Jews by their enemies in the Persian Empire was similarly a battle of self-defense. Thus while the Diaspora situation both is and is not parallel to the situation of Israel as they initially enter the Promised Land, the inter-textual typology leads the reader to see the parallels as well as the differences. The situation in Esther, like that faced by Israel in the Book of Joshua, does not teach future generations to engage in violence themselves but to trust God to preserve the nation from the violence of others. As implied above, a similar conclusion would pertain to Ezra-Nehemiah.

Conclusion

Goldingay is right about a certain form of anti-Ezra-ism in Yoder. It is tied to Yoder's understanding of diaspora as mission and is prooftexted by a (mis?)reading of the Babel narrative and Jeremiah 29. But this is not necessary and is therefore not, logically speaking, the "left hand of his Christology." Yoder's view can be rehabilitated with a more nuanced reading of the relationship between the post-exilic temple community and the still-exilic and/or Diaspora existence of the majority of Jews. This would be furthered by the acknowledgment of an element, however tentative of the "already" character of the return even if the primary accent is on the "not-yet" rather than the "already." Yoder does not need to be anti-Ezra in order to maintain his pacifist Christology and his valuing of diaspora as a normative image for church and synagogue. But given these sorts of modifications, Yoder's approach to the Old Testament has as much to contribute to the Stone-Campbell tradition as do his insights on ecclesial practice.

Endnotes

[1] Gary Hall, "The Old Testament in the Early Stone-Campbell Movement," in *Evangelicalism & the Stone-Campbell Movement*: Volume 2, *Engaging Basic Christian Doctrine*, ed. by William R. Baker (Abilene, TX: Abilene Christian University Press, 2006), 245.

[2] Unlike most of the rest of the authors in this volume, I write as an Old Testament scholar and an admirer of John Howard Yoder, not as a Yoder expert. Besides the Bible, the two books which most influenced me in my development as a young Christian were *The Cost of Discipleship* by Bonhoeffer and *The Politics of Jesus* by John Howard Yoder. John Nugent is responsible for re-introducing me to Yoder only relatively recently.

[3] Cf. John C. Nugent's recent unpublished doctoral dissertation, "Old Testament Contributions to Ecclesiology: Engaging and Extending the Insights of John Howard Yoder" (Calvin Theological Seminary, 2009), for an attempt to reconstruct that narrative in detail.

[4] For an insightful reading of the Primary History (Genesis through Kings) for its political theology, see J. G. McConville, *God and Earthly Power: An Old Testament Political Theology: Genesis-Kings* (New York: T & T Clark, 2006). McConville's primary target is Oliver O'Donovan's *The Desire of the Nations: Rediscovering the Roots of Political Theology* (Cambridge: Cambridge University Press, 1996), which valorizes the Monarchy.

[5] Yoder, "If Abraham Is Our Father," in *The Original Revolution: Essays on Christian Pacifism* (Scottdale, PA: Herald Press, 1971; reprinted, Wipf and Stock, 1998), 91-111.

[6] Ibid., 93.

[7] Ibid., 102.

[8] Ibid., 107.

[9] Ibid., 106.

[10] See for example, Craig G. Bartholomew and Michael W. Goheen, *The Drama of Scripture* (Grand Rapids: Baker, 2004).

[11] See Paul J. Kissling, "The Old Testament in the Stone-Campbell Movement Today: Proposals for Change," in *Evangelicalism & the Stone-Campbell Movement*, 2: 274-286.

[12] Yoder notes Lind's attempt to revise the understanding of Holy War: "One core part of the task, the most strategic in some ways, is the revision that Millard Lind is undertaking. What was actually the shape of the war story in the formative experience of ancient Israel? When properly understood, does that meaning point toward or away from Jesus?" in Millard C. Lind, *Yahweh is a Warrior: The Theology of Warfare in Ancient Israel* (Scottdale, PA: Herald, 1980), 18.

[13] Ibid.

[14] Kissling, "The Old Testament in the Stone-Campbell Movement Today," 274-286.

[15] While the Babel episode does result in humanity spreading across the world as they were commissioned by God immediately after the flood (Gen. 9:1, 7), the diversity of languages and cultures arises from the confusion of the languages at Babel. The narrative in Genesis is not in chronological sequence, i.e., the nations described in chapter 10 are the result of the confusion of languages described in chapter 11. For the likely reason for this chronological disruption, see my *Genesis*, Volume 1, (Joplin, MO: College Press, 2004), 379. Yoder regards the diversity of languages and cultures as the Lord's intention from the beginning. See *Jewish Christian Schism Revisited* [hereafter *JCSR*], eds. Michael G. Cartwright and Peter Ochs (Grand Rapids: Eerdmans, 2003), 188-189.

[16] Yoder's translation. "See How They Go with Their Face to the Sun," in *JCSR*, 202, fn. 60.

[17] Ibid., 193-94.

[18] Ochs, "Commentary" on chapter 10, in *JCSR*, 203-204.

[19] John Sailhamer, "Biblical Theology and the Composition of the Hebrew Bible," in *Biblical Theology: Retrospect and Prospect*, ed. Scott J. Hafemann (Downers Grove, IL: InterVarsity, 2002), 25-37.

[20] Much of what follows is drawn from my article, "Can John Howard Yoder's Ethics Embrace the Entire Old Testament as Scripture?" *Theological Reflections* 8 (2007): 10-22.

[21] John Goldingay, *Israel's Gospel, Old Testament Theology*, Volume 1 (Downers Grove, IL: InterVarsity, 2004), 764, which refers to the version of Yoder's "See How They Go with Their Face to the Sun" that was published in *For the Nations* (Grand Rapids: Eerdmans, 1997), 141.

[22] Ibid.

[23] In some places Yoder locates the fall of the church with its fall away from its Jewish roots to the time of Justin Martyr and the Jewish response to him. See "It Did Not Have to Be," in *JCSR*, 61: "We do not know for *sure* of *any* rabbi trying to drive a wedge between himself and the *nozrim* before Justin began driving his wedge between himself and the Jewish church. If Justin's need for Gentile respectability had not led him to be ready to split the church, we cannot be sure the rabbis would have reciprocated in kind."

[24] Yoder, "See How They Go," in *For the Nations*, 74, fn. 57.

[25] Yoder, "See How They Go," in *JCSR*, 188.

[26] Yoder, "See How They Go," in *For the Nations*, 75.

[27] Ibid.

[28] Yoder, "Exodus and Exile: The Two Faces of Liberation," *Cross Currents* 23 (Fall 1973): 306.

[29] The problems with this terminology are widely known. It defines the continuing history of Judah in terms of the relatively small number of people who returned to the land during the Persian era.

[30] Daniel L. Smith-Christopher, *A Biblical Theology of Exile*, Overtures to Biblical Theology (Minneapolis: Fortress, 2002).

[31] Ibid., 40.

[32] Ibid., 45.

[33] On the new exodus typology in Ezra-Nehemiah, see Mark A. Thronvielt, *Ezra-Nehemiah*, Interpretation (Louisville: John Knox, 1992).

[34] "The people of Israel, the priests, and the Levites have not separated themselves from the peoples of the lands with their abominations, from the Canaanites, the Hittites, the Perizzites, the Jebusites, the Ammonites, the Moabites, the Egyptians, and the Amorites" (Ezra 9:1, NRSV). It seems unlikely that this is a literal list. While Moabite, Ammonite, and perhaps Egyptian women were potential marriage partners in Ezra's time, most likely the other peoples listed are not to be taken literally, but listed to parallel the situation in the time of Joshua.

[35] Tamara Cohn Eskenazi, *In an Age of Prose: A Literary Approach to Ezra-Nehemiah*, Society of Biblical Literature Monograph Series 36 (Atlanta: Scholars Press, 1988).

[36] Ibid., 2.

[37] Ibid.

[38] Ibid.

[39] Ibid.

[40] Notably Eskenazi draws a strong contrast in this regard between Ezra-Nehemiah and 1 Esdras.

[41] Alain Epp Weaver, *States of Exile: Visions of Diaspora, Witness, and Return* (Scottdale, PA: Herald Press, 2008), 60-61.

[43] Referenced in "Jesus the Jewish Pacifist," in *JCSR*, 89, fn. 18: "It was more than a witticism when Steven Scharzchild wrote me, 'The Maccabees are in your Bible, not in ours.'

[The editors have been unable to locate a copy of this document, but Schwarzchild was well known for offering this quip in a variety of settings.]"

[44] Yoder, "See How They Go," in *For the Nations*, 75: "The prophesied hope of return to Jerusalem, which would ultimately be implemented not by politicking elders but by messianic miracle, needs to be further interpreted."

[45] The Scripture indexes in Yoder's books are unfortunately not always detailed enough.

[46] Yoder, "On Not Being in Charge," in *JCSR*, 172.

[47] I owe this suggestion to Alexander Mamonov, a TCMI student from Ukraine.

Chapter Seven

KINGDOM WORK
John Howard Yoder's Free Church Contributions to an Ecumenical Theology of Vocation

JOHN C. NUGENT

Einer Billing persuasively argues that one cannot discern Luther's theology of vocation without recovering a sense of his entire theological system.[1] In many ways, this is how theologies of vocation must be. There is no "biblical doctrine of work" that can be lifted from the pages of Scripture and translated into the contemporary context.[2] Luther's doctrine of vocation, like that of his predecessors and successors, follows necessarily from his wider views of creation and fall, church and world, salvation and eschatology.[3] This is why mature theological traditions, whether Catholic, Lutheran, or Reformed, have highly refined views of vocation.

May the same be said of the comparatively young Free Church tradition?[4] To my knowledge, a Free Church theology of work has yet to be offered.[5] This tradition has not, however, been entirely silent. John Howard Yoder, arguably the most influential twentieth century Free Church thinker, has written extensively on this topic. Though Yoder never offered a formal theology of vocation, he advocated a coherent theological framework that both addresses this topic from a distinctly Free Church perspective and contributes much to wider ecumenical conversations about work.[6] I call Yoder's contribution an *"ecumenical Free Church"* perspective because, although his insights flow from and reflect his Free Church commitment to a separation of church and state, there is nothing particularly sectarian about his constructive proposal. Whether by choice or not, when it comes to separation of church and state in the post-Christendom West, we're all free church now.

Yoder wrote his only essay dedicated to this topic, "I Choose Vocation," when he was twenty. Beyond this two-page popular piece, we have only brief references scattered throughout his writings.[7] Fortunately, Yoder is consistent and concise in his treatment of vocation. He usually begins by critiquing standard Protestant and Catholic views that presuppose the Constantinian compromise and fail to reflect a biblical doctrine of the powers, creation, and state. He continues by hinting at the shape of a Post-Constantinian theology of work, which includes two key emphases: an eschatological rather than Constantinian view of history, and the foundational importance of Christ's reign and its universal implications. These two areas constitute the heart of Yoder's theology of work. In this essay, I discuss each of them in detail and conclude by summarizing the key components of Yoder's vocational project and evaluating its contributions to the wider ecumenical conversation.

The Constantinian Captivity of Vocation

Yoder stands well within the Free Church tradition in maintaining that one of the most significant turning points in world history was when the minority church of the first few centuries became the majority church of the Roman Empire. For Yoder, Constantine is the symbolic figurehead for this transition.[8] He acknowledges, however, that this symbol should not be pushed literalistically; Christians started making peace with the empire long before Constantine and it was not until after his death that Christianity eventually became the empire's official religion.[9] Nonetheless, this epochal shift profoundly influenced social ethics with deep reverberations into our own time. When tracing its effects on the doctrine of vocation throughout history, Yoder paints with broad strokes that are sure to frustrate those who insist upon historical precision.[10] This lack of precision should not be confused with historical ineptitude. Yoder is a historical theologian by training and has performed careful analysis in his field of specialty.[11] Rather we should remember that Yoder only makes passing references to his view of vocation (no more than a few pages at a time) and that he presumes scholarly consensus on his basic view of the historical periods involved. For this reason, Yoder's contribution to a theology of vocation is not his account of the specific vocational theologies of various eras, per se, but how he interprets them as part of a wider historical movement colored by Constantinian impulses.

Yoder describes the decline and fall of vocation by observing that when the empire sponsored Christianity and most citizens became at least nominally Christian, all professions deemed necessary for the smooth operation of the empire were effectively baptized, without conversion. In Yoder's words, "since there are no more confessing heathen, every profession must be declared Christian."[12] The problem, of course, is that Scripture does not furnish Christian counsels for operating the empire, and specific gospel commitments conflicted with specific tasks that were deemed essential for imperial stability.[13] Loving one's enemy, repeatedly forgiving wrong-doers, countering evil with kindness, and renouncing top-down power could not realistically be brought to bear, so it seemed, on imperial policy.

Yoder laments that the church did not, at this point, stringently analyze whether this merger was biblically appropriate. Rather, it assumed that God willed this partnership and went about justifying it theologically. The church's solution was simple: since the gospel's radical requirements cannot realistically be lived by all without collapsing the empire, they must not be mandatory for all Christians. Theologians then developed a system of morality that could reasonably be expected of all people, regardless of their professions, and relegated the gospel's less realistic components to the sphere of special calling or vocation.[14]

Since the gospel could not furnish the basis for a majority ethic, the medieval church sought guidance from human reflection on God's creation, that is, from natural law.[15] Guidance for civil order was therefore rooted in general revelation whereas guidance for monastic order was rooted in gospel. Exceptional individuals are called to live lives pointing to heaven whereas the majority is supposed to keep things running smoothly on earth. The former task was strictly voluntary; the latter was mandatory for all and enforced by the sword.[16] Thus, according to Yoder, the post-Constantine, pre-Reformation doctrine of vocation revolved around religious separateness and effectively granted autonomy (or at least an exemption from gospel mandates) to the vocational sphere.[17]

The Magisterial Reformers, in Yoder's telling, only partially addressed the limitations of the medieval Constantinian synthesis. Following Luther, they rightly affirmed the value of "non-religious" vocation.[18] The monastic ideal, though not required of all, had been elevated to a special status that rendered "secular" professions inconsequential from a faith perspective. Conceived as such, monasticism came to represent the kind of works-righteousness that Luther sought to eradicate from the church.[19] Part of Luther's solution was to recognize that God calls all believers to serve him with their professions as long as those professions contribute to the good of society as he understood it. Furthermore, an essential way to show love to one's neighbors is to serve them in the public realm via one's profession, whether as prince, soldier, or banker.[20]

It was no stretch for Luther to imbue the individual's vocation, calling, or station in life with religious significance. Luther believed that God was Lord over all and that he rules the church with gospel standards and the world with lesser standards more appropriate to those in rebellion. That being the case, Christians were called to serve God in personal and ecclesial spheres according to the teachings of Christ and in public and governmental spheres according to principles inherent in their respective professions. These principles have to be discerned, in medieval manner, via reasoned reflection on the orders of creation and society, that is, via natural law. Yet Yoder could not tolerate this or any kind of dualistic ethic that restricts the gospel's relevance. Though he commends Luther for acknowledging a qualitative separation between church and world, he rejects the suggestion that Christians must adhere to world-friendly standards when on the world's turf. The autonomy that Constantinianism granted to vocation remained unchallenged by Luther, even though repackaged.[21]

Such autonomy was better addressed, albeit not to Yoder's complete satisfaction, by the heirs of John Calvin.[22] The Calvinist tradition challenged Luther's choice to place the "public sphere" outside the jurisdiction of God's Word; though it, too, conceded that the gospel's radical demands were not sufficient to rule a rebellious world. Rather than look strictly to creation, natural law, or each vocation itself for guidance, they turned to the Old Testament. In it, God provides concrete guidance for worldly governance. Yoder is not satisfied with this approach, however, because it continues to render certain spheres of life unchallenged by the gospel of Jesus Christ. Though it boldly affirms that Christ has changed the course of world history, it leaves many spheres functionally unchanged.

The results, according to Yoder, were disastrous. When it became apparent that the Old Testament, as it was often read, yielded the same ethical results as natural law, Scripture became superfluous. Identical ethical conclusions were reached by deistic and later atheistic reflection.[23] Once Christ is bracketed, Yoder points out, the ethical mores of many Christians, deists, and atheists become essentially the same. This sameness could be narrated positively insofar as it allows believers and unbelievers to work together smoothly in order to develop shared "public" ethics. Yet, without the difference that the gospel makes, what do Christians really have to add to the conversation?

It is worth noting that Yoder qualified his critique of the Magisterial Reformers. He did not believe that they sought to grant complete ethical autonomy to various vocations. After all, they instructed statesmen and declared certain professions unchristian. But the outcomes of declaring the orders of creation independent of Christ were the secularization of the creation orders and the autonomy of the state, which became master of its own house.[24] So an ethic that seemed viable in a Christendom context was later exposed as short-sighted in a post-Christendom milieu.

Having survived the Reformation, the Constantinian vision of vocation still dominates many mainstream Christian traditions today, by which Yoder means the heirs of the Magisterial Reformation.[25] He sees in their work two contradictory emphases. On the one hand, when it comes to politics, economics, and education, Yoder sees them operating within a Christendom framework wherein Christians are responsible for taking charge in neo-theocratic manner to help things turn out right. On the other hand, when determining ethical standards within vocational responsibility, they trade a specific Christian ethic for a generic universal one derived from the natural order. From Yoder's perspective, however, if following Jesus gives Christians such superior insight that they ought to be in charge, then that charge should involve applying their superior, Christologically-informed insights to social ethics. Yoder knows, of course, that such thinkers have theological reasons for not doing this. He acknowledges, for example, H. Richard Niebuhr's trinitarian strategy of linking the Father and Spirit's work with nature and experience so as to locate his social ethics in a purportedly balanced theological framework that corrects overly Christological emphases.[26] Yet such correction is itself problematic, according to Yoder, on historical-theological grounds: "'Trinity' did not originally mean, as it does for some later, that there are three kinds of revelation, the Father speaking through creation and the Spirit through experience, by which the words and example of the Son must be corrected; it meant rather that language must be found and definitions created so that Christians, who believe in only one God, can affirm that that God is most adequately and bindingly known in Jesus."[27]

Moreover, scholars like Niebuhr would not feel obligated to find theological justification for bracketing Christ's demands if they were not already committed to a Constantinian vision of church and world. For Yoder's narration to stand, then, he needs to demonstrate biblically why Christians should not be willing to sacrifice gospel mandates in order to love their neighbors via retributive justice or top-down coercive power. This demonstration is rooted in Yoder's doctrine of the powers.

The Difference the Powers Make

Yoder's critique of Constantinianism is connected to his exousiology.[28] He did not presume to be pioneering a new doctrine of the powers (*exousiai*), but drawing upon what he perceived to be an emerging consensus among New Testament scholars.[29] The identity of these powers is not clear in Scripture and that is intentional. The Apostle Paul refers to them differently in varying contexts as a way of discussing the unquantifiable and uncontrollable forces that exert sometimes helpful, sometimes harmful influence on human affairs. In Pauline texts, this term is used with reference to and in conjunction with sister concepts like principalities, thrones, dominions, angels, archangels, elements, heights, depths, law, and knowledge.[30] Its scope is wide enough to include religious, intellectual, moral, political, educational, and economic structures.[31] Though Yoder does not make this connection explicit, this view of the powers is broad enough to encompass all realms typically associated with vocation.[32]

It is crucial for Yoder to establish the origin, current state, and destiny of the powers. His account begins with Colossians 1:15-17: "[Christ] is the image of the invisible God, the firstborn of all creation; for in him all things in heaven and on earth were created, things visible and invisible, whether thrones or dominions or rulers or powers—all things have been created through him and for him. He himself is before all things, and in him all things hold together" (NRSV). The powers were thus created good in order to serve God's purposes in Christ for his created order. Unfortunately they did not remain good. This is why the majority of New Testament passages about them presuppose their fallenness. In Scripture, we find them seeking to separate humans from God's love (Rom 8:38), ruling over those who are disobedient (Eph 2:2), binding humans in servitude to their rules (Col 2:20), and holding humans under their tutelage (Gal 4:3).[33]

The powers' fallen status does not, however, render them useless. God still employs them, despite themselves, to do good. Though they stand in rebellion to God, he sovereignly orders them to do his bidding. For this reason, Christians are called to be subject to the governing powers (Rom 13:1).[34] God's providential use of the powers and our consequent subjection to them does not, however, make them admirable or imitable. Since they fail to serve God as they should and enslave humankind instead, God is subjecting the powers to himself. This subjection began in earnest at the cross where Christ disarmed and made a public example of the powers (Col 2:15-16). It will be finalized at the consummation when Christ hands the kingdom to the Father after destroying all rulers and powers and subjugating them under his feet (1 Cor 15:24-25). In the meantime, God wills that through the church his wisdom may be revealed to rulers and powers in heavenly places (Eph 3:10). Thus the church's proper relation to the powers is neither righteous rebellion nor absolute submission. Rather, believers must accept the reality of their subjection to the powers in light of the more determinative reality of Christ's victory and remain steadfast in their witness to that victory.[35]

Though all powers are fallen, all powers are not equally compatible with God's original intentions for creation. Consider, for example, the state. Yoder defines the state somewhat narrowly as "the fundamental phenomenon that society is organized by the appeal to force as ultimate authority."[36] According to this definition, there is no state where there is no appeal to force, which means there could be no state prior to the Fall. Yoder tests this claim by imagining a hypothetical prelapsarian society with no sinful self-affirmation and asking whether violence and retribution would be needed.[37] His answer is that, whereas some sort of order would be needed, something akin to the good powers and principalities originally created through Christ, violence would be superfluous. Instead, a form of distributive justice would function to ensure that each person receives his or her share. Since each person would accept his or her share as sufficient, violence would not be necessary to sustain order and maintain boundaries. Thus, God did not create violence and the sword-bearing state it requires; human rebellion did.[38]

Since God, in Christ, originally created good powers to maintain an order that is fully compatible with the gospel and governed by love, a social ethic that is rooted in creation should be identical with that enjoined by Christ. Indeed, Christ's ethic, not the diluted universal ethic of Constantine, is truly natural and fully aligns with the grain of the universe.[39] Although Yoder does not unpack what a Christocentric protology might look like, he seems to suggest that one is possible. Such theologizing from creation would avoid conflating creation and fall and, instead, would interpret creation in closer connection to the new creation revealed partially in Christ's first coming and anticipated fully at his return. If Yoder is right about this, a Constantinian social ethic can no longer gain moral respectability by rooting its claims in creation. It cannot authorize Christians to act violently as a function of the state on the grounds that God "created" the state to use violence to keep evil in check. It cannot rebuke Christians who renounce state-sponsored violence as if they are declaring evil what God had declared good. It cannot categorize the sword as God's created method for dealing with some spheres of creation and the cross as his means for dealing with others. The question "What sphere am I operating in now?" can no longer serve as the first and most determinative question of Christian social ethics. Yoder's doctrine of the powers therefore resituates the state and its sword and reconfigures the practice of theologizing from creation. If right, Yoder has dislodged the capstone of Constantinian doctrines of vocation and created space for a fundamentally different approach that is grounded in a fundamentally different view of history.

An Eschatological View of Vocation

For Constantinian ethics, Christian responsibility entails setting gospel ethics aside so the world will be willing to include Christians in their efforts to contribute positively to historical progress. Christians are therefore invited to infiltrate the power structures that are poised to get things done effectively and efficiently. The assumption underlying this invitation is that such structures are the most fundamental and powerful means of truly making a difference in the world and that the meaning of history's direction is whatever progress they make to improve the overall quality of social life.[40]

Yoder argues that the biblical view of history is quite different. Since Abraham, God has been creating a people whose life together bears the true meaning of world history because God's people order their lives in ways that point to God's purposes for all creation.[41] The well-being of this world is tied to the faithfulness of this people to carry out their task since God has scattered them throughout the world in order to draw all nations to himself. In Yoder's words,

> In spite of the present visible dominion of the "powers" of "this present evil age," the triumph of Christ has already guaranteed that the ultimate meaning of history will not be found in the course of earthly empires or the development of proud cultures, but in the calling together of the "chosen race, royal priesthood, holy nation," which is the church of Christ. The church is not fundamentally a source of moral stimulus to encourage the development of a better society—though a faithful church should also have this effect—it is for the sake of the church's own work that society continues to function. The meaning of history—and therefore the significance of the state—lies in the creation and work of the church.[42]

Israel's prophets prepared God's people for a future divine in-breaking when God's purposes for them and the world would become reality. The church confesses that this in-breaking began with Christ's first coming and will be completed at his return. Yoder's theology of work is unintelligible outside of this confession. His eschatological framework is best understood as two overlapping ages: the old age of the world, which points backwards toward human history before Christ, and the new age that began with Christ, which points forward to the fullness of God's kingdom.[43] The old age did not, however, end with Christ's ministry. It perseveres and will do so until Christ returns to consummate his reign. The overlapping of these ages has created, in effect, a third age that stems from the beginning of the new until the end of the old. This age, from Pentecost to Parousia, is the age of the church.

It is important, Yoder emphasizes, to acknowledge that Christ's lordship even now encompasses not only the church but all history and all powers.[44] This has implications for both the state and the saints. The state remains part of the old age and is confined to the divine service of maintaining "a pragmatic tolerable balance of egoisms" in this world.[45] In so doing, the state renders the old age more bearable and allows the saints to continue their distinct mission: to bear faithful witness to the new age of Christ's reign.[46] To the extent that the church embodies God's kingdom as a kind of first fruits, it already shares in Christ's eschatological reign—it already is, according to Yoder, the "new order in which men live together in love."[47]

It is crucial for Yoder to identify the agency behind the consummation of Christ's reign and its implications for ecclesial efforts.[48] There will be new heavens and a new earth, evil will be defeated, and God's kingdom will come in its fullness; but making this happen is not the church's responsibility. Christ has already secured victory and only divine intervention will bring its completion. The church must therefore resist all efforts to force God's kingdom by way of human progress.[49] Instead, it must follow Christ in suffering for the sake of love, pursue the way of the cross and the power of the resurrection, and preserve society in the old age by living in the new.[50] Though the church lacks control, these actions are powerful because they *signify* the work of Christ. Yoder explains this power of signification as follows:

> The relation between our obedience and the achievement of God's purposes stands in analogy to the hidden lordship of Him who was crucified and raised. It is reasonable because there is the continuing relevance of *the sign*. When Jesus washed the feet of His disciples He made no abiding contribution to the hygiene of Palestine. Nevertheless, this act took a position in the world which has in itself both spiritual and ethical value. Similarly, when Christians devote themselves to the care of the seriously ill, of the mentally retarded, of the improductive [sic] aged, the fruitfulness of this service cannot be measured by any statistical index of economic efficacy. Whether evaluated from the perspective of the individual or the society, the meaning of this deed is what it signifies, the reality for which it is *the sign*, namely, that this man is here to be the servant of his neighbor. His presence and his posture, *not* his productivity, are the referent of the sign.[51]

The church's most fundamental contribution to world history is thus to be a sign, foretaste, and herald of God's in-breaking kingdom. It is what God has determined the world needs and it is what he appointed the church alone to do. It is the church's all-encompassing vocation.

The Difference the Church Makes

This eschatological framework positions us to appreciate Yoder's constructive vocational project because the latter follows logically and necessarily from the former. This project may be delineated in terms of three ecclesial modes: servant, sign, and support.

Church as Servant

If Christ's reign has truly begun, then all humans and all powers are already Christ's subjects. These subjects fall into two categories: obedient servants and rebellious servants. In Yoder's words, "church and world are not two compartments under separate legislation or two institutions with contradictory assignments, but two levels of the pertinence of the same lordship. The people of God is called to be today what the world is called to be ultimately."[52] Christ is therefore the norm not only for the church but also for the world.[53]

The challenge, of course, is discerning how Christ's obedient servants ought to mediate Christ's reign to the disobedient world. Christians have not been called to punish the disobedient or to coerce them into submission (Rom 12:17-21; 1 Cor 5:12-13); they have been called to respect the world's unbelief and to proclaim his lordship faithfully. Yet without the various forms of empowerment that accompany genuine faith, the unbelieving world is incapable of following Christ.[54] On what basis, then, may the church relate Christ's reign to the world? Whereas Yoder agrees with Luther that the church cannot rule over the world with the gospel, he disagrees that Christians should look for a different means of ruling. Rather, they should choose not to rule the world but to serve it.[55] This answer, however, does not entirely satisfy. If Christians fail to rule on Christ's behalf and the world subsequently ignores Christ who is its norm, then the powerful will rule at the expense of the weak and the church will be guilty of acquiescence.

Yoder dismisses this charge on several grounds. First, there are ways of making a difference in the world without ruling it. Christ has taught his people that service is not weakness. It is not the absence of power but an alternative form of power. Servanthood, in Yoder's view, "brings to bear powers which, on balance, are stronger than the sword alone: the power of the truth rediscovered when obscured, the power of the dissenter willing to suffer, the power of the people to withhold confidence, the attraction of an alternative vision, the integrity that accepts sacrifice rather than conformity to evil."[56] The choice is therefore not between making a difference or not making a difference, but between making a lasting difference by the power of Christ or making a fleeting difference some other way.

Second, though Constantinian thinkers accuse the servant church of irresponsibility, Yoder argues that God's people can focus on their unique vocation because they know that Christ is Lord of all and that he uses other servants, even rebellious ones, to carry out other tasks.[57] No servant is called upon to do everything, and truly faithful servants trust that their master is best positioned to delegate or personally fulfill various responsibilities outside of their responsibility. The Jewish people, who also confessed God to be king over all nations and all people to be answerable to him, have always operated under this assumption. Yet they never took it upon themselves to strategize about how they might rule over the nations.[58] The burden is on Constantinian thinkers to demonstrate that Christ somehow made a change in this regard.

Third, Yoder frequently quotes Luke 22 where Christ strictly prohibits his people from ruling over others, saying, "The kings of the Gentiles lord it over them; and those in authority over them are called benefactors. *But not so with you*; rather the greatest among you must become like the youngest, and the leader like one who serves" (vv. 25-26).[59] It would be one matter if Christ left it ambiguous as to how Christians should posture themselves before others, but he did not. Moreover, in neither testament does God authorize his people to rule over the unbelieving world on his behalf. The way of Christ and his people is anticipated not only in the servant songs of Isaiah, but also in the overall direction of the Old Testament narrative as Yoder interprets it.[60] This is why those who have taken it upon themselves to rule on Christ's behalf have had to look away from his teaching and example for authorization and guidance.

This servant status therefore dictates the motive, position, and posture of all professions Christians may occupy. The primary motive for Christian work in the world is to serve Christ by serving the world in ways that point to Christ's reign. The proper position must therefore be one a servant can occupy without abandoning the nature of his or her role as Christ's servant. To carry out tasks that militate against Christ's way and work in the world is self-defeating.[61] Christians do not derive their working posture from their employers; they have already received it from their Lord. So whether one serves as CEO or secretary, one must truly serve ones cowork-ers and community. One must not lord over others but serve alongside them. Christians should not consider this posture to be only delimiting. Though there will be positions to which believers will be inclined to con-scientiously object, there will also be roles in which Christians will desire conscientiously to participate.[62] Christians ought to gravitate toward roles that strategically position them to serve others in the community.[63]

Church as Sign

Does assuming this servant posture mean the church has nothing to say to the world? It is often claimed that if Christians are against running the world, then they have no right to speak about how it should be run.[64] Yoder refuses, however, to be muzzled.[65] Whether it submits to Christ or not, the world remains under Christ's lordship and, since proclaiming Christ's reign and its implications is central to the church's vocation, Christians must not remain silent.[66] Such proclamation is not, however, the church's "prophetic" task. Because Scripture presents prophecy primarily as an *in-house* call to faithfulness, Yoder deems it more appropriate to regard Christian procla-mation *to the world* as an extension of Christ's kingly role.[67] The king has defeated his enemies and has been enthroned on high; it is therefore the good pleasure of his heralds to announce that good news to all. But if living the norms of Christ requires faith and Yoder refuses all norms outside of Christ, how can the church possibly address the world? Yoder's answer lies in his understanding of church as sign. The church carries out its voca-tion of pointing the world to Christ's reign by being and planting signs of his lordship throughout the world.[68] Though Yoder acknowledges that this happens in multiple ways,[69] I focus here on the two he stressed most.

First, the church's *life together* is a sign insofar as it is ordered in every way by Christ's reign. Ecclesial practices are instrumental in this order-ing. Yoder routinely selects five particular practices to represent how the church signifies Christ's reign to the world: baptism, breaking of bread, uni-versality of charisma, open meeting, and binding and loosing. Here is not the place to unpack the details of Yoder's portrait of these practices,[70] but it is worth briefly noting how Yoder defines them and how the world may recognize them. Baptism is the boundary-breaking, field-leveling practice of initiating persons into the faith community, recognizable to the world as egalitarianism. The breaking of bread constitutes eating a common meal around a common table, recognizable to the world as economic sharing. The universality of charisma is how God equips each member to contribute to the common good of the church, recognizable to the world as nonhierarchical social process. Open meetings are gatherings in which all members are given equal opportunity to speak, recognizable to the world as a form of democratic procedure. Finally, binding and loosing is the method by which the community sensitively confronts sin among its members, recognizable to the world as conflict resolution. Thus, in Yoder's estimation, the church is a truly public and truly political entity whose way of life is recognizable and therefore imitable by the wider world. When the church remains faithful in these practices, it serves as a powerful sign of the way the world was created to be and is destined to become now that Christ is Lord.

Second, the church serves as a sign as its members enter public spaces occupied primarily by unbelievers. Christians do this as families in neighborhoods, students in public schools, patrons in local shops and, most germane to the focus of this essay, employees in the workforce. God has dispersed his people throughout these venues to proclaim Christ's reign. Christians proclaim Christ in the "workplace" not simply by earning money to support the congregational budget, filling positions that are inherently evangelistic in nature, or cultivating a relational pool of potential converts. They also do so by showing their fellow workers the difference that Christ has made in their particular field of specialty. In Yoder's words,

> If we reclaim the doctrine of vocation in light of the practices and social vision that we are studying, then the specific ministry of the Christian banker or financier will be to find realistic, technically not utopian ways of implementing jubilee amnesty; there are people doing this. The Christian realtor or developer will find ways to house people according to need; there are people doing this. The Christian judge will open the court system to conflict resolution procedures and resist the trend toward more and more litigation; this is being done. Technical vocational sphere expertise in each professional area will be needed not to reinforce but to undercut competently the claimed sovereignty of each sphere by planting signs of the new world in the ruins of the old.[71]

Elsewhere Yoder speaks of medical and social workers who transform "cases" into persons, businessmen who place community service over profit, teachers who transmit what students truly need beyond simply what is outlined in the curriculum, labor managers who seek right answers rather than selfish gain, and cogs in bureaucratic machines who change the character of bureaucracy by their personal attitudes and neighborliness.[72] As servant signs in the workforce, Christians are called not to sacrifice the norms established by Christ in order to bring about a better world, but to announce that the new world has already begun in Christ and to showcase the implications of that world for every vocational niche.[73]

Church as Support

Yoder bemoans what he considers the common evangelical practice of trusting the regenerate individual to bridge the gap between gospel and the so-called "public sphere." The church has given its members little guidance for vocational morality and encouraged them to enter positions of considerable top-down power. The assumption is that the individual whose heart has been changed by the gospel will use such power unselfishly, creatively, and industriously for good. Yoder agrees that this happens, but argues that it is far too small an answer and is often beset by multiple shortcomings, such as (a) providing no substantial information about better ways to use power, (b) ascribing little significance to the insights of those not in power, (c) fostering too great an evaluation of worldly power and prestige in society, and (d) dodging the fact that even the least selfish heart cannot clean up a fundamentally vicious structure. The main problem, according to Yoder, is that "the insight or role definition of the banker, the businessman, the legislator, the educator, the soldier is not sufficiently sanctified that he or she can read off the surface of the social order a definition of the duties of the child of God in that slot, as the frequent celebration of the effectiveness of the sanctified important individual would lead us to try to do."[74]

The solution to this problem, Yoder suggested, is the support of the Christian community. One way congregations may support the professions of their various members is by way of paradigm. Multiple aspects of various professions converge at specific points with ecclesial practices. At these points of convergence local churches model for their members the gospel's implications for appropriate activity. Congregational practices may thus serve as paradigms for leadership that is not self-serving but other-empowering, apprenticeship that is not demeaning but enriching, and stewardship that is not wasteful but fruitful. Members learn these practices in congregational life and translate them into vocational protocol.

Congregations also support their members through mutual admonition.[75] Members should converse with one another regularly about how they discharge their vocational responsibilities and help one another keep their respective offices from gaining independence from the reign of Christ. Sometimes member support will help someone muster the nerve to make a bold and potentially costly move; other times it provides key insights that never would have dawned upon particular workers since those insights are only gained outside of their professions. The preached Word also helps Christian workers accurately perceive and criticize the present structures within which they work. In sum, local churches provide their members an invaluable reference group to help them both see the pertinence of Christ's reign for their professions and bear faithful daily witness to that reign.

Congregations provide such support without lording it over their members because they have learned from the gospel how to discern God's will. The practices of open meeting and universality of charisma remind local churches that they do not exist to make decisions on behalf of others by legislating in advance what professions are valid or not. Rather, congregations must remain open to the Spirit's leading in unexpected ways to address new situations. Yoder thus claims that there are better and worse ways of posing vocational questions. For instance, believers should avoid asking "Could a Christian be a lawyer?" and should ask, instead, "Are the things a lawyer does in modern America the things a person who proposed to follow Jesus might do?"[76] Yoder advocates such openness even to positions associated with the violence he adamantly renounced in light of Christ's reign. Rather than ask, "Can a Christian join the police force?" he recommends asking, "Is a particular Christian *called* to be a policeman?" If so, he must provide evidence of this calling.[77] Christian discernment and openness to God's future lends itself not to legalistic prohibition but to creativity and stewardship.

It would appear, however, that congregational support would be limited to persons who profess Christ and to positions that Christians might conceivably occupy. Yoder disagrees. No person or position stands outside of Christ's reign, and the church's example impacts everyone. For instance, though Yoder argues that Christians have no business wielding the sword, he affirms that the church is best positioned to render advice concerning its legitimate use. God does not allow authorities to wield the sword indis-criminately whenever they see fit, but only as a last resort intended to limit further violence.[78] Moreover, the state's sword-wielding power may only be used for the purpose of keeping evil in check so that people of good will can pursue good. When the state uses the sword, instead, to construct an ideal social order, it usurps the unique role of Christ and heads down the same path as the demonic state of Revelation.[79] How will statesmen know this if Christians do not tell them?

Sometimes, however, the church will find that gospel language does not communicate Christ's lordship relevantly to those who do not profess his lordship. In such cases, Yoder does not recommend addressing unbe-lievers on some basis outside of Christ. Rather, he advocates addressing them via "middle axioms,"[80] which are alternative categories and concepts that mediate Christ's lordship in language that communicates to those who lack ears to hear the gospel due to prior presuppositions. Yoder does not believe this strategy betrays the gospel: "What we ask of him does not cease to be gospel by virtue of the fact that we relate it to his present avail-able options. It is rather the gospel itself in relation to his present situation, that situation in turn being determined largely by his earlier disobedience . . . . To his Christian brethren the Christian addresses a testimony whose sole norm is Jesus Christ and whose adequate basis is the faith commit-ment of the brother spoken to. Outside the circle of faith, the presupposi-tion cannot be the commitment of the individual spoken to and challenged, but only Christ's objective claim on him."[81] In such ways, the church sup-ports not only the faith community but also the unbelieving world and it supports them both in terms of Christ's lordship alone.

Summary and Conclusion

Having noted Yoder's critique of Constantinian doctrines of vocation and located his own position within a post-Constantinian framework, I now summarize Yoder's theology of work and evaluate its contributions to wider ecumenical conversations. Yoder's view of vocation may be sum-marized in ten emphases:

1. Christians have received a single all-encompassing vocation, which is to announce and bear witness to Christ's reign in the context of Christian community to all creation.

2. Like all other aspects of their lives, Christians must view their professions as extensions of their single aforementioned vocation.
3. The Christian view of work should be rooted in an eschatological—not Constantinian—view of history and so its mood should not be realistic but apocalyptic.[82]
4. Christian involvement in various professions thus aims not to bring God's kingdom through social progress and engineering, but to point faithfully to the kingdom Christ has already brought and continues to bring.
5. Christ's lordship should dictate the choice and shape of Christians' professions since it is the norm for all social life.
6. The appropriate posture for Christians in any profession is that of a servant, not a master.
7. The ethical source for all vocations is the gospel, not some natural or creational source conceived of as distinct from or in contradiction to the gospel.
8. The political life of the church models proper participation in various professions.
9. The support of the local church body is necessary to keep the professions of its members properly situated under Christ's lordship.
10. A spirit of creativity and stewardship should dictate the Christian's choice of vocation, not pre-determined legalistic prohibition.

A thorough evaluation of Yoder's theology of work would involve a rigorous biblical testing of his interpretation of the powers, state, creation, eschatology, Christology, and other related topics. Indeed, it would entail critical engagement of Yoder's entire theological project—an engagement that far exceeds the scope of this essay. Instead, I relate a few strengths and weaknesses of Yoder's proposal from an ecumenical perspective. The focus of my evaluation is the viability of his project as a means of uniting Christians from various traditions around a post-Christendom vision of vocation.

A glaring weakness of Yoder's project, from an ecumenical perspective, is his roughshod review of prior doctrines of vocation. As noted earlier,

Yoder does not engage specific thinkers at length, but makes sweeping generalizations about "mainstream" Reformation traditions. As a result, Yoder not only fails to gain some insights that may be gleaned from careful study of specific thinkers, but he alienates potential dialogue partners who, in turn, make sweeping generalizations about him. It must be remembered, however, that the coherence of Yoder's constructive project does not depend on the incoherence of his predecessors' positions, but on the biblical support for his own.

Favoring Yoder's project is an emerging consensus that the alliance between church and state symbolized by Constantine is no longer a desirable arrangement. Though thinkers from various traditions may narrate past alliances more charitably than Yoder does, there is widespread agreement that their usefulness has diminished. It is not clear to me, however, that mainstream evangelical scholars are finished grappling with how deeply the social ethics they have inherited are indebted to Constantinian presuppositions (e.g., the questionable identification of the state with the ideal prelapsarian created order). In thrusting such issues to the forefront of vocational deliberation, Yoder adds significantly to the current conversation.

Similarly, by seeking to root his doctrine of vocation squarely in Scripture, Yoder opens up space not simply for a Free Church theology of work, but also for a truly ecumenical position shared by all who are willing to renounce the polarization caused by the Constantinian compromise—a compromise which led some to identify with a Christendom posture and others with its mirror-image opposite. Since Christians from multiple traditions acknowledge the pitfalls of linking normative Christian theology to a temporary social configuration of the church, a fresh, self-consciously post-Constantinian return to Scripture may uncover helpful truths that have long been obscured.

Yoder's own position, it must be acknowledged, fails to embody a simple return to Scripture. Nowhere in the New Testament is the church taught to speak to non-Christian powers in order to call them to align their lives according to Christ's lordship using middle axioms or any other techniques. Nor does the New Testament provide examples of Christians who did so. So it seems that Yoder set forth not a biblical but a plausible framework by which to imagine how the church might serve God by addressing pagan power structures without compromising gospel convictions.

Whereas nothing in the New Testament prohibits such address, nothing specifically commends it.

Finally, Yoder contributes positively to the wider ecumenical conversation by bringing fresh ideas into a stultifying stalemate between long-entrenched positions. In raising the possibility that a gospel-grounded ethic may address all professions and social structures, Yoder unsettles the simplistic assumptions that purity requires quiescence and responsibility requires compromise. His ecumenical attempt at public theology thus makes possible a robust conversation between the Free Church and other theological traditions.

Endnotes

[1] Einer Billing, *Our Calling*, trans. Conrad Bergendoff, Social Ethics Series (Philadelphia: Fortress Press, 1964), 4.

[2] This much is admitted by Alan Richardson in *The Biblical Doctrine of Work*, Ecumenical Biblical Studies 1 (London: SCM Press, 1952). This does not mean, however, that Scripture entirely ignores human work. Rather, work is presupposed and addressed in an ad hoc rather than systematic or consciously reflective way.

[3] The classic statement of Luther's doctrine of vocation is Gustaf Wingren, *Luther on Vocation*, Concordia Heritage Series (Philadelphia: Muhlenberg, 1957). Wingren states his view more concisely in "The Church and Christian Vocation," in *This Is the Church*, eds. Anders Nygren, et al (Philadelphia: Muhlenberg Press, 1952).

[4] The designation "Free Church," also referred to as the "Believers' Church," does not refer to a single tradition, but to a diverse family of traditions that share common ecclesial sensibilities often associated with the left wing of the Protestant Reformation. Representatives include Baptists, Quakers, Brethren, Mennonites, Disciples of Christ, Pentecostals, and Churches of Christ. In "Where Two or Three Are Gathered: Communion Ecclesiology in the Free Church," *Perspectives in Religious Studies* 31 (Fall 2004): 259, Curtis Freeman identifies five common traits of such churches: (1) freedom of governance (non-hierarchical order, congregational piety), (2) freedom of worship (non-prescribed liturgy, spiritual worship), (3) freedom of faith (non-binding confession, gathered community), (4) freedom of conscience (non-coercive authority, soul liberty), and (5) freedom of religion (non-established religion, separation of church and state). Foundational works concerning this tradition include Frank Littell, *The Free Church* (Boston: Starr King Press, 1957); Donald Durnbaugh, *The Believers' Church* (Scottdale, PA: Herald Press, 1968); and James Leo Garrett, Jr., ed., *The Concept of the Believers' Church* (Scottdale, PA: Herald Press, 1969).

[5] Miroslav Volf has published what he considered to be a "new" pneumatological understanding of work that would seem to provide a promising start (*Work in the Spirit: Toward a Theology of Work* [New York: Oxford University Press, 1991; reprinted Wipf & Stock, 2001]). Unfortunately, for our purposes, Volf does not build off of a distinctly Free Church foundation. For criticism of Volf's claims of novelty, see Lee Hardy's review

of *Work in the Spirit* in *Calvin Theological Journal* 28 (Apr 1993): 191-196. Gordon R. Preece grants many of Volf's critiques of the vocation tradition and seeks to assimilate them within a Reformed approach in *The Viability of the Vocation Tradition in Trinitarian, Credal and Reformed Perspective: The Threefold Call* (Lewiston, NY: Edwin Mellen Press, 1998).

[6] Helpful introductions to Yoder's life, thought, and influence include Craig A. Carter, *The Politics of the Cross: The Theology and Social Ethics of John Howard Yoder* (Grand Rapids: Brazos, 2001); and Mark Thiessen Nation, *John Howard Yoder: Mennonite Patience, Evangelical Witness, and Catholic Convictions* (Grand Rapids: Eerdmans, 2006).

[7] Yoder, "I Choose Vocation," *Mennonite Community* 2 (Oct 1948): 6-7. Other works include *Body Politics: Five Practices of the Christian Community Before the Watching World* (Nashville: Discipleship Resources Press, 1992), 25-27 and 52-53; *Christian Witness to the State* (Eugene, OR: Wipf & Stock, 1998), 20, 27-28, 56-57, and 88; *Discipleship as Political Responsibility* (Scottdale, PA: Herald Press, 2003), 45; *For the Nations: Essays Public and Evangelical* (Grand Rapids: Eerdmans, 1997), 184-186 and 233-235; *The Fullness of Christ: Paul's Vision of Universal Ministry* (Elgin, IL: Brethren Press, 1987), 39-40; *The Original Revolution: Essays on Christian Pacifism* (Scottdale, PA: Herald Press, 1971), 118-121; *The Politics of Jesus: Vicit Agnus Noster*, 2d. ed. (Grand Rapids: Eerdmans, 1994), 8-9; *The Priestly Kingdom: Social Ethics as Gospel* (Eugene, OR: Wipf & Stock, 2000), 83, 109-110, 138-139, 162, and 210; and *The Royal Priesthood: Essays Ecclesiological and Ecumenical* (Scottdale, PA: Herald Press, 1998), 56-64, 80-82, 94-95, 113-114, and 117.

[8] Yoder's misgivings about this shift permeate his work. A few representative pieces include "Christ the Hope of the World," in *Original Revolution*, 148-184; "The Disavowal of Constantine: An Alternative Perspective on Interfaith Dialogue," in *Royal Priesthood*, 242-261; and "The Constantinian Sources of Western Social Ethics," in *Priestly Kingdom*, 135-150.

[9] Cf. Yoder "Disavowal of Constantine," in *Royal Priesthood*, 245; and "Constantinian Sources," in *Priestly Kingdom*, 135.

[10] For example, Luther is the only specific thinker Yoder consistently names throughout his narration. Less frequently he mentions Calvin and the Niebuhrs.

[11] Cf. Yoder, *Anabaptism and Reformation in Switzerland: An Historical and Theological Analysis of the Dialogues between Anabaptists and Reformers*, Anabaptist and Mennonite Studies (Kitchener, Ontario, 2004).

[12] Yoder, "Otherness of the Church," *in Royal Priesthood*, 58.

[13] Yoder, "Why Ecclesiology is Social Ethics," in *Royal Priesthood*, 123.

[14] Ibid., 117.

[15] Yoder, "Otherness of the Church," in *Royal Priesthood*, 58.

[16] Yoder, *Christian Witness to the State*, 80.

[17] Though Yoder's typology of vocation is rather simplistic, he was aware that the medieval church's legacy was not. He affirms in several places that, despite its Constantinian shaping, the medieval church also carried forth a great deal of the gospel's radical otherness. Cf. "Otherness of the Church," in *Royal Priesthood*, 58.

[18] Yoder, "Otherness of the Church," in *Royal Priesthood*, 59.

[19] Yoder, *Fullness of Christ*, 39.

[20] Ibid.

[21] Ibid., 40; and "Otherness of the Church," in *Royal Priesthood*, 60-62.

[22] Yoder, "Radical Reformation Ethics in Ecumenical Perspective," in *Priestly Kingdom*, 109; *Christian Witness to the State*, 57 and 210, fn. 9.

[23] Yoder, "Otherness of the Church," in *Royal Priesthood*, 60.

[24] Ibid., 59.

[25] Yoder, "A People in the World," in *Royal Priesthood*, 81-82, fn. 20.

[26] Yoder, "Why Ecclesiology is Social Ethics?" in *Royal Priesthood*, 114.

[27] Yoder, *Politics of Jesus*, 99.

[28] Yoder spells out his exousiology in *Politics of Jesus*, ch. 8; *Discipleship as Political Responsibility*, ch. 1; and *Christian Witness to the State*, ch. 2. That he was influenced by Hendrikus Berkhof's *Christ and the Powers* is evident in that he translated it into English (Scottdale, PA: Herald Press, 1977).

[29] E.g., Hendrikus Berkhof, G. B. Caird, G. H. C. MacGregor, and Markus Barth. Cf. *Politics of Jesus*, 136. This list continues to grow in our time, especially due to the influence of Walter Wink.

[30] For powers language in the New Testament, see Matt 24:29; Luke 12:11; Rom 8:38, 39; 13:1-4; 1 Cor 2:8; 15:24-26; Eph 1:20-23; 2:1, 2; 3:10; 6:12; Col 1:15-17; 2:15, 16; Titus 3:1; and 1 Pet 3:21-4:1.

[31] Yoder, *Politics of Jesus*, 142-143.

[32] Yoder implies this connection in *Politics of Jesus* when he commends a healthy doctrine of the powers as the best context within which to discuss the "orders of creation" (144). The mainstream traditions, in Yoder's narration, commonly recommend the orders of creation over against the gospel as the means by which Christians ought to discern proper vocational ethics.

[33] Yoder, *Politics of Jesus*, 141.

[34] The word commonly translated "authorities" three times in Romans 13:1 is *exousiai* or powers. For Yoder's commentary on this particular passage, see *Politics of Jesus*, 193-211.

[35] Yoder's position may be illustrated by comparison to the common Christian view of the human body. Christians are called to accept the powers' authority over them much like they accept the limitations of perishable bodies. I do not mean a Gnostic renunciation of physicality, but a nuanced acceptance of the reality of sickness, disease, and disability. Believers neither relish these liabilities nor actively perpetuate their advancement. Rather they learn to live with them, seek to ameliorate their negative consequences, and strive to use them for good. Furthermore, Christians live in relative peace with these limitations because Christ has triumphed over them and will renew our bodies when he consummates his reign. As far as I can tell, Yoder himself does not employ this analogy.

[36] Yoder, *Christian Witness to the State*, 12.

[37] Ibid., 83.

[38] Yoder sees the true origins of the state in society's fearful response to Cain's murder of Abel. After God banishes him from tending the soil, Cain fears the vengeful reflex of society (Gen 4:14). He assumes that, independent of divine intervention, the wider world citizenry will be morally outraged at his conduct and will take it upon themselves to bring him to deadly justice. God shares Cain's concern both for Cain's sake and for wider society. He thus protects Cain and all future humans who commit such "capital offenses" by harnessing for his purposes the fear of vengeful retaliation that could be worse than the original offense incurred. The mark of Cain points to this circle of vengeance within which Cain finds protection. God did not create such vengeance mechanisms that would later be institutionalized in various forms of "the state." Rather, he used them to keep a bad situation from getting worse. Cf. Yoder, "Noah's Covenant and the Purpose of Punishment," in *Readings in Christian Ethics*, Volume 2, *Issues and Applications*, eds. David K. Clark and Robert V. Rakestraw (Grand Rapids: Eerdmans, 1996), 473; and "Voice of Your Brother's Blood," in *He Came Preaching Peace* (Scottdale, PA: Herald Press, 1985), 61-62.

[39] Yoder affirms that cross-bearers are those who are truly "working with the grain of the universe," in "Armaments and Eschatology," *Studies in Christian Ethics* 1, no. 1 (1988): 58.

[40] For Yoder's response to the charge of irresponsibility, see "Peace without Eschatology," in *Original Revolution*, 80-88.

[41] Yoder, "Why Ecclesiology Is Social Ethics," in *Royal Priesthood*, 116-117.

[42] Yoder, *Christian Witness to the State*, 13. Yoder does not mean here that the world exists to somehow help the church maintain its religious order. He means that the church is God's means of extending God's salvific offer to all creation and that the powers best serve God by maintaining a level of order throughout the world so the church may carry out its task with the least amount of unnecessary hindrances.

[43] Yoder, "If Christ Is Truly Lord," in *Original Revolution*, 56-58 and 63-64.

[44] Yoder illustrates Christ's present universal reign most dramatically in an illuminating reading of Revelation in "To Serve Our God and to Rule the World," in *Royal Priesthood*, 127-140.

[45] Yoder, "If Christ Is Truly Lord," in *Original Revolution*, 79.

[46] Yoder, "To Serve Our God," in *Priestly Kingdom*, 131.

[47] Yoder, "The Original Revolution," in *Original Revolution*, 18.

[48] Yoder, "If Christ Is Truly Lord," in *Original Revolution*, 64-67.

[49] Yoder labels such efforts heresy in ibid., 73.

[50] Ibid., 60-61 and 87.

[51] Yoder, "Christ, the Hope of the World," in *Original Revolution*, 160-161 (original emphasis).

[52] Yoder, *Body Politics*, ix.

[53] Yoder, *Christian Witness to the State*, 17.

[54] Yoder, "Why Ecclesiology Is Social Ethics," in *Royal Priesthood*, 116.

[55] Yoder, *Body Politics*, 74.

[56] Yoder, "Biblical Mandate for Evangelical Social Action," in *For the Nations*, 191.

[57] Yoder, "Otherness of the Church," in *Royal Priesthood*, 56.

[58] Yoder lists five reasons why the Jewish people never sought to take over the Gentile world: (1) God is sovereign over world history and is not dependent on them to fulfill his goals; (2) the Messiah's task was to subdue the nations and it would be presumptuous for them to usurp his responsibility; (3) the Maccabeans and other Zealot groups failed miserably when assuming this function; (4) God sometimes uses pagan nations as his means of punishment (even of his own people) so that rising against them could interfere with God's work; and (5) the innocent suffering of God's own people contributes in a concrete way to the positive progression of God's purpose in world history. "See How They Go with Their Face to the Sun," in *For the Nations*, 67-68.

[59] E.g., Yoder, "Biblical Mandate," 191, and "Are You the One Who Is to Come?" in *For the Nations*, 208.

[60] Yoder, "Behold My Servant Will Prosper," in *Karl Barth and the Problem of War and Other Essays on Barth*, ed. Mark Thiessen Nation (Eugene, OR: Cascade Books, 2003), esp. 151-159. For depth level analysis of Yoder's full Old Testament narration, see my Ph.D. dissertation, "Old Testament Contributions to Ecclesiology: Engaging and Extending the Insights of John Howard Yoder" (Calvin Theological Seminary, 2009), esp. chs. 3-4.

[61] Later I unpack how Yoder recommends discerning when such is the case.

[62] Yoder, *Christian Witness to the State*, 20.

[63] Yoder, "Christian Case for Democracy," in *Priestly Kingdom*, 162.

[64] E.g., Reinhold Niebuhr. Yoder's *Christian Witness to the State* is dedicated to answering this objection. In this work he engages Niebuhr on p. 7.

[65] Yoder goes so far as to say that addressing the social order in a relevant way is obligatory. *Christian Witness to the State*, 8.

[66] Yoder, *Christian Witness to the State*, 21.

[67] Ibid., 36.

[68] Yoder, "The Spirit of God and the Politics of Men," in *For the Nations*, 234.

[69] E.g., the world experiences the church directly whenever it comes into contact with the church's servant work in the community and indirectly through the children of Christians who do not themselves proclaim Christ but who have nonetheless been shaped by Christ's reign during their upbringing. Cf. *Christian Witness*, 20-21.

[70] Cf. Yoder, *Body Politics*. Articles that list all five practices include "Firstfruits: The Paradigmatic Public Role of God's People" and "The New Humanity as Pulpit and Paradigm" in *For the Nations*; and "Sacrament as Social Process: Christ the Transformer of Culture," in *Royal Priesthood*. Yoder has written additional articles and books about a few of these practices and has referred to them at different times as the apostolic model, the order of the faith community, the shape of grace, the marks of the church, and sample civil imperatives. He also makes it clear that he does not intend this list to be comprehensive in "The New Humanity as Pulpit and Paradigm," 43.

[71] Yoder, *Body Politics*, 27.

[72] Yoder, *Christian Witness to the State*, 20.

[73] Yoder, "Are You the One Who Is to Come?" in *For the Nations*, 209-11.

[74] Yoder, "Biblical Mandate for Evangelical Social Action," in ibid., 184-86.

[75] Ibid., 185-86.

[76] In Thomas L. Shaffer's *Moral Memoranda from John Howard Yoder: Conversations on Law, Ethics, and the Church between a Mennonite Theologian and a Hoosier Lawyer* (Eugene, OR: Wipf and Stock, 2002), v.

[77] Ironically, as Yoder points out, this situation was reversed in the Middle Ages. The minority who were drawn to gospel standards claimed a unique calling and those going against the gospel required no exceptional justification. Cf. *Christian Witness to the State*, 56-57.

[78] Yoder, *Christian Witness to the State*, 37.

[79] Ibid.

[80] Ibid., 32. Yoder used the language of middle axioms early in his writings, but does not continue to use such language. His later use of the five practices, however, functioned in an analogous way. As noted above, Yoder emphasized that the world could recognize and learn from ecclesial practices without having to learn an in-house tongue. I agree with Branson Parler's perceptive essay in this volume that Yoder's emphasis on the communicability of these practices does not constitute a reduction of them to that which communicates to unbelievers. That which communicates without translation serves as a bridge leading to additional meanings, some of which require faith.

[81] Yoder, *Christian Witness to the State*, 25 and 29.

[82] Here I set eschatology against "Constantinianism" and not "theologizing from creation" because it is not clear to me that Yoder is against theologizing from creation as much as from a Constantinian form of natural theology that collapses creation and fall rather than interpret creation in light of Christ or new creation.

Chapter Eight

Spinning the Liturgical Turn
Why John Howard Yoder Is Not an Ethicist

Branson Parler

Liturgy is a hot topic.[1] For some who focus on the intersection of liturgy, theology, and ethics, Yoder is read with suspicion and accused of being reductionistic insofar as he reduces worship and the sacraments to social processes and theology to ethics or sociology.[2] In this essay, I deal specifically with the concerns of Paul Martens, who worries that the mature Yoder positions the church in such a way that it may slide easily into secularism, thus opening the church to an easy assimilation into the surrounding world.[3]

Two key issues are at stake in this conversation. First is the question of continuity and development in Yoder's thought throughout his life. Second, and more importantly, is the question of whether Yoder should be read as reductionistic regarding the sacraments. Contra Martens, I contend that Yoder ought to be read as an "expansionist" rather than a reductionist with respect to the sacraments and worship. According to Stanley Hauerwas and Samuel Wells, modern thought often bifurcates ethics and liturgy. Their account of this divorce is helpful insofar as it sharpens Martens's critique by asking if Yoder perpetuates or problematizes the modern dichotomy between worship and ethics. I contend that Yoder will not allow liturgy to be conceived as something separate from the everyday life of the church. This is a good thing to the extent that it prevents dichotomies between worship and ethics, theology and sociology, liturgy and life. Moreover, this is a persistent theme in Yoder's thought from beginning to end. Thus, insofar as ethics is understood in modernity as independent of theology and liturgy, Yoder is not an ethicist.[4] Rather, Yoder helps us get beyond unhelpful dichotomies so that we can see how liturgy informs our life and how all aspects of life are liturgical.

Sacrament as (Nothing More Than) Social Process: Critique of Yoder

Paul Martens critiques Yoder's position on liturgy, the sacraments, and the language used for the church. Since Martens is a close reader of Yoder, his discussion of Yoder's thought helpfully drives the discussion forward. Moreover, Martens's desire to avoid reductionism and serve the church by guarding against a drift toward secularism is surely commendable. Martens contends that the sacraments are a touchstone for Yoder's overall theological direction, and he worries that Yoder's thought develops in such a way that Yoder risks (unintentionally) undermining some "very basic Christian convictions."[5] To substantiate his critique, Martens provides a diachronic analysis of the development of the sacraments in Yoder, dividing Yoder's thought into three stages.

In the first stage (pre-1979), Yoder addresses two key practices of the church: binding and loosing and the universality of charisma. With respect to the former, Yoder connects forgiveness and moral discernment, such that Matthew 18:15-20 describes not only church discipline but how discernment should happen within the body of Christ. Regarding the latter, Yoder argues against the notion of ministerial hierarchy within the church by appealing to the ministerial giftedness of each member of the local body. Martens highlights that, at this point, Yoder identified neither practice as worship or sacramental, as he will later on.

In the second stage (1979-91), precipitated in part by Paul Ramsey's address on liturgy and ethics, Martens observes that Yoder now relates these two practices to worship, where worship is construed as the "communal cultivation of an alternative construction of society and history."[6] Martens notes that Yoder here defines worship in "essentially moral/empirical terms."[7] This definition prepares the way for Yoder's innovations. First, he places binding and loosing (and later the other two practices) alongside baptism and the Lord's Supper as a sacrament. Second, Yoder (following Barth) describes the church as "an alternative community with a modeling mission," such that the wider world around can see and, in some sense, follow the way of life exhibited by the church. Thus, the sacraments are foretastes of what the world as a whole should be.[8] According to Martens, Yoder is not sufficiently clear at this point as to whether these sacraments are only internally intelligible or whether they also make sense to those outside the church.

In the third stage (1991-94), Martens argues, Yoder reduces the sacraments to nothing more than social processes in order to avoid both Catholic sacramentalism and Zwinglian rationalism. In the end, Yoder trades the language of theology for sociology. The world no longer has to learn a foreign language (that of Christian theology or the biblical narrative) but may simply observe the "obvious efficiencies and values of the form of the church's social community as polis."[9]

Although Martens recognizes the helpful aspects of Yoder's thought (the sacraments are communal, communicable, and concrete), he concludes that Yoder may be "presenting a form of Christianity that is but a stepping stone to assimilation into secularism."[10] Thus, he offers four critiques. First, Yoder seldom addresses the sacraments in a way that is in line with the Mennonite confessions of faith. Second, Yoder sees the church as only ethical, only empirical; there is no mystery, and the church is simply a secular social community. Third, Yoder translates all theological language into sociological language. Finally, Martens wonders if, in the last stage of his work, Yoder presents a "demythologized or reductionistic Christianity."[11] In sum, Martens is worried that Yoder views the church as nothing more than an ethical body that can be described in sociological language and for which the sacraments are no different from secular social processes. If Martens is right, then Yoder stands in need of correction. Martens is wrong, however, because his critique presumes a problematic binary framework and reads Yoder as opting for only one side of it (e.g., sociological language over against theological language, or ethical or secular over against liturgical), whereas a chief concern of Yoder is to point the way beyond these false dilemmas. In doing so, Yoder addresses the very problem that Martens is worried about: a reductionistic view of the sacraments.

Beyond Binaries

Before moving to Yoder's treatment of the sacraments, it is necessary to think about how to position his thought in relation to modern ways of construing the relationship between ethics and liturgy. For Stanley Hauerwas, liturgy, theology, and ethics are always of a piece.[12] To think we can do one without the other is modernity's mistake. As Hauerwas and Wells argue, modern thought is characterized by binary logic that divorces ethics from liturgy and worship, as well as theology.[13] They highlight four faulty assumptions with which we should dispense in order to overcome these binary oppositions.

First, ethics is about the real; worship is about the unreal.[14] Thanks in part to Kant, worship is routinely associated with the nebulous noumenal (about which we cannot really say anything or know anything truly), while ethics has to do with the "real world," the here and now world of space-time action. In this way, Kant positioned moderns to think wrongly that ethics is possible without worship and vice versa.

Second, worship is about beauty; ethics is about the good.[15] Or, put differently, ethics is practical and objective, and worship is not. Ethics deals with "the functional, the instrumental, and the transferable, leaving worship muddling along in the backwaters of goodness, truth, and beauty."[16] Ethics presumes to deal with the universalizable and attempts to ground itself in a foundationalist epistemology, looking down on worship as something unjustified and unjustifiably particular in that it lives by doxology.

Third, ethics has to do with the external; worship has to do with the internal.[17] This is another way of conceiving the public/private split, such that Christians and non-Christians alike have often considered questions of power, economic sharing, and racial reconciliation to be "public" issues, whereas the public and political are conceived as fundamentally different from the private and religious activity of worship.

Fourth, it is often thought that worship is about words; ethics is about action.[18] In contrast, Hauerwas and Wells point out that both ethics and worship are about words *and* action. Thus, the church does not merely repeat words, listen to words, and read words; the church gathers, prays, baptizes, remembers, shares, praises, and goes forth. In the end, Hauerwas and Wells want us to grasp that any sharp distinction between liturgy/worship and ethics is problematic.

The way that Hauerwas and Wells crystallize these points is helpful because, when reading Yoder on liturgy and ethics, we are forced to ask: Was Yoder working from a modern, Kantian standpoint, where social ethics and sociology are capable of being divorced from liturgy and theology? How one answers this question shapes how one casts his project and how one views the charges of reductionism. Did Yoder assume that liturgy and ethics were fundamentally different and thus cast about for a helpful way to relate these two distinct and unrelated things? Or did Yoder attempt to show how ethics is always already liturgy and how liturgy is always already ethics?

"Sacrament as Social Process": Yoder on the Sacraments

Yoder's treatment of the sacraments is summarized in "Sacrament as Social Process: Christ the Transformer of Culture."[19] This article and its expansion as *Body Politics* are chief examples of what Paul Martens finds problematic in the mature Yoder. Consequently, we must grapple with exactly what Yoder is doing here. For purposes of charting Yoder's continuity and development, it should be noted that although this article was first published in 1991 and re-published in 1994 (Martens includes it in the 1991-1994 period of Yoder's thought), it originated in a 1986 lecture and develops suggestions Yoder first made in 1980.[20] In this text, Yoder outlines five practices of the church that he labels "sacraments." According to Yoder, the commonality between these practices "is that each of them concerns *both* the internal activities of the gathered Christian congregation *and* the ways the church interfaces with the world."[21] The five practices are binding and loosing (fraternal admonition), the universality of charisma (the fullness of Christ), the Spirit's freedom in the meeting (open meeting), breaking bread (the Lord's Supper), and induction into the new humanity (baptism). While at least the first three are not typically thought of as worship or liturgy, Yoder identifies all five as such. He then lists nine implications of these practices[22]:

1. Each action is wholly human, not esoteric, but also an act of God "in, with, and under the human practice."
2. These practices are *social*, such that language of sociology (not philosophy or semantics) is most appropriate.
3. These practices can be paradigmatic for other social groups.
4. They are not "religious" or "ritual" activities at bottom, but "public" phenomena.
5. These practices are "enabled and illuminated by Jesus of Nazareth, who is confessed as Messiah and Lord."
6. These practices focus on the believing community as the primary agent of change, rather than isolated individuals.

7. None of the five practices was new in and of itself, but each was taken up by Jesus and the early church, such that their meaning and source of power were indeed new.

8. These practices do not depend on one specific meta-ethical discourse, whether deontological, consequentialist, or virtue ethics.

9. These practices transcend traditional dichotomies, including "Protestant/Catholic," "radical/liberal," and "revelation/reason."

Yoder concludes by noting that all of these practices are evangelical in that they communicate good news. They are *good* insofar as they are communicated as helping, saving, and shalom, and they are *news* insofar as they communicate what would not and could not be known if someone did not say it and live it.[23] The church does not simply speak an in-language to which outsiders must first convert before these practices become intelligible at all. Rather, each of them is "an a posteriori political practice that tells the world something it did not know and could not believe before. It tells the world what is the world's own calling and destiny, not by announcing either a utopia or a realistic goal to be imposed on the whole society, but by pioneering a paradigmatic demonstration of both the power and the practices that define the shape of restored humanity. The confessing people of God is the new world on the way."[24]

Yoder's understanding of these sacraments thus breaks down any conception that would see the "religious" or "theological" on one side, and the "public" or "sociological" on the other. The sacraments are an example of Yoder taking the language of a problematic binary opposition and trying to work it apart from the inside out. He is speaking to those *with* the operative binary "religious versus public" and so trying to get beyond it, *not* opting for one side of it. As the church pioneers culture,[25] it undercuts the idea that we can segment any part of life apart from the reign of Jesus and it underscores that cruciform living goes with the grain of the universe.[26]

Two Guidelines for Reading Yoder

At its foundation, Yoder's view of liturgy, ethics, and theology is rooted in doxology: to sing with those in Revelation 5 the praise and confession that the Crucified Lamb is Lord of the cosmos. Doxology, declares Yoder, is more than liturgy, ethics, or dogmatics, taken on their own. Rather, doxology is a

"way of seeing; a grasp of which end is up, which way is forward."[27] Yoder's
concern here, as he addresses the guild of Christian ethicists, is to remind
them that ethics is never an "autonomous discipline"; it never takes place
apart from a doxological orientation toward some object of ultimate worship and "is not separable from theology without denaturing both."[28] Thus,
the attempt to construct ethics apart from its context within the fullness of
human life is just the rebound effect of the problematic Kantian dichotomy
between theology/worship and ethics outlined earlier. Ethics, says Yoder,
ought to be driven by doxology, such that "moral being and behaving are
primordially proclamation or celebration."[29] Moreover, Yoder is concerned
to preserve a clear coherence between liturgy and life. In "Hermeneutics
of Peoplehood," he calls for a unity of worship and morality.[30] There he
declares, "Worship is the communal cultivation of an alternative construction of society and of history."[31] Yoder is calling Christians to recognize that
worship is never just "religious," but always positions us with respect to
how we relate to God, to others (society), and to our calling in God's time
and mission (history).[32]

Part of Yoder's genius is his ability to see beyond the binary oppositions
of many modern theological dilemmas (e.g., faithfulness versus relevance,
the "religious" versus the "political").[33] Part of the difficulty in interpreting Yoder is that he had no other language to use, and so he often used the
language and logic of his contemporaries in a way that pointed beyond
them. For example, many of his book titles and subtitles attempt to point
the way beyond a public/private or politics/religion dichotomy even as
they include language that risks being misunderstood: *The Politics of Jesus,*
Discipleship as Political Responsibility, "Social Ethics as Gospel," "Essays
Public and Evangelical," and "Five Practices of the Christian Community
before the Watching World." Yoder's thought is best comprehended, not by
importing the binary logic of theology/sociology, worship/ethics, liturgy/
life, cult/culture, church/politics, or sacred/secular into our reading of his
work, but by seeing how Yoder helps deconstruct those binaries from the
inside out. Most of the aforementioned titles and subtitles will be misread
if one presumes the binary logic that is often at work in the thought processes of the modern reader. Yet Yoder rejected the sacred/secular dualism
that permeates contemporary discussions of these topics.

Thus, the first guideline for reading Yoder rightly on this matter is that
liturgy and ethics, theology and sociology, are not two distinct and different

things, but two aspects of the same thing. When theological language is conceived as something over against and absolutely distinct from sociological language, we import a problematic modern dualism into the text of Scripture and the heart of the church. Yoder appears to be reductionistic in his approach to the sacraments only if his readers come to the text with a dualism between liturgy and ethics. Rather than drawing this line and saying that Yoder does not make the sacraments religious or transcendent enough, one should consider whether Yoder is focusing on the way in which *all* of life is liturgical (including the sacraments and liturgy of the church). When readers bring to Yoder's work their Kantian hangovers (which we all do, to some extent), they miss the extent to which every theological statement for Yoder is also liturgical, ethical, and sociological, and vice versa. Rather than perpetuating the modern divorce between liturgy and ethics, Yoder problematizes that division.

A second guideline for reading Yoder is that *we should take Yoder as an expansionist (not a reductionist or antagonist) except in areas where we have very good textual or contextual reasons to do otherwise.* That is, we must be careful to note when Yoder positions himself as an expansionist with respect to the broad Christian tradition, and when he positions himself as an antagonist or reductionist. For example, in the second edition of *The Politics of Jesus,* the mature Yoder is careful to note that his project is not meant as a denial of the traditional view of Jesus, but an attempt to open the tradition to see how *it* was being reductionistic in light of the richness of Scripture, Nicea, and Chalcedon: "The element of debate in the presentation may make it seem that the 'other' or 'traditional' element in each case—Jesus as sacrifice, God as creator, faith as subjectivity—is being rejected. It should therefore be restated that—as perusal of the structure of our presentation will confirm—no disjunction is intended. I am rather defending the New Testament against the exclusion of the 'messianic' element. The disjunction must be laid to the account of the traditional view, not of mine. It is those other views that say that because Jesus is seen as sacrifice he may not be seen as sovereign, or that because he is seen as Word made flesh he cannot be seen as normative person."[34]

Yoder notes in the epilogue of the second edition that he is often accused of being "reductionistic" by critics who see him as offering the politics of Jesus *over against* creedal orthodoxy, rather than arguing that this expanded view of Jesus is precisely what that tradition should entail.[35]

But Yoder is not trying to take a position in a debate whose parameters he accepts (e.g., conservative creedal orthodoxy versus liberal social gospel). Rather, he is trying to expand our view so we can see why the logic of the debate does not make sense biblically and theologically in the first place. To those locked in the logic of the debate, Yoder may appear reductionistic when in fact he is an expansionist, pointing out the rich complexity of both Jesus and the nature of the gospel. I would submit that Yoder most often serves as an expansionist, someone who wants to broaden our horizons about who Jesus is and what the gospel is all about. When he does intentionally deny or antagonize a doctrinal position (e.g., transubstantiation), it is often not because in and of itself a doctrinal position is inherently wrong or necessarily incoherent, but because it closes down the broad view of what God is doing. It divorces life from liturgy, and Jesus from our everyday lives.

Liturgy for Life: The Lord's Supper

These two guidelines—reading Yoder as moving beyond binaries and Yoder as expansionist—can be seen when one looks at his treatment of the Lord's Supper. Rather than demonstrating a problematic drift toward secularism, Yoder's discussion of this particular sacrament can serve as a test case that illuminates his persistent emphasis on the integration of liturgy and life.

In contrast to Martens's argument that Yoder's thought shifts significantly on the sacraments, Yoder in fact describes the central task in discussing the sacraments the same way in 1966 as in 1986/1991: to break down the notion that liturgy/sacraments and ethics are two unrelated things that we must now try to relate.[36] The early Yoder states, "Preoccupied to reject certain aspects of the Catholic practice, the reformers were willing to agree with the assumption that the mass was a ritual distinct from the rest of life."[37] Likewise, the mature Yoder sees "motivational" or "moral" approaches to worship as problematic because "they begin with the problem of a qualitative distance between the two realms of liturgy and ethics and maintain that a bridge of some kind needs to be built."[38] Yoder's polemic against both Roman Catholic and Zwinglian Protestant views of the Lord's Supper moves along the same lines in both his early and late work: both positions divide the sacraments as a "religious ritual" from the everyday life of the Christian community.[39] Interestingly, he even uses exactly the same terminology ("Catholic sacramentalism" and "Zwinglian rationalism") in

1966 and 1994. This makes problematic Martens's claim that the mature Yoder "has now moved some distance from his initial beginnings in 1967."[40] Though Yoder certainly nuanced his thought over time as he engaged new interlocutors, his critique of and solution to the schema of liturgy and life remain essentially the same. The problem is that they are conceptualized as essentially unrelated, which creates the pseudo-problem of trying to relate them, whereas Yoder's solution is to discern how they are essentially related from the very beginning.

Moreover, Yoder is more than capable of emphasizing the multifaceted meaning of the sacraments, when that is his assigned task. According to Yoder, there are at least sixteen layers that have developed throughout history around the celebration of the Lord's Supper.[41] This list demonstrates that Yoder did not think of the sacraments as social processes *over against* any other possible meaning. Instead, as with many topics, Yoder seeks to enrich our understanding by setting forth the complexity of the topic at hand. Of the sixteen layers he identifies, Yoder sees the following eleven as clearly rooted in Scripture:

1. Thanksgiving (Eucharist)—Every time a meal is celebrated, thanksgiving is offered up and the bread is distributed to all those who share the table.
2. Celebration of Passover—The annual Jewish celebration is both a meal and an act of worship.
3. Sharing—The sharing of food—what one eats and with whom one eats it—is significant not only in Jewish law and culture, but in virtually all human societies.
4. Memorial—The Lord's Supper is about remembering Jesus.
5. Celebration—Because the risen Lord appeared to his disciples in the context of meals, the Lord's Supper is also a celebration of the presence of the resurrected Jesus.
6. The Love Feast—One of the most basic ways the early church shared with one another was sharing a meal together.
7. Communion of goods—The early church shared not only meals and "spiritual" blessings, but wider material goods so that there were no needy people among them.
8. Unity of the body—In correcting the Corinthians (1 Cor 10:14-17), Paul highlights "the loaf as a unity, the body of Christ as a

unity, and the meal as a unity representing the body of Christ and represented by the loaf."[42]

9. Reminder of the death of Christ—Because of this, we must examine ourselves so that we do not participate in an unworthy manner (1 Cor 11:27).

10. Hope—Since this is a proclamation of the Lord's death "until he comes" (1 Cor 11:26), it is not only about remembering the past, but looking expectantly to the Lord's return.

11. A proto-sacramental understanding—In the Gospel accounts, the focus on the elements ("This is my body, this is my blood") is in the context of the meal, but Yoder says that "we see already beginning inside the New Testament the development of something like what will later be called 'the sacrament'; i.e., a symbolic act whose meaning is more than the act itself."[43]

This list is significant because, based on what Yoder does here, Martens's thesis about Yoder's reductionistic view of the sacraments needs some revision. This list shows that Yoder can and does treat the Lord's Supper in a more traditional Mennonite/Anabaptist way, with an emphasis on remembrance of Jesus' broken body and shed blood, as well as the fellowship and unity of the gathered community. Moreover, for Martens's thesis about Yoder's development to hold, Yoder would need to reject or significantly modify every entry on this list. Although Martens could contend that this list simply represents the first stage of Yoder's thought, it would require more work to show that Yoder rejects or modifies all of the above, whether explicitly or implicitly. Given the obvious biblical rootage of this list, it seems highly unlikely that Yoder would do so.

Furthermore, in context of this list, Yoder overtly argues for an expansionist view of this particular sacrament. In his discussion of the Lord's Supper as love feast, Yoder states, "It is pointless to ask whether the Christians in eating in their homes were continuing one or only one of the others of the above meanings: *why were they not doing all of the above?*"[44] Yoder notes that eating together is always, at base, certainly eating together; but he notes that eating together is always *more than* eating together—it is always already liturgical, always already social-economic.[45] In this, Yoder has more than sufficient evidence in the Gospels and Acts, where one of the key issues is with whom Jesus will or will not eat, and with whom the early Jewish Christians will or will not eat. Therefore, this is an area where we should see Yoder as expansionist—not a reductionist—with respect to both his own Mennonite tradition and the broader Christian tradition.

What then is Yoder's problem with the debates about the precise nature of the Lord's Supper and Christ's presence with respect to the traditional Roman Catholic and Protestant (and even Anabaptist) positions? He might ask: *If* liturgy and ethics have already been divorced, if the "religious" is conceived of as *other than* the "social," then have not *those* Christian traditions reduced the Lord's Supper to "a ritual distinct from the rest of life"?[46] It is not that there are no biblical grounds for seeing the Lord's Supper as rich and complex; there are. It is a time of remembering Christ's death, sharing in Jesus' body and blood, celebrating his resurrection, thanking God for his past work in Christ and hope for the future, and so on. But, Yoder argues, the problem with both Catholic and Protestant practice of the Lord's Supper is that it "remained a ceremony within the church, with no direct connection to what bread and drink commonly mean. It would occur to no one, upon unfolding the meaning of that common meal, as explained in Protestant practice, to sell a piece of land and contribute it to the church so that everyone would have enough."[47] Yoder's view of the Lord's Supper, then, is complex and multi-layered: social, theological, economic, and ecclesiological. His injunction to us is not to reduce but to enrich.[48]

If Yoder leans too far to the social-economic meaning of the Lord's Supper, it is not to move from a one-dimensional "religious" view to a one-dimensional "social-economic" or "secular" view, but to highlight the ignored aspects of the Lord's Supper that are in Scripture but have been neglected in our practice. Yoder is often in dialogue with those who saw the sacraments as *only* religious, with no inherent social, economic, or political meaning. Because of these conversation partners, we would expect to see Yoder placing more emphasis on the social, economic, and political meanings of the sacraments, which is exactly what we find. Thus he argues that "the need is rather to overcome the separation of the sacrament from the daily life of the body which was at the very root of the development of sacramentalism."[49] In any case, Yoder can be a remedy to a view of liturgy that asks about the "social, practical, and public" *implications* of liturgy.[50] To Yoder, this is like asking about the "social, practical, and public" implications of the gospel. The gospel is not "religious" with social implications, it is religious/social/public through and through (Eph 2:11-22). Likewise, the sacraments and liturgy are always already social, ethical, economic, and public; whereas the social, ethical, economic, and public are always already liturgical. Rather than seeing Yoder as a mere ethicist, focusing on ethics or sociology at the expense of theology or liturgy, he should be seen as breaking down the false barriers between liturgy and ethics, liturgy and life. Beyond these barriers, Yoder calls us to see how our life practices are always oriented either toward or away from God's kingdom, either moving with or against the grain of the universe.

Language, Liturgy, and the Sacraments

This still leaves a key concern of Martens unanswered, namely, that Yoder sees paradigmatic practices as the chief mode of communication from church to world.[51] Hence, "language and text are rejected; empirical and sociological practices remain the only possible means of uninhibited communication."[52] Martens argues that since Yoder characterizes the sacraments as social processes, they fit with his notion of communication via paradigmatic practices. Again, as an historical aside, Yoder characterized the church as "paradigm" and provided detailed description of this notion as early as 1973, which makes it problematic that Martens sees this as developing only around 1984.[53] In any case, because Yoder emphasizes communication by paradigmatic practices rather than peculiar language, Martens worries that he ends with a merely empirical, ethical church that is nothing more than a secular, social community. Beyond the points already made about reading Yoder in this way, three further points should be noted about Yoder's emphasis on the church as paradigm.

First, Yoder often makes claims about the church as paradigm in a debate whose terms he does not necessarily accept, but that he uses anyway. In "Firstfruits," Yoder is asked to address the question of the "public good" at the inauguration of the Institute for the Study of the Public Good at Christian Theological Seminary. Yoder is intent here, as elsewhere, to break down the notion that Christians are a private "religious group" that speaks an in-language and lives in ways that are inherently incommunicable to the broader public, such that Christians need to set aside their particular language and way of being in the world in order to truly communicate in the public square.[54] By contrast, Yoder references the five sacraments, noting that we do not need to change our practices *or* our language for these practices to be accessible to non-Christians. Rather, "that action is public by nature, with no need for it to be translated or buffered or diluted."[55] Yoder's point is *not* that we can do away with the language of Christian theology or the biblical narrative when speaking to the non-Christian world. Indeed, part of his point is to say that the church is not required, by definition and a priori, to leave its own language behind as a condition for communicating with outsiders! Rather, echoing Barth, Yoder highlights the "confessional and Christological logic of the claim that *the order of the faith community constitutes a public offer to the entire society.*"[56] Thus, church and world are not defined by whether they are religious, political, or secular, but by whether or not they acknowledge Jesus as Lord of the cosmos. Belief and unbelief are not on two different planes but are two different ways to orient our lives. In this sense, there is no secular city, only the city of God and city of man, only "allegiances in opposite directions, and social relationships patterned according to the contrasting logics of self-interest and Christ-like love."[57]

Second, Yoder shied away from an overemphasis on language because he was a missionary. As such, he saw all language, even Christian language, as always provisional and always undergoing translation. In a clear dig at Hauerwas, Yoder states,

> Some have warned me that it is dangerous to borrow such worldly words as "egalitarianism" or "freedom" since those concepts are not only hard to define but are the property of the liberal establishment, which is an oppressive elite. These friends are right in thus warning me. If I were to think that those contemporary terms have a univocal normative meaning, and if I were proposing that they simply be "baptized," I should have sold out. But those warning friends are wrong if they suggest that some other, less liberal words (for example, "virtue," "narrative," and "community") would be safe from abuse. The right corrective is not to seek fail-safe words never yet corrupted but rather to renew daily the action of preempting the extant vocabulary, rendering every creature subject to God's rule in Christ. What is needed is to surface the criteria whereby we can tell whether, in the appropriation of each new language, the meaning of Jesus is authentically reenacted or abandoned.[58]

Yoder was enough of a missiologist to know that one must go beyond simply latching onto particular words to the difficult task of figuring out a way to faithfully translate both concepts *and* practices from a host language and culture into a receptor language and culture.[59] This means that even words that we take as basic need to be consistently clarified, critiqued, and corrected. The need to do so never stops because language and culture never stop. This is what Yoder does, for example, in *The Politics of Jesus,* where he revisits the terms "Lord," "Son of God," and "Messiah," to help us understand more fully what it means to call someone "Son of God" in first-century Jewish thought.[60] So when Yoder uses "secular" words like egalitarianism, democracy, and socialism to talk about the sacraments, he underscores that *"each of these terms needs to be taken in a way different from their secularistic and individualistic uses."*[61] As far as I can tell, Martens (and other critics) seldom take note of these important (and explicit) interpretive caveats. Consequently, I would revise Martens's claim that Yoder rejects language and text, and instead see Yoder as emphasizing the contingent and translatable nature of all language, including Christian language, as we continue to find ways to say with our lips and lives that Jesus is Lord. The task for the missionary church is not *whether* we will do translation, but whether it will be faithful or unfaithful translation.

Finally, Yoder affirms Christ as Lord of the cosmos and Lord of the church. Because creation and redemption are not to be set at odds with one another, and because the politics of Jesus reveal the grain of the universe, Yoder is not surprised when unbelievers sometimes move with that grain, while Christians sometimes do not. Moreover, when Yoder argues that his five sacraments can "be spoken of in social process terms easily translated into nonreligious terms,"[62] this should be understood as a statement about our description of these sacraments, not about their grounding in who God is. After all, as noted earlier, these practices are ultimately rooted in God's action and enabled and illumined by Jesus.[63] But Yoder's concern here is to hedge against the liturgical turn in ethics, where the focus is all about the liturgy (in the traditional sense), such that we become occupied with speaking a "religious language" that is not *also* social, ethical, and political. That is, Yoder wants a robust and complex view of liturgy to match our robust and complex God. Hence, it is legitimate to describe baptism in terms of racial and socio-economic reconciliation (after all, Paul does) and to describe dialogue in the Holy Spirit as the basis of real democracy. But this is not to grant these things ontological, epistemological, or linguistic independence from Jesus' Lordship. Rather, it is to highlight that the Spirit sometimes moves ahead of or beyond God's entrenched church, coming not only in familiar forms, but also in the guise of strangers like Martin Luther King Jr. or Gandhi.[64] We should not be surprised to hear parables of the kingdom bursting through in unexpected places or to find them being spoken of in terms of mundane social processes.[65] Although Yoder's critics worry that his mature thought turns away from the particularity of the church, Yoder worries that his critics turn the liturgy (in the traditional sense) into a self-perpetuating phenomena that underscores the *unintel-ligibility* of our language and practice before the watching world. That is, we emphasize liturgy for the sake of emphasizing the specialness of the church as an end in itself. But Yoder is not ultimately interested in being against the nations for the sake of being against the nations; he wants to be against the nations in a way that is ultimately for the nations.

Conclusion

I have offered here an alternative to Martens's view of Yoder on the sacraments. If I am correct, there is more consistency and continuity in Yoder's overall work than Martens allows for. Moreover, far from being reductionistic, Yoder actually offers a robust account of the inherent relationship between the sacraments and the life of the Christian community. Yoder therefore continues to be helpful because Christians continue to construct problematic dichotomies and continue to fall into the trap of divorcing liturgy and life. The sacraments are a critical element of the church's inner constitution as well as a paradigm for the world to see and join. They are no more secular or religious, public or private than the proclamation that Jesus is Lord.

Endnotes

[1] I use "liturgy" interchangeably with "worship," recognizing that liturgy can refer both to the specific activity of the church on Sunday as well as the "work" of the church's daily life together. For discussions of liturgy, see *The Blackwell Companion to Christian Ethics*, eds. Stanley Hauerwas and Samuel Wells (Oxford: Blackwell, 2004); Walter Brueggemann, "Always in the Shadow of the Empire," in *The Church as Counterculture*, eds.

Michael L. Budde and Robert W. Brimlow (Albany, NY: SUNY Press, 2000), 39-58; Rodney Clapp, *A Peculiar People: The Church as Culture in a Post-Christian Society* (Downers Grove, IL: InterVarsity Press, 1996), esp. 114-125 and 172-186; *Liturgy, Time, and the Politics of Redemption*, eds. C. C. Pecknold and Randi Rashkover (Grand Rapids: Eerdmans, 2006); Catherine Pickstock, *After Writing: On the Liturgical Consummation of Philosophy* (Oxford: Blackwell, 1998); Paul Ramsey, "Liturgy and Ethics," *Journal of Religious Ethics* 7, no. 2 (1979): 139-171; and David L. Stubbs, "Ending of Worship: Ethics" in *A More Profound Alleluia: Theology and Worship in Harmony*, ed. Leanne Van Dyk (Grand Rapids: Eerdmans, 2005), 133-153. Also, the entire issue of *Liturgy* 20, no. 1 (2005) is devoted to examining how liturgy shapes and forms us in context of other cultural liturgies.

[2] The charge of reductionism is raised from various angles by Michael G. Cartwright, "Sharing the Household of God: Learning to Read Scripture with the Anabaptists," *Mennonite Quarterly Review* 74, no. 4 (2000): 593-621; Paul Doerksen, "Share the House: Yoder and Hauerwas Among the Nations," in *A Mind Patient and Untamed: Assessing John Howard Yoder's Contributions to Theology, Ethics, and Peacemaking*, eds. Ben C. Ollenburger and Gayle Gerber Koontz (Telford, PA.: Cascadia Publishing House/ Scottdale, PA: Herald Press, 2004), 187-204; Thomas Finger, "Did Yoder Reduce Theology to Ethics?" in *A Mind Patient and Untamed*, 318-339; Nathan Kerr, *Christ, History, and Apocalyptic: The Politics of Christian Mission* (Eugene, OR: Cascade, 2009); Paul Martens, "The Problematic Development of the Sacraments in the Thought of John Howard Yoder," *Conrad Grebel Review* 24, no. 3 (2006): 65-77; and A. James Reimer, "Mennonites, Christ, and Culture: The Yoder Legacy," *Conrad Grebel Review* 16 (1998): 5-14.

[3] Martens, "Problematic Development of the Sacraments."

[4] For an account of this development, see Stanley Hauerwas and Samuel Wells, "Why Christian Ethics was Invented," in *The Blackwell Companion to Christian Ethics*, 28-38; and Steve Long, *The Goodness of God* (Grand Rapids: Brazos, 2001), 53-104.

[5] Martens, "Problematic Development of the Sacraments," 65.

[6] Yoder, "The Hermeneutics of Peoplehood," in *The Priestly Kingdom: Social Ethics as Gospel* (Notre Dame: University of Notre Dame Press, 1984), 43.

[7] It would be a problem if Yoder had said that worship is "only" or "nothing more than" the communal cultivation of an alternative construction of society and history. Elsewhere, Yoder clearly sees worship and doxology as more than a merely moral/empirical action. E.g., "To Serve Our God and Rule the World."

[8] Martens, "Problematic Development of the Sacraments," 69.

[9] Ibid., 71.

[10] Ibid., 73.

[11] Ibid.

[12] E.g., Hauerwas, *The Peaceable Kingdom* (Notre Dame: University of Notre Dame Press, 1983), esp. 106-111; "Worship, Evangelism, Ethics," in *A Better Hope: Resources for a Church Confronting Capitalism, Democracy, and Postmodernism* (Grand Rapids: Brazos Press, 2000), 155-161; and Hauerwas and Samuel Wells' introductory essays in *Blackwell Companion to Christian Ethics*.

[13] Hauerwas and Wells, "Christian Ethics as Informed Prayer," *Blackwell Companion to Christian Ethics*, 3-12. On this point, see also James K. A. Smith, *Desiring the Kingdom: Worship, Worldview, and Cultural Formation* (Grand Rapids: Baker Academic, 2009).

[14] Hauerwas and Wells, "Christian Ethics as Informed Prayer," 4.

[15] Ibid., 5.

[16] Ibid.

[17] Ibid., 6.

[18] Ibid.

[19] Yoder, "Sacrament as Social Process," in *The Royal Priesthood: Essays Ecclesiological and Ecumenical,* ed. Michael G. Cartwright (Grand Rapids: Eerdmans, 1994), 359-373.

[20] Editor's Introduction to "Sacrament as Social Process," in *Royal Priesthood,* 359. Cartwright notes that Yoder's suggestions in this direction were made in the Stone Lectures at Princeton Theological Seminary in February 1980. Mark Thiessen Nation specifies that "Sacrament as Social Process" is the fourth and portions of the fifth lecture, significantly reworked ("Behold My Servant Shall Prosper," in *Karl Barth and the Problem of War and Other Essays,* ed. Mark Thiessen Nation [Eugene, OR: Cascade Books, 2003], 149, fn. 1).

[21] Yoder, "Sacrament as Social Process," in *Royal Priesthood,* 361. For similar points, see also "Why Ecclesiology is Social Ethics" (1980), in *Royal Priesthood,* 102-126; *Body Politics: Five Practices of the Christian Community before the Watching World* (Scottdale, PA: Herald Press, 1993); and "Firstfruits: The Paradigmatic Public Role of God's People" (1992), and "The New Humanity as Pulpit and Paradigm" (1994), in *For the Nations: Essays Public and Evangelical* (Grand Rapids: Eerdmans, 1997).

[22] The following list is summarized from Yoder, "Sacrament as Social Process," in *Royal Priesthood,* 369-372.

[23] Yoder, "The Sacrament as Social Process," in *Royal Priesthood,* 373.

[24] Ibid.

[25] I am indebted to John Nugent for this way of phrasing Yoder's position.

[26] Yoder, "Armaments and Eschatology," *Studies in Christian Ethics* 1, no. 1 (1988): 58.

[27] Yoder, "To Serve Our God and Rule the World," in *Royal Priesthood,* 129.

[28] Yoder, "The Experiential Etiology of Evangelical Dualism," *Missiology: An International Review* 11, no. 4 (1983): 458.

[29] Yoder, "To Serve Our God and Rule the World," in *Royal Priesthood,* 136.

[30] Yoder, "The Hermeneutics of Peoplehood," in *Priestly Kingdom,* 43.

[31] Ibid. I find it hard to believe that Yoder is reductionistic and that he means that worship is *only* this historical-constructive task, as Kerr charges in *Christ, History, and Apocalyptic,* 171-72. Kerr elsewhere notes that Yoder's account of doxology stands in contrast to this. I think Kerr ought to take Yoder's definition here as operating under Yoder's broader account of doxology, rather than in contrast to it.

[32] This way of framing things explains why Gerald Schlabach sees Augustine as an "Augustinian interlocutor," in "The Christian Witness in the Earthly City: John H. Yoder as Augustinian Interlocutor," in *A Mind Patient and Untamed,* 221-244.

[33] Yoder, *The Politics of Jesus* (Grand Rapids: Eerdmans, 1972). Yoder spells out these binaries in chapter 1: "The Possibility of a Messianic Ethic." Further citations in this essay will be from Yoder, *The Politics of Jesus,* 2d ed. (Grand Rapids: Eerdmans, 1994).

[34] Yoder, *Politics of Jesus,* 226.

[35] Ibid., 227.

[36] See Yoder, "The Mandate to Share," in Lectures presented in Montevideo and Buenos Aires, 1966, John Howard Yoder papers in the Archives of the Mennonite Church, box 117, and "Sacrament as Social Process," in *Royal Priesthood,* 361. As noted earlier, the latter essay was first given as a lecture in 1986 and first published in 1991.

[37] Yoder, "The Mandate to Share," 3.

[38] Yoder, "Sacrament as Social Process," in *Royal Priesthood,* 361.

[39] Yoder, "The Mandate to Share," 1-6, and "Sacrament as Social Process," in *Royal Priesthood,* 364-66.

[40] Martens, "Problematic Development of the Sacraments," 71.

[41] Yoder, "The Lord's Supper in Historical Perspective," Assembly Congregation, Goshen, Indiana, Nov. 26, 1978. John Howard Yoder papers in the Archives of the Mennonite Church, box 117. The following list summarizes Yoder's points.

[42] Ibid., 3.

[43] The remaining five extra-biblical layers (on Yoder's read) are: (12) a remedy for sin, a "medicine for immortality," (13) a general theory of sacraments behind any one act, (14) transubstantiation as a repetition of the miracle of the incarnation, (15) the mass itself is a sacrifice that participates in the removal of sin, and (16) the mass as a ritual that can be performed by the priest alone, without the congregation.

[44] "Lord's Supper in Historical Perspective," 2 (emphasis mine).

[45] Yoder, "Sacrament as Social Process," in *Royal Priesthood*, 364-365.

[46] Yoder, "The Mandate to Share," 3.

[47] Ibid.

[48] He might repeat that "the disjunction must be laid to the account of the traditional view, not of mine." *The Politics of Jesus*, 226.

[49] Yoder, "The Mandate to Share," 6. Elsewhere Yoder distinguishes between "sacramental" and "sacramentalistic." The former is fine, while the latter is problematic (*Body Politics*, 44).

[50] Yoder, *Body Politics*, 46.

[51] This theme can be seen in the first two essays of *For the Nations:* "Firstfruits: The Paradigmatic Public Role of God's People," 23-28, and "The New Humanity as Pulpit and Paradigm," 43.

[52] Martens, "Problematic Development of the Sacraments," 71.

[53] Ibid., 68. See Yoder, "The Biblical Mandate for Evangelical Social Action," in *For the Nations,* 184-189. As stated in the introductory footnote to the essay, Yoder initially gave this as an address to the constitutive meeting of Evangelicals for Social Action in November of 1973.

[54] See also Yoder, "But We Do See Jesus," in *Priestly Kingdom,* 46-62; and "On Not Being Ashamed of the Gospel: Particularity, Pluralism, and Validation," *Faith and Philosophy* 9 (July 1992): 285-300.

[55] Yoder, "Firstfruits," in *For the Nations*, 27.

[56] Ibid.

[57] Gerald Schlabach, "Christian Witness in the Earthly City," in *Mind Patient and Untamed*, 232.

[58] Yoder, "Sacrament as Social Process," in *Royal Priesthood*, 370.

[59] Yoder, "The Racial Revolution in Theological Perspective," in *For the Nations*, 121.

[60] Yoder, *Politics of Jesus*, 24-27.

[61] Yoder, "Sacrament as Social Process," in *Royal Priesthood*, 370 (emphasis mine).

[62] Ibid., 364.

[63] Ibid., 369-370.

[64] Yoder makes this point well before 1991-1994. For example, "The Racial Revolution in Theological Perspective" was initially given at the conference "The Christian and the World Revolution" in 1967 and later published in *For the Nations*, 97-124, as well as "The Power Equation, the Place of Jesus, and the Politics of King," which was originally presented in 1981 and later published in *For the Nations*, 125-147.

[65] Alain Epp Weaver, "Parables of the Kingdom and Religious Plurality: With Barth and Yoder toward a Nonresistant Public Theology," *Mennonite Quarterly Review* 72, no. 3 (1998): 411-440.

Chapter Nine

The Ecumenical Movement and the Faithful Church

John Howard Yoder

It is the purpose of the following pages to deal seriously with the problems raised for the churches of the Anabaptist tradition by the movement known as "ecumenical." It is a highly significant fact, worthy of being noted at the very outset, that evangelical Christians see any problem at all at this point. Roman Catholics and Jehovah's Witnesses have no difficulty with such questions, for they believe, consistently and in line with their doctrine of the church, that it is possible to be a Christian only within their own organization. Catholicism makes some exceptions to this rule, in the sense that Catholic doctrine makes room for people outside the Roman church to be Catholics without knowing it, by virtue of their ignorance and good intentions; but it remains clear that the existence of other churches and of Christians with other convictions is no basic challenge to the convictions of a sincere Catholic, and no problem for his church.

Since Mennonites and other evangelicals of the Anabaptist-Free Church tradition have never taken the position that they are the only Christians, they cannot honestly be content with the same indifference or the self-righteousness with which an organization claiming to be "the only true church" can face the ecumenical movement. We recognize full well that, for some good reasons, many have been hesitant to bring this problem into the open. Nonetheless, the imperative of brotherly unity outweighs the good reasons for caution and demands that the question be faced. In this study we must therefore first of all be acquainted with events in the rest of

Christendom; we must then attempt to evaluate those events and to determine what we should have to do with them, in light of Scripture, and, in a secondary way, in the light of the Anabaptist tradition. This pamphlet aims to contribute to the beginning steps of such a process of study. We describe first very briefly the history and the present organization of some of the movements which attempt to unite various churches, and then ask how they should be evaluated.

The word "ecumenical" comes from a Greek noun *ecumene* (this spelling is not a direct transliteration but has become customary) meaning "that which is inhabited." In Luke 2 the word is translated "the whole world," and means, practically speaking, the whole known world, the Roman Empire. The adjective "ecumenical" was first applied to a series of gatherings of bishops which were held in the Roman Empire when Constantine began tolerating Christians. The first, held in Nicea in 325, dealt with the deity of Jesus Christ, and led gradually to the development of the orthodox doctrine of the Trinity. These meetings were different from the "synods" which were held frequently in the various provinces of the empire, in that "all the world" was represented. Strictly speaking, this was of course not the case; already at the time of Nicea there were separatist churches, and the later councils, by making doctrinal decisions by a bare majority, often created new divisions; but they came to be called "Ecumenical Councils" by Catholic historians because their decisions, enforced by the empire and the hierarchy, were considered as valid for Catholicism. Most Protestant and Free Churches also accept these doctrinal decisions as "orthodox"; thus "ecumenical" came to be a symbol of times when the church was united in doctrine and organization.

We may note in passing that much confusion, not only in "ecumenical" affairs but also in basic Christian theology, has resulted from the failure of historians and theologians to recognize that these early councils were not truly ecumenical, and that the way they were called together and the way they deliberated were hardly worthy of a Christian body. Nor would the Protestant and Free Church theologians who accept the councils' decisions about the Trinity or the two natures of Christ be equally willing to accept their other decisions.

The word "ecumenical" was then picked up and given a new meaning in modern times, when Christians began to be concerned about the fact of division among Christians. Their efforts did not aim first of all so much at uniting "all the world" as at overcoming barriers between denominations; but their movement nevertheless began to be referred to with the name "ecumenical." The related terms, "ecumenics," which means the study of the unity and the divisions of the church, and "ecumenicity," which means the state of being interested in unity, are all new coinings, and are all derived from the new meaning given to the word in recent years.

Efforts to unite divided Christendom are as old as the schism between the Roman and the Greek Orthodox Catholic churches. Here, however, it will only be possible to deal with what has been attempted in modern times.

An early effort at interdenominational fellowship and co-operation began in the middle of the nineteenth century, as a result of revivalist work in England and on the European continent. The Evangelical Alliance was set up in 1846, uniting Christians (but not churches) of all denominations, especially those of the Free Churches and of "evangelical" (i.e., doctrinally conservative) leanings. After several world conferences held intermittently for a half century the Alliance became less active, limiting its activities to the fostering of local interdenominational co-operation on a free-church and evangelical basis, and to the planning of an annual joint Week of Prayer. The Alliance exists to our day, though its international organization has been changed by events we shall report later.

The first root of today's ecumenical movement is found in the revival work of D. L. Moody. Moody's activity was nondenominational, and he brought forth, with his preaching and with the retreats and other activities growing out of his revivals, a generation of zealous and consecrated young people desirous of spreading the Gospel. These young people had great enthusiasm, little doctrinal background, and little interest in denominational peculiarities. The Student Volunteer Movement recruited young people for missions with the challenging slogan, "The Evangelization of the World in This Generation." The Student Christian Movement had similar ideals and much of the same leadership.

When these young missionaries began to reach the field, their enthusiasm was soon dampened by their discovery of the problem of division of the churches. Converts on a Methodist mission field would be told to baptize their children; if they moved to a Baptist mission field a few villages away, rejoicing that they would find fellowship there, they would be told they should not have baptized their children. If the field to which they moved was under an Anglican Mission, it was questioned whether they themselves were validly baptized and had any right to commune. In America these differences had not been taken too seriously; on a mission field they became much more troubling to the converts, and a source of offense for unbelievers. These divisions were of long standing, but they were seen for the first time to be an offense against the Gospel, because of the world-wide perspective, the youth and ambition, and the lack of denominational conviction of many of the young missionaries. Such problems led various missionary organizations to meet, and in 1910 there was formed the International Missionary Council, an organization which has been active and effective ever since in the common study of missionary problems. It is now moving toward union with the World Council of Churches, with which it has been sponsoring some joint projects for a number of years. Some Mennonite mission agencies are associated with the International Missionary Council.

In addition to the strictly missionary side of Moody's influence, we have already mentioned the Student Christian Movement. Meeting each other across national and denominational borders, Christian students often discovered a degree of unity in their common faith and commitment which was hard to reconcile with denominational division. While the Student Christian Movement could never become a church or a council of churches, it could bring to the consciousness of educated Christians the problem of division among Christians, and could also train several generations of leadership: persons who through their work in international Student Christian work became acquainted with problems of interchurch relations and with the leaders of the various churches.

The second root of the modern ecumenical movement was the peace movement. At the time when World War I broke out there was a meeting in Constance, on the Swiss border, of an international conference whose aim was to promote international friendship through the churches. The conference had to disband in order for the participants to get home before travel became impossible, but it contributed both to the later ecumenical movement and to the formation of the first Christian peace movement to become really significant outside the Historic Peace Churches. Two participants in the Constance conference, Friedrich Siegmund-Schulze of Germany and Henry Hodgkin of England, vowed as they parted that neither would take up arms; from that agreement has grown the International Fellowship of

Reconciliation. This organization, not being a church, has certain organizational and sometimes doctrinal weaknesses; but it has brought a witness for the peace position, within the churches not committed to nonresistance, which the better-organized and doctrinally more evangelical peace churches were not bringing. For most of the period between the two World Wars, Siegmund-Schulze led both the peace movement and the ecumenical movement in Germany.

The third root of the modern ecumenical movement was distinctly American. This does not mean that similar motives did not exist elsewhere, but nowhere except in American Protestantism were the problems and the proposed answers so clear and so simple in the minds of their advocates. First of all, only the United States (and Canada) had a denominational situation in which no church had official government support, so that all stood on the same footing. Secondly, America had a very simple, very optimistic kind of theological modernism, according to which all orthodox doctrine was out-of-date, so that naturally differences in doctrine could have no meaning. And thirdly, America is more prone to the "bigger-the-better" mentality, which could combine with the fact that there were no serious doctrinal or legal differences between the denominations, to produce the conclusion that all American Protestant churches should combine in one great organization with a message of social welfare. This was largely the mentality behind the formation of the Federal Council of Churches before World War I. One Mennonite group joined this organization but was soon obliged to withdraw, since the organization was clearly not impartial either theologically or ethically. Theologically its leanings were toward an un-Biblical liberalism, and ethically it favored World War I as a necessary step toward social welfare.

After World War II the Federal Council joined with a great number of other interchurch organizations, dealing with women's work, men's work, youth work, missions, education, etc., to form a new organization, the National Council of the Churches of Christ, commonly referred to as the NCC. The National Council, as did the Federal Council, represents a cross section or a common denominator of American theological orientation; but since the theological atmosphere has changed considerably since the 1910s in the direction of greater respect for Biblical thought, it is by no means as extremely liberal in theology nor as one-sided in ethical thinking as the Federal Council had been.

Before going farther we will do well to note a difference between American and European ecumenical thinking which has persisted to our day. For American thinking, all denominations are on an equal basis, and the problem is how to bring their organizations together into some kind of union. For the kind of thinking which has predominated in Europe, all denominations are not on an equal basis; in each country or province one church is supported by the state and the other "free churches" are so small as to be insignificant organizationally; the problem is to establish friendly relations between churches in various nations. In the American ecumenical movement the effort has been to minimize differences, if necessary by minimizing the importance of doctrinal fidelity; in the international ecumenical movement the question of organizational union has been so far off that the tendency is first to study the differences, and the particular heritage of each church, and the result has often been to revive an interest in the distinct position of each of the various historic confessions.

A further distinction should be noted between expressions of Christian unity which faced the denominational problem and those which tried to ignore it. Most early efforts were nondenominational; i.e., they united individual Christians with no reference to church affiliation (Evangelical Alliance, Young Men's Christian Association, Student Christian Movement). With time it became clear that such organizations could do much good but did not solve the problem of division. More recent efforts have centered on interdenominational relations, carried on between organized church groups on the official level.

The Modern Ecumenical Movement Takes Form

After having seen the roots of the ecumenical movement we may go on to study its growth, especially in the period following the first World War.

First of all, a number of organizations which already existed grew in strength, in world-wide membership, and in interest for Christian unity. The International Missionary Council, founded in Edinburgh in 1910, the Young Men's and Young Women's Christian Associations, and the World Student Christian Movement became, in the period between the wars, accepted parts of the international Christian landscape, becoming continually better acquainted with one another, and having sometimes and in some places the same individuals as leaders. The Young Men's Christian Association, now over one hundred years old, began as a prayer meeting and grew into an agency of evangelism and fellowship among young people; thus, like the Missionary Council and the Student Christian Movement, it is also rooted in an atmosphere of revival.

The organization which had hoped to serve the cause of peace, whose meeting at Constance, Germany, in 1914, was broken up by the opening of hostilities, before the group had even given itself a name, was finally formulated in 1915 as the World Alliance for Promoting International Friendship Through the Churches. This organization was not formed of churches, but of individual Christians, joined within each country in a National Council. After the close of the war it held annual meetings, dealing with international problems such as the question of war guilt, the Kellogg-Briand Pact, and war reparations. It brought together many notable personalities, including men from the Eastern Orthodox churches, who could not have participated if it had been an organization of churches; but gradually it began to suffer from its lack of connection with the churches themselves. It began to decrease its activity in the 1930s, many of its functions being taken over by the "Life and Work" movement.

"Life and Work" was the result of attempts made by Nathan Söderblom, Swedish Lutheran Bishop of Uppsala, to maintain international Christian fellowship during World War I. His attempts to hold an international meeting with representatives from the churches of the belligerent nations were unsuccessful, though a meeting of people from neutral nations was held in 1917, which carried on a study of the question of international law. Meetings held in 1919 and 1920 paved the way for the "Universal Christian Conference of Life and Work" finally held in Stockholm in 1925.

The best description of this movement is the name it carried in German and French: "Ecumenical Council for Practical Christianity." Without dealing with problems of church order and theology, it attempted to unite the churches in the areas of service, ethics, and the study of the social order. This made it possible for many to participate in the discussions, to gain international acquaintances and face problems together, whose churches would by no means be able to agree on doctrinal matters. There was disagreement at Stockholm as to whether Christians are to "build the kingdom of God on earth" or not, but the awakening of interest in social work, in Christian citizenship, in education and economics, went on nevertheless. Until 1930 "Life and Work" had no American branch, being identified directly with the Federal Council of Churches.

More and more the study activity of "Life and Work" began to concentrate on the problem of the state. This study was given increased seriousness by Hitler's accession to power in Germany, and was also deepened by the recognition of the "Life and Work" leadership that it was no longer possible to deal with social problems without being clear on some basic matters of doctrine. An extensive study program, well underway already in 1934, led finally to a conference held at Oxford, England, in 1937, on "Church, Community, and State."

At the same time another movement, bearing the name "Faith and Order," had been dealing with the question of Christian unity in another way. This movement had begun with the negotiations which had been necessary to bring the Society for the Propagation of the Gospel, a mission agency of the Church of England, into the Edinburgh mission conference of 1910. The Church of England (known in America as the Protestant Episcopal Church) is highly interested in questions of sacrament and church order. For it, the most important characteristic of the church is that it has orthodox doctrine and validly ordained ministers and dispenses valid sacraments. Thus the problem of Christian unity is that the different churches have different doctrinal viewpoints and different views of ordination and sacraments. The first thing to do was for the various churches to get acquainted with one another's viewpoints in these areas.

The initiative in this work was borne until 1920 chiefly by leaders of the Anglican church; then a more representative "Continuation Committee" was formed. Study conferences on a large scale were held in 1927 in Lausanne and in 1937 in Edinburgh. The purpose was not to form a new church, but to establish acquaintances, compare views, and learn at what points there was already agreement about the nature of the church and its doctrine, and just what the real disagreements were.

Already in the early 1930s the suggestion had been made that the two movements, "Life and Work" on one hand and "Faith and Order" on the other, should be brought closer together. "Life and Work," which had begun by avoiding theological problems, was beginning to realize that they could not be avoided; "Faith and Order," studying only theological problems, could further mutual acquaintance but then could go no farther. The fact that both met in Great Britain in the summer of 1937 provided the occasion for these proposals to be dealt with, with the result that in the following year both organizations fused to form the Provisional Committee of the World Council of Churches in Process of Formation. Ten years later, in Amsterdam, the formal organization of the World Council of Churches took place with delegates from 147 churches participating.

Before the official formation of the World Council, a number of subsidiary organizations had already begun work. What is now the Department of Inter-Church Aid distributed considerable financial and other help to churches which had suffered during the war. Still earlier work had been done for refugees and prisoners of war, and refugee work continued on after the war. The Study Department and the Ecumenical Institute carried on both advanced study and education in educational matters. The Commission of the Churches on International Affairs attempts, as had the earlier World Alliance, to study and witness on behalf of the churches in the field of international relationships. Now the World Council has other departments dealing with youth work, women's work, laymen's work. The Study Department, now called the Division of Studies, has enlarged its program, and is preparing an extensive study of the problems of adjustment faced by the "younger churches" in parts of the world which are undergoing rapid social change, as well as other projects dealing with the problems of war and the state.

At the same time that churches began to become acquainted with one another across denominational lines, there took place a certain revival of interest in the particular positions of each denomination. One result was the formation of international federations, alliances, and conferences grouping together churches from all over the world on confessional lines. Such organizations are not new; the Reformed-Presbyterian group was founded in 1875, the International Congregational Council in 1891, the World Methodist Council in 1881, the Baptist World Alliance in 1905; but they grew in importance between the wars and especially after 1945. Mennonites held three World Conferences between the wars, which however were limited in participation and in subject matter; two were quadricentennial celebrations and one dealt with the refugee problem. Since the war three Mennonite World Conferences were held.

Whether organized within or between confessional groups, "ecumenical" activities have often tended to lose sight of certain problems which are difficult to deal with in organizations. One of these problems is that a denomination (to say nothing of loosely bound groups such as the Lutheran or the Reformed-Presbyterian world fellowships) is seldom doctrinally united; the differences which exist within a denomination are often, unless that denomination is very young or has a very rigid discipline, more significant than the formal differences which separate it from other denominations. Those tendencies in doctrine and social views which were most liberal were often held by those who, because the peculiarities of their own denomination seemed unimportant, were most interested in ecumenical activity. Thus the opinion has become very widespread that ecumenical interest is generally connected with liberalism in doctrine. This is not really the case. Not only did most of the currents which eventually led to the ecumenical movement have evangelical roots, as we have already shown; some of them were interesting only for conservatives. The study of "Faith and Order" was never really interesting for liberals, and even in "Life and Work" a movement toward theological orthodoxy began in the 1930's, to the consternation of many of the founders of the movement. This conservative tendency grew continually until it was possible for the main theme of the Evanston Assembly of the World Council in 1954 to be the Christian Hope, a topic which is of interest only to those who are committed to Biblical and historic Christianity.

Nevertheless, there have been, especially in America, grounds for reservations on the part of the theologically conservative, as to the doctrinal soundness of the participants in the ecumenical movement. This could not be otherwise; for the movement's reason for being lies in the fact that Christians disagree. The only way to avoid contact with Christians with whom one disagrees would be to have no conversation with them. The conviction that interchurch relations are ultimately possible only between churches accepting a certain minimum doctrinal basis led to the formation, in church circles variously known as "evangelical," "fundamentalist," and "conservative," of the National Association of Evangelicals, a rapidly growing organization with special interests in Christian education, publications, aid to foreign churches, evangelization, representation of church and mission interests in Washington, and other activities of a nondenominational character which may usefully be carried on on a strictly Biblical basis. Several Mennonite and related church groups are affiliated with the National Association of Evangelicals or subsidiary organizations. The National Association of Evangelicals has its international counterpart in the World Evangelical Fellowship, an organization including parts of the old Evangelical Alliances.

Stating Our Problem

After our brief survey of the various movements and organizations interested in bringing together churches or Christians of different denominations, we must begin to approach the task of evaluating those movements, Scripturally first of all, and then also with reference to the Anabaptist-Mennonite heritage.

It would be an error, however, to ask too hastily the purely organizational question: "Should our church join this or that movement or organization?" The answers often have been hasty, because the question has been unclear. What do we mean by "joining"? When an individual joins a church, by confession and baptism, he is (or should be) making a commitment which involves irrevocably his whole being, because it is a part of his belonging to Christ. When the same individual joins a book club, subscribes to a magazine, enters a school, or contributes to a class letter, he is also making commitments; but they are neither irrevocable nor all-inclusive. It would be foolish to place these various kinds of "joining" on the same level; yet that is just what is often done when many think that all kinds of relationships with any kind of interchurch agency must be subject to the same standards of orthodoxy and sanctification as church membership.

The first question to ask is not "whether to join" or "what to join"; it is much simpler. Do we believe seriously that there are other Christians in the world than ourselves? If so, do we really take account of that fact in our thinking? When we think and speak and pray about "the Church," do we include them? Exclude them? Ignore them?

For centuries it has been possible for Mennonites to ignore this problem. They would never have said that there were no other Christians in the world; yet the barriers of persecution and language, and later of custom, occupation, and geography made it possible to keep from raising seriously the question. If, however, we face the question, we must also seek an answer; for it is clear that the unity of all believers is a Scriptural command, just as clear as the other commandments which we Mennonites tend to emphasize, and often even more important in the eyes of the apostolic writers.

If we reject the solution of the Roman Catholics, Jehovah's Witnesses, and Mormons, we must at the same time refuse to go to the other extreme. There are people in the world who are decidedly not Christians, who

nevertheless want to be considered as such. For their own good as well as
for that of the church they should be brought, with love and patience, to
understand that they need first to be reconciled with God before they can
enjoy the fellowship of the church. There are also certain kinds of behavior
and certain doctrines, accepted and even advocated in good conscience by
sincere Christians, which are condemned by Scripture and have no place in
the Christian brotherhood. The "ecumenical problem" does not only have
to do with other Christians; it has to do with other Christians with whom
we seriously disagree.

Before going on to investigate various attempts at solving this problem, we do well to remind ourselves that we are discussing the Ecumenical
Movement and the Faithful Church. This is the only way to approach our
question in all its seriousness; for we want earnestly to be faithful—personally, congregationally, and in the broader brotherhood. Yet we must
remember, lest we be not only pharisaical but clearly dishonest, that we
are not a faithful church. No Biblical Christian can affirm that he, his congregation, or his broader brotherhood is fully faithful. We are not ready to
ask on what terms we can accept other Christians as fellow believers until
we have remembered on what terms God has accepted us. Perfect sanctification is the goal and the standard of God's fellowship; it is not its pre-
requisite. It will be a good Anabaptist way of thinking, and a good check on
whether the answer we find to the ecumenical question is evangelical, if we
ask: "Where would we be if God took that attitude toward us?"

One approach to the problem would be to say that the Christian with
whom we disagree is automatically out of our fellowship, just as a disobedient and unrepentant member of our own church would be excommunicated.
But the New Testament knows nothing of automatic excommunication, or
of people who, without a hearing, are to be treated as if they were excommunicated. Excommunication is, in the faithful church, the result not of disagreement but of persistent and unrepentant disobedience. It is applied
only after a lengthy process of attempted reconciliation which Jesus Himself
prescribed in detail. There is no ground in Scripture for excluding from fellowship any individual with whom that attempt at reconciliation has not
been made.

Another approach would be to accept division as normal; to recognize with regret that we disagree, but continue going each his own way.
This would, however, mean, paradoxically, that we have no right to remain

separate. For if the principles to which we hold are true only for us, they are not worth the trouble. If they are true before God, then they are true also for the brother, however misinformed and incomplete his faith and obedience might be, and our responsibility is to inform him of them. If our brother can be a Christian without knowing and doing these things, continuing to go his way, then so could we. Our beliefs are not true if they are not for the brother.

The second way in which this "each his own way" approach is wrong is that it is a result of fear. If we are willing to keep our peculiar convictions to ourselves, it might well be that we are not sure they can stand examination by outsiders. If we attempt to share them with other Christians, we shall have to demonstrate to them that they are clearly Biblical. Often the reason we are not ready to press our beliefs on others is that we are not too sure of them ourselves.

It seems that neither of these approaches, which we have attempted to use in the past, is satisfactory. Neither answers the question, "What is the church of Christ, if both we ourselves and those other Christians with whom we disagree are in it, but have no fellowship with one another?"

By asking the question, and attempting to exclude the answers which are not satisfactory, we shall not be likely to stumble upon the right answer. It can be found only if we search in Scripture. We must ask whether the New Testament knows anything about the "ecumenical problem" and, if it does, we must find, and accept, its answer.

The Witness of the New Testament

When an attempt is made to bring the question of church unity to the Bible for an answer, the first reaction is often one of doubt. Division, we tend to think, is one problem the New Testament knows nothing about. The apostles all were in agreement, the organization was young, and the Holy Spirit was guiding; how could the New Testament church have had the problems which arise from disagreement, age, and spiritual lethargy?

This reaction, as normal as it may be, is mistaken. For the New Testament church, from the very beginning, dealt with, and solved to a great degree, the problem of Christian unity, in the face of difficulties as great as those of our time.

"Denomination" means literally a "naming." In this literal sense of the word, the group of "Hellenists" in the church at Jerusalem, whose complaints led to a reorganization of the church (Acts 6), was already a denomination. They seem, if Stephen and Philip, their two major leaders, are typical, to have had a different view of the importance of the temple and of Jewish conceptions of purity from that held by the rest of the church.

Even more literally, the church at Corinth was divided into "denominations." One group named itself for Paul, one for Peter, and one for Apollos (1 Cor 1:12). Then there was already an "interdenominational" group, the Christ party. Judging from what we know elsewhere about Peter, Paul, and Apollos, we may suppose that the differences had to do with the attitude to be taken toward Greek wisdom and toward Jewish law; perhaps also with different styles of preaching and such matters of personality. Furthermore, there were economic divisions, which may or may not have coincided with the groupings around individual leaders, by which the brotherhood was so seriously divided that the love feast was no longer being celebrated in unity.

When the Apostle Paul wrote to his churches, he made no attempt to appear impartial. He did not seek to give the impression that there was no difference between Apollos and himself, or that people were free to choose as they liked between his teaching and that of Apollos. On the contrary, he spoke of his own work as the laying of a foundation on which everyone else must build (1 Cor 3). He criticized openly Peter's compromising attitude to the problem of Jewish law (Gal 2). And yet he did not instruct the "Paul people" to take over the church. He ordered the entire church to unite, to overcome both doctrinal and economic differences in Christian love, and to deal rapidly with the problems of discipline which were being neglected. In other words, the unity of the church at Corinth was not to be created by the central authority of one group of leaders, even if those leaders were in the right; *Christian unity is not to be created, but to be obeyed.*

In the realm of missions the situation was no better, as a careful analysis of the books of Acts and Galatians will show. At the one extreme were the "Judaizers," for whom a pagan, to become a Christian, first had to become a Jew. These people were Pharisees, even within the church (Acts 15:5). At the other extreme were the "Hellenists," who were the first to carry the Gospel to the half-Jewish Samaritans (8:4), to the pagans who participated in Jewish worship (8:27 ff.), and to complete pagans (11:20 ff.). They were also the first to be called Christians (11:26), and the first to go deliberately about the sending of missionaries (chapter 13). This wing of the church was joined and led by the converted Pharisee, Paul.

Between these two extremes there were two other shadings. James, the Lord's brother, was himself not opposed to evangelization of the pagans, as we see by his friendly attitude to Paul (Acts 15 and 21); yet he was close enough to the Judaizing party that he was acceptable to them as a leader of the Jerusalem church, and it was possible for people who traveled around sabotaging Paul's mission work to come under the cover of James's name (Gal 2:12). Then there was Peter, who agreed in principle with Paul (when he was free to do as he liked, he ate with the Gentile Christians—Gal 2:12 and 14; Acts 15:7 ff.), but was more closely connected to the Jerusalem church than Paul, since representatives of that church, or of the Judaizing party within it, could force him to separate himself from the Gentiles, against his own convictions. Peter bore the missionary initiative for the Jerusalem church ever since he had been the first apostle to baptize a pagan (Acts 10) and especially since he had left Jerusalem, leaving the leadership of the church to James (12:17).

It is thus evident that there existed not only differences of viewpoint and emphasis within the early church, but also real differences of principle, which were so great that there was real doubt in the apostle's mind as to whether the Judaizers had understood the Gospel at all. This difference of principle expressed itself in the existence of two "mission organizations," Paul sent by Antioch and Peter sent by Jerusalem. Once an attempt was made to divide the mission work between them (Gal 2:7 ff.), but it was unsuccessful because they could not strictly separate the work among Jews from that among Gentiles. The result was a tendency to divide churches, which was just what was happening in Antioch (Gal 2:12).

What did Paul do about this situation, which resembles so closely that of the churches in our day? By far the easiest solution would have been for him to accept the division which the others were causing, and to go on unhampered with his work among the Gentiles and those Jews who would be willing to abandon their law. Paul did not depend on the Jerusalem church for his authority as an apostle (Gal 1:11-2:9); his branch of the church was Spirit-filled, growing; his theology was right. Why not leave the Judaizers and the Jerusalem church, with their distortion of the Gospel, with their lack of evangelistic zeal, to themselves, to wither up and gradually become extinct? It would have been by far the most convenient solution, personally and with respect to problems of organization and discipline, to let the split take place at the initiative of his opponents.

This is just what Paul did not do. Without ever giving in on what mattered (we note, for instance, his refusal to circumcise Titus), he constantly went out of his way to maintain relations with those who "were apostles before me" (Gal 1:17). When the problem at Antioch became difficult, Paul took the initiative in bringing about the Jerusalem Conference; all over the mission field he collected money for the home church, even though he wasn't sure the brethren at Jerusalem would even accept the money from him (Rom 15:31). To prove his good faith he went to the temple, and thereby got himself into prison.

Paul had absolutely no reasons of convenience for going to all this trouble. The only explanation is that he must have had real reasons of faith, theological reasons, for acting as he did. The only possible explanation is that, for the Apostle Paul, the unity of all believers, including the attempt to maintain unity with those who seek division, whose doctrine is wrong, and whose view of the church is distorted, was the will of God. The essence of the Lord's Supper is lost by division (1 Cor 11); the essence of the Gospel is the destruction of the barrier between Jews and Gentiles (Eph 2:3); the essence of discipleship is to follow Christ in the humility which enables unity (Phil 2); the purpose of the various ministries in the church is unity (Eph 4; 1 Cor 12). Even when the work of the church was done for the wrong reasons, Paul could rejoice (Phil 1:18). This deep concern for unity was not a new idea with Paul; Jesus had said that the unity of the believers was necessary if the world were to accept Him (John 17:23).

When we ask how Paul could go so far and sacrifice so much for the cause of unity without also losing true doctrine and pure life, the answer is that such matters were dealt with on an individual basis in the local congregation. Even where Paul was clearly in the right, he did not impose his views on the churches, but left the supervision of doctrine and morals in the hands of the local elders (Acts 20:28), trusting that the Spirit would lead every congregation to the same conclusions (Gal 5:10; Phil 3:15). Even in a clear case of sexual disorder the action was to be taken locally (1 Cor 5).

Not only was discipline applied locally; it was applied individually. The discipline procedure prescribed by Christ applies to one person at a time (Matt 18). This command of Christ is not respected when whole groups are excluded from fellowship, be it because they are Gentiles (Gal 2), because they are poor (1 Cor 11), or on any other such "denominational" basis. The New Testament has "close communion," in the sense that those who do not belong to the church do not participate in communion; but that "close communion" applies to one person at a time, excluding only those who themselves have refused correction.

Christian Unity in Christian History

Having observed the way in which the church of the New Testament responded to the problem of division among Christians, we may look to the later history of the church to see what was done with the same problem. Our interest will turn especially toward the position of the Anabaptists, after a summary survey of certain previous approaches.

In the first centuries of the post-apostolic church, the primary expression of church unity and the primary means of dealing with problems of doctrine and discipline was the synod. A meeting of the ministers or perhaps of only the bishops of a given area would be called by one of the bishops, often the bishop of the largest congregation or of the congregation in the largest city. The geographical boundaries of a synod were not firmly fixed; the number of churches invited to send ministers would depend on the nature of the problem; nor was the frequency of meeting fixed. These synods, meeting in such an unsystematic and occasional way, gradually solved, in the relative unity, some of the church's earliest problems. The two earliest heretical tendencies within the church, Gnosticism with its search for "wisdom" outside of Christ, and Ebionitism with its effort to get Christ into Jewish tradition, were eventually defeated, the canon of the New Testament was fixed, and the so-called "Apostles' Creed" came into general use as a résumé of accepted truths. When, however, a division took on larger dimensions, these synods were no longer successful in restoring unity; each group held its own synods, and the only contacts between the groups were in literary polemics or individual conversations. The idea that the Christian Church was united in the early centuries before the schism between eastern ("Orthodox") and western ("Roman") Catholicism comes from a one-sided and inaccurate Catholic report of early church history. In reality there was no time when serious differences in matters of life and doctrine did not divide the church.

When Christianity became the favored religion, and then the official religion, of the Roman Empire, a new approach began to be used. Now travel was easier and it was possible to bring together all the bishops of the world (i.e., of the world then known, the Roman Empire) in an "Ecumenical

Council." Decisions were made by majority vote, subject to the approval of the emperor, and then they became imperial law; and the minority could be forced, by banishment and other punishments, to submit. This was a very effective method; it enabled the official church to maintain a high degree of formal unity. But it was not very Christian. For one thing, the procedure in the councils was itself far from the normal process of seeking the leading of the Holy Spirit. At Nicea, where the doctrine of the Trinity became law, the compromise phrasing which enabled the two parties to agree was provided by the Emperor Constantine himself, who was not even a baptized Christian. At later councils the emperor would send his favorite bishop with a bodyguard of soldiers to ensure that the proper decision would be made. Nor did this method really bring about unity. The councils of the fourth century, which decided how to state the doctrine of the Trinity, could not prevent the Arian churches, because they were more missionary, from winning the Gothic tribes outside the Roman Empire and holding their allegiance for centuries. The councils of following centuries, while they defined the humanity and the divinity of Christ in the terms now considered orthodox, did not prevent the more missionary-minded Nestorians, who were condemned for distinguishing too clearly between the divine and human natures of Christ, and a group of "Monophysite" churches, from winning the peoples along the eastern border of the empire, from Armenia to Ethiopia, and farther east on into India and China. Especially in our day, when the essentially missionary nature of the church is being rediscovered, we should learn to challenge the method and rethink the results of these councils.

Hand in hand with the development of the imperially called councils came the growth of the hierarchy of bishops. In case of disagreement, matters of doctrine or discipline were settled by the local bishop. If he could not bring about a settlement, the matter was "appealed" to another bishop. Gradually there was worked out a system of "courts of appeal" in which one bishop in each area had higher authority than the others (the archbishop); five or six bishops in the largest cities or the oldest congregations were still higher in importance ("metropolitans" or "patriarchs"); and the bishop at Rome was highest of all (the pope). This did not happen, as many non-Catholics think, primarily because the popes were always crassly grasping for power. It happened also because a highest court of appeal was needed, once the episcopal system had been established; it happened because it

was in the interest of a local bishop to appeal to the pope against the decision of his archbishop; it happened also because the popes were often wise
and made the right decisions; it happened because, when the empire col-
lapsed, the popes showed themselves to be good social administrators and
even good generals; it happened because, when Charlemagne revived the
western Roman Empire, he needed a high priest to crown him. But however it happened, we remain convinced that the hierarchy of bishops is no
more satisfactory than the imperial councils as a means of expressing and
maintaining Christian unity. The external unity of the church, in its alliance with the state, was preserved; but the life of the church had to find
other paths, whether within the system (the monastic orders), on its borders (the tierce orders, the Beghards, the mystics of the Middle Ages), or
frankly outside it (the Bogomils, the Albigenses, the Waldenses, and finally
the Reformation).

Whatever were its faults, and however much it failed to unite all
Christians in a spiritual way, medieval Catholicism at least had two positive achievements. It was truly international, and there was room within it
for a degree of freedom in certain doctrinal matters. These two values were
lost in the Reformation. State-church Protestantism, whether Lutheran or
Reformed, felt obliged to solicit the support of local government in order
to resist the imperial government which favored Roman Catholicism. The
result was permanent division on national lines. Since the division centered upon a question of doctrine, both the Protestant confessions and, in
reaction, Catholicism became far more strict in the definition of orthodoxy
and in the persecution of new ideas. It is within this situation that we find
the Anabaptist movement and must ask whether it had a better answer to
the problem of Christian unity.

One way of understanding the Anabaptist movement is to say that
it broke off from other churches in the effort to form a faithful church.
"Break-in-order-to-be-faithful" was their principle. This principle then can
continue to bring about divisions, such as the score of different branches
which existed in the Netherlands in the century after Menno's death; such
as the Amish, or Mennonite Brethren, or Reformed Mennonite groups.
According to this viewpoint, division itself is, at least in many circumstances, a sign of faithfulness.

This viewpoint could be criticized from a historical point of view. We
could observe that such divisions have seldom been successful in maintaining

for more than a few generations the faithfulness they sought. We could observe that those groups which, by their division, have maintained the clearest witness and the clearest nonconformity, have at the same time been ineffective at other points. But for the present we have another question to ask, namely: "Is this 'break-to-be-faithful' view true of the first Anabaptists?"

The decisive move of Ulrich Zwingli, placing the church in Zurich under the control of the city-state authorities, was made in 1523. In October, 1523, Simon Stumpf and Conrad Grebel objected publicly to Zwingli's attitude. In December of the same year it was so clear that Zwingli was determined to persist in this wrong position, that Grebel once, in mock debating style, put forth the thesis: "Whoever believes, thinks or says that Zwingli is acting as a pastor should, believes, thinks, and speaks godlessly." And yet Grebel did not start a new church. For more than a year Grebel and the friends who gathered with him waited. While waiting they went back, again and again, to Zwingli and his fellow ministers, trying to win them to their view that the church should be separate from the world. They did this with relation to the question of the abolition of the Mass; they did it with the proposal that Zwingli should provoke new elections in order to have an evangelical majority in the city council; they did it finally with respect to the question of believers' baptism.

When it was clear that they could not talk with Zwingli, Felix Manz wrote to the city council, late in December, 1524, addressing the council members as "Dear Lords and Brethren," and appealing to them, "in virtue of the common name which we all together bear" (that is, the name of Christians), to examine fairly the Biblical grounds for refusing to baptize infants. A meeting was held for this purpose, after which the council not only decided in favor of maintaining the traditional baptismal practice, but also declared that the friends of Grebel and Manz should not meet together, and even expelled four of them from the canton. Only at this date, after it was clear that neither Zwingli nor the council, even though both claimed to be Christian, could really be called upon to deal with disagreements on a Christian basis, i.e., before the criterion of Scripture, did the small group move, on January 21, 1525, by the institution of baptism on confession of faith, to establish a separate church. The process of attempting to break through to Zwingli and the council, after there was really little hope left, had taken a year and a half; and in the revolutionary days of the 1520s, a year and a half was a long time.

Zwingli explained later that Grebel and Manz had always wanted a division; according to him they only attacked the institution of infant baptism so that, having rejected it, they could "rebaptize," and thus form a sectarian group. Not only is this historically inexact because, as Zwingli himself testified, the group's intention was to win the whole church to their views, but also because, as far as we know, the idea that if infant baptism is not valid, therefore adults should be baptized, was an idea that Grebel, Manz, and Blaurock themselves had not thought of until, in January, it was clear that the break was already irreparable. From the point of view of the men who, from then on, were called Anabaptists, the break in fellowship did not come with their institution of baptism and the Lord's Supper; it came when Zwingli and the council, in the face of protest and repeated appeals for reconsideration, resorted to violence rather than to Scripture to deal with a disagreement. Far from using the "break-to-be-faithful" principle, the Anabaptists refused, for over a year, to accept a break that was already there. Once, in fact, when Zwingli asked Felix Manz why he didn't go ahead on his own to set up the kind of church discipline he wanted, Manz answered that he could not because Zwingli was the bishop. So far went the "Anabaptists'" respect for the existing church.

Although the break had come in Zurich, and, from Zwingli's viewpoint, all his friends in the other Swiss and South German cities should also consider them as out of fellowship, the Anabaptists refused to agree that a breach which came about in Zurich would also apply elsewhere. In the other cities to which they came—Schaffhausen, Basel, Strasbourg—they went to the church leaders, and proposed to them first the establishment of Scriptural church discipline, and second the institution of Scriptural baptism. Sometimes they got a serious hearing. At Waldshut their ideas were accepted. In most places, however, Zwingli was able to intervene and prevent any serious discussion. When the competent church leaders refused, the Anabaptists asked to have an organized debate. Only when it was abundantly clear that all roads were barred and no contact possible did they go on their own to organize their own congregations. The one place where that was not done, and where, under the leading of a local person, they refused to use the church building which was offered them, was St. Gall, where within a few months the movement broke away from Grebel and Manz and degenerated into excesses of much the same kind as may be observed in extreme forms of modern Pentecostalism. These excesses were not a direct continuation of Anabaptism, as Zwingli claimed; but it is not sure that they had no connection with the "break-to-be-faithful" attitude of Wolfgang Ulimann, the leader in St. Gall.

Even when the breach of fellowship was definite and extended all over Europe, the Anabaptists did not accept it as final. Repeatedly they came back both to church and to state leaders with the same argument: "If you claim to be Christian, and accept Scripture as authority, you must discuss with us; for we want only to be Scriptural." In the small space of Reformed Switzerland and southern Germany, and the short time from the birth of Anabaptism until 1540, more than a score of debates were held, almost always at the initiative of the Anabaptists. They were never successful in winning the state-church authorities (twice they resulted in the return of the Anabaptists to the state church), but they demonstrate that the Anabaptists went to great lengths in seeking to overcome division. Even when they were forced to accept division, as is the case in the Schleitheim articles, where it is said that separation from the world will include not attending "papistic or antipapistic" churches, this separation was a far less radical one than the refusal of a hearing and the persecution with which the "papistic and antipapistic" churches responded.

This does not mean that the Anabaptists were optimistic about the chances for an understanding with the state-church leaders, nor that they ever thought there could be an understanding between the church and the world. But it does mean that, if there must be a break within the church, between the unfaithful church and the faithful church, the initiative must come from the unfaithful side. God has taken the initiative to reconcile the world to Himself. If there is a break, it comes from the world's refusal, not from God. If the break must reach even into the church, even then the faithful church does not take the initiative. The faithful church will discipline; she will expel, if necessary, one at a time, disobedient individuals. She will not, in so far as the choice is hers, withdraw from the body of believers.

We have gone into this question in some detail, because of the widespread opinion which would understand the Anabaptists as the advocates of the "break-to-be-faithful" attitude. Yet there would be many other aspects of the Anabaptist witness to study. In fact there are good grounds for saying that the Anabaptists were the first ecumenical movement, in the positive sense of that word. Alone of all the churches of the Reformation, they were truly international. Not only did they maintain contacts all the way from England to Macedonia, but with their rejection of the state church and of war they broke down the greatest barriers to Christian fellowship which have operated in modern times. Alone of all the churches of the Reformation, they insisted that the church is essentially missionary, and that she must be separate from the world, even if that world be Christianized; this is an idea which Lesslie Newbigin, one of the bishops of the United Church of South India, thinks is a new discovery, and which is gradually becoming one of the accepted principles of ecumenical discussion. Alone among the churches of the Reformation, the Anabaptists refused to define their faith exclusively in terms of hierarchy or a confession. To be a Christian according to Lutheran orthodoxy one must accept the Augsburg confession, which was originally a political document. To be a Christian according to Anglican orthodoxy one must join the Anglican organization, whose liturgy and doctrine are fixed by the British Parliament. To be a Christian according to "Anabaptist orthodoxy" you need neither sign nor join anything; you just practice Biblical baptism, communion, and discipline in your local congregation, and accept Scripture as the criterion for all future discussion. Alone among the churches of the Reformation, the Anabaptists refused to accept division as final and came back again and again to discuss.

Not only was the first "ecumenical" concern in modern times that of the Anabaptists; when such a concern has been fruitful in later times, it has again been in similar fellowships. The Quakers in the seventeenth century, the Moravians and the Brethren in the eighteenth, the revival and the British Brethren (George Muller) in the nineteenth—all these were groups which, in their work, if not always in their doctrine, agreed with the Anabaptists that the church is not a hierarchy nor a branch of the state, but a separated, disciplined, missionary fellowship. Even the Student Christian Movement, the Young Men's Christian Association, and the modern peace movement, which, as we have seen, had a significant part in the growth of the modern ecumenical movement, gained their vitality from the fact that they had some of these same ideals.

Conclusion

After having discussed the ecumenical movements and the problems of Christian unity from several angles, we are obliged to draw some conclusions from the facts we have seen, and especially from the fact that both the

New Testament church and the early Anabaptists were much more deeply concerned about this problem than most Mennonites and evangelicals in general have been in the recent past. The proposals which are submitted here, without much argument, attempt to apply to the present situation the lessons which can be learned from the past. They are only tentative, and would need to be discussed before they could be acted upon; but they are submitted in the conviction that Christian unity is just as clearly a Biblical imperative as are evangelization, nonresistance, and nonconformity, and that, however delicate the question may be, it demands open discussion and action.

The New Testament and the witness of the Anabaptists seem to agree that it is the duty of the evangelical Christian to seek to establish and maintain brotherly relationships with anyone who confesses Christ. They agree further that "brotherly relationships" means much more than is generally understood; they require not only polite mutual recognition or even "inter-communion" (the term used in ecumenical circles for the mutual acceptance, by two denominations, of the validity of each other's sacraments); brotherly relations meant, to both the New Testament and the Anabaptists, unity in disciplined discipleship—something much more difficult to attain than the mere mutual recognition of separate denominations. Unity does not mean that we approve of the present belief and behavior of another Christian; it means that we lay upon him the claims which Christ lays upon those who confess His name; we ask of him Christian obedience, Biblical baptism, separation from the world, and the rest of what the Gospel implies.

If there is to be a breach in fellowship between us, that breach cannot be at our initiative. If the fellow Christian with whom we discuss is willing to "return the compliment," and to lay upon us, according to his convictions, the claims which Christ lays upon His disciples, we must converse with him. If our concepts of Christ's claims are different, even contradictory, that means we must keep on conversing and appealing to Scripture, and that there will be little that we can usefully do together in a practical way beyond keeping up our conversation; but as long as his convictions are sincere and he is willing to admit Scripture as our court of appeal, we have no right to take the initiative in breaking off relations with him. He can, however, take the initiative, in a number of ways; he can, for instance, make it clear that for him there are other authorities besides the Bible which are binding. With Roman Catholics, Adventists, Jehovah's Witnesses, Christian

Scientists, and Mormons, this additional authority is so clear that the possibility of real conversation is practically nil. We may well come to the point where conversation is no longer possible because of certain postulates, not Scriptural in origin, which the other party refuses to let be called into question. This may happen, for instance, in the case of theological liberals, for whom a modern philosophy or a certain view of science or history is not open to question; or in the case of some orthodox Lutherans, for whom man always remains first of all a sinner, and the state is fully autonomous in its own realm. It may also be that, for reasons not in our control, the other party will refuse to accept our good faith. In such cases we must accept, reluctantly, and only for a time, the break.

The other point at which fellowship can be broken is the point where, without contesting the rightness of the claims we lay upon him, someone simply decides not to obey. This is the normal situation foreseen in Matthew 18; it calls for successive appeals to repentance and reconciliation, but may eventually come to excommunication. Once again, even though the excommunication is pronounced by the church, the initial breach of fellowship was the responsibility of the unfaithful individual.

It would be wrong to leave this analysis without the reminder that the above paragraphs have made one unjustified assumption. They have assumed that "we" are right and "they," the other Christians with whom we converse, are wrong. If we face honestly the fact that this assumption is only theoretical, and that in fact "we" have something to learn just as surely as we have something to teach, then the need for conversation becomes all the more clear.

The extent to which it may be possible to do things together will depend entirely upon the degree of agreement already reached. Less unity is needed to converse than to commune; less unity is needed to evangelize together than to baptize together; less to advocate morality than to apply discipline; less to attack liberalism together than to agree together on what is sound doctrine. The essential for obedience in this realm is to go neither farther nor less far than existing agreement permits. If we refuse to converse because we cannot commune, we fail to go the first mile (to say nothing of the second) toward restoration of fellowship, as did the Apostle Paul and the Anabaptists. If, on the other hand, we commune where there is actually only sufficient unity for conversing, we cheapen both unity and truth and do our brother no good.

In general this would tend to mean that a certain minimum degree of contact such as we have been calling "conversation" should be possible on a relatively broad basis, and more extensive collaboration in evangelism and teaching within narrower limits. Now the striking fact is that in Mennonite practice in the last century the opposite has been the case. In many places Mennonites are members of local ministerial associations or participate in joint evangelistic activities with other churches; in countless cases Mennonites have studied in non-Mennonite theological schools of every sort without even raising any questions as to what that meant in terms of faithfulness to their own ideals, even though it may have meant they were acquiring for life ideas completely foreign to their own heritage. And yet at the same time there has been, and still is, great suspicion attached to efforts to converse with and witness to other Christian bodies. We somehow have the idea that it is less dangerous to receive the witness of others than to give them our own. To receive one's education in a Presbyterian or Baptist seminary is just receiving an education; to enter an interchurch organization in order to testify to Presbyterians and Baptists would be "fellowshipping with unbelievers" or "losing our distinctive witness."

One attempt to decide upon the limits within which it is useful for Christians of varying convictions to associate has been the doctrinal criterion of Fundamentalism. According to this view, it is possible to work together with anyone who accepts the inspiration of the Bible, the doctrines of the Trinity and the natures of Christ, and the virgin birth. This answer has the advantage of being simple; a check list of four or five points permits deciding immediately who is "safe." But at the same time it is unsatisfactory, first of all because it oversimplifies, forgets that there are a great number of different possible levels of agreement and possible collaboration. With some persons and churches we can agree on much more than that; with others on less, but still without being able to deny their real belief.

Secondly, the fundamentalist criteria are unsatisfactory because they represent a very particular choice of crucial points, which were especially necessary for the debate with Modernism in the 1910s but are not by any means the crucial points in all other debates at all other times and places. Many churches would get a perfect grade on the fundamentalist check list, while holding very unclear, or even wrong, views on separation from the world, the Christian attitude toward nationalism and war, and baptism. In fact, the National Association of Evangelicals, to which some Mennonite groups belong, is unclear on all these points, which in many times and places are more crucial than a philosophical doctrine of the Trinity. The section of the National Association of Evangelicals which promotes Christian day schools is committed to an understanding of Christian faith and nurture which is drawn from state-church conceptions of Christian nurture and is difficult to reconcile with the Anabaptist view of believers' baptism. The National Association of Evangelicals also has a special section dedicated to recruiting military chaplains, a highly questionable activity, not only from a nonresistant point of view, but also because, even apart from its military character, the chaplaincy operates as a state church. It is sometimes hard to see what is the use of having a check list requiring people to accept the Biblical view of the cross of Christ if that acceptance does not issue in a Biblical view of the cross of the Christian.

Thirdly, the fundamentalist criteria are based on the supposition that doctrine is the most important test of faith. As we have seen, it was this supposition which largely guided the Anglican founders of the "Faith and Order" movement in its early days. It is highly doubtful that the New Testament church believed this; it is absolutely sure that the Anabaptists did not. The Anabaptists accepted in their midst men who sometimes were too original and too daring in the attempt to rethink traditional doctrine in the light of discipleship. They accepted them, without accepting their doctrinal deviations, because of their conviction that discipleship mattered first. Likewise, the Anabaptists accepted separation from the state churches, with whom they agreed about everything on the fundamentalist check list; once again, because discipleship comes first.

One often hears the term "superchurch" used in the argument against the ecumenical movement. Much of the time the word is used like the word "communist"; as a red herring, an attempt to replace thought by emotional reactions. In such cases the Christian thing to do is to forgive the person who uses such emotional arguments, and otherwise not to be bothered by them. Yet the word also does point up a real danger. There is unavoidably a tendency for any organization to grow in power, to make claims on more authority than it really has, to disregard differences among its members and take one-sided positions contrary to the convictions of some of those whom it claims to represent. Any interchurch organization stands before this temptation, just as does every conference, mission board, school, publishing house, and relief organization. We may justifiably ask that there be safeguards against this tendency wherever we enter interchurch conversations or collaboration.

With this background, it might be possible to submit for discussion a number of concrete proposals.

(*a*) Mennonite participation in meetings of the Historic Peace Churches (with Brethren and Quakers) and of the Church Peace Mission (with pacifists from non-peace churches) should continue. There we should contribute something of our understanding of the church's relation to the world, and of the purely Biblical basis of a valid peace testimony, which some other groups lack; at the same time we might have something to learn in the way of concern for social justice.

(*b*) Mennonite participation in the activities of the National Association of Evangelicals and affiliated agencies should continue if it is possible to find safeguards against the organization's "superchurch" tendencies. At present the lines of organizational responsibility are not fully clear; since it is possible for individuals, congregations, or whole denominations to join the group, it is not fully clear how all the interests of the various kinds of constituents are safeguarded. Actions like lobbying in favor of the McCarron Act or the chaplaincy, or the advocacy of the death penalty for narcotics distribution and for treason, seem clearly to overstep the bounds of what an interdenominational organization should do if Mennonites are to feel free within it.

(*c*) On the same basis, Mennonite contacts with the World Council of Churches should be possible and useful. The clear organization and the clearly limited authority of the World Council, its constitutional incapacity to speak for anyone but itself, its official declaration that no member church is committed to any view of the church, or even to recognizing as churches the other member churches, and its policy of not directly seeking to bring about on its own authority any union of churches, are encouraging safeguards against the "superchurch" tendency. Its growing willingness to discuss the problem of war and to criticize the state-church past and rethink the question of the relations of church and world makes for an openness to the specific witness of Mennonites such as has not existed in such circles for centuries. Apart from the North American churches, the leadership and membership of the World Council are surprisingly free of theological liberalism. Churches all over the world, especially in Europe, are groping and struggling for insights, with respect to church and world, state and war, which their own denominational backgrounds cut them off from, but which were seen with great clarity by the Anabaptists already centuries ago. The question raised by Mennonite contacts with the World Council of Churches is not whether we will fellowship with unbelievers. The question is whether, following the example of the New Testament and the Anabaptists, we will give to misinformed and seeking believers the help they are looking for and which only the heirs of the Anabaptist tradition can give; and whether we will seek, as this tradition itself demands, whatever correction, admonition, and instruction may be received from the encounter with fellow confessors of the Lord's name under the norm of Scripture and the guidance of His Spirit.

Chapter Ten

IS THERE HISTORICAL DEVELOPMENT OF THEOLOGICAL THOUGHT?

JOHN HOWARD YODER

Our question can be stated most simply and dramatically by the juxta-position of three Johannine statements: "There is still much that I could say to you, but the burden would be too great for you now. However, when he comes who is the Spirit of Truth, He will guide you into all truth: for He will not speak of His own authority, but will tell only what he hears; and he will make known to you the things that are coming. He will glorify me, for everything he makes known to you he will draw from what is mine" (John 16:12-14).

It is evident from this text that the early Christians not only conceived of the development of doctrine, but that they in fact expected new truths to be revealed to them as a part of the promised workings of the Holy Spirit. There is here no conception of a canon which is already closed or will soon be closing. The reference to "things that are coming" would indicate that the prophetic speaking of the Spirit is to be expected until the end of the age. Thus from the very beginning, it is characteristic of faith in Jesus Christ to expect to continue to be led through history. This testimony is not simply a pointer to the past, receding irreversibly: Jesus rather promises the con-tinuing guiding presence of the Paraclete giving meaning to discipleship in every age. "For my part, I give this warning to everyone who is listening to the words of prophecy in this book: Should anyone add to them, God will add to him the plagues described in this book: should anyone take away from the words in this book of prophecy, God will take away from him his share in the tree of life and the Holy City, described in this book" (Rev 22:18-19).

If it he true that God has spoken, revealing His will and purpose, then unfaithfulness will consist in "changing the book," in adding to or subtracting from the deposit of that which God has charged His spokesman to say.

Between these two statements, we have the testimony of the Epistles of John:

"This is how we can make sure that he dwells within us: we know it from the spirit he has given us. But do not trust any and every spirit, my friends: test the spirits, to see whether they are from God, for among those who have gone out into the world there are many prophets falsely inspired. This is how we recognize the Spirit of God: every spirit that acknowledges that Jesus Christ has come in the flesh is from God, and every spirit which does not thus acknowledge Jesus is not from God. This is what is meant by 'anti-Christ'. . . Anyone who runs ahead too far, and does not stand by the doctrine of Christ, is without God: he who stands by that doctrine possesses both the Father and the Son" (1 John 3:24-4:3; 2 John 9).

Here we find the two statements linked. On the one hand the promised presence of the Spirit, which says new things whereby the church will be instructed, is simply presupposed. But then there are other spirits as well, so that the speaking of the spirits needs to be tested, and the testing is by the standard of Jesus Christ's coming in the flesh. To "run on ahead" beyond that foundation is apostasy. Yet this warning is only meaningful within the context of the assumption that there will be new and continuing revelations of truth. The phrase, "every spirit," certainly does not mean that there is more than one Holy Spirit of God; it does however indicate a plurality of spirit manifestations which the church may be moved to accept.

What we have seen here in the Johannine writings could abundantly be confirmed with parallel statements elsewhere in the New Testament, but for this there is here no need. Now it will not do to recognize these statements in the order of what we take to be their importance or their authority. This kind of reorganization is done by some who discern here a movement from the "freer" expectation of the gospel writer to the "narrower" conclusion of the book of the Apocalypse. Such a liberal critic will interpret this narrowing and hardening process as regrettable, and will call upon us to turn to the original liberty of the spirit, overcoming the stiffening which was the work of the second generation, and already a sacrifice of Spirit liberty.

On the other side, reasoning in a very similar way, there would be those Protestant scholastics who would wish to interpret the promise of Jesus in the Gospel of John as limited uniquely to the inspiration of the apostolic writings, so that with the closing of the New Testament canon, stated symbolically by the last words of Revelation 22, there can be henceforth no equally valid workings of the Spirit of God.

Whether we approach it from the right or the left, such a sifting of the biblical statements is illegitimate. We must therefore take the witness of the Johannine literature as a whole. We must affirm at once that there is a call to faithfulness and a mandate to change: That there is at once a promise of new leading and a demand that the church retain her identity with her past confession. The classical modern statement of this conviction is the testimony of the British radical Puritan John Robinson: "I am verily persuaded, the Lord has more Truth yet to break forth out of His Holy Word . . . . I beseech you, remember, 'tis an Article of your Church Covenant, that you be ready to receive whatever Truth shall be made known to you from the written Word of God . . . It is not possible the Christian World should come so lately out of such thick antichristian Darkness, and that Perfection of Knowledge should break forth at once."

Here we find at the same time both statements: The Lord has more truth to reveal: yet it will be out of the pages of Scripture that it will be made manifest, and by the standard of Scripture that it will be judged, all of this amidst the struggle to emerge from "Anti-Christian darkness."

How now can we work in a theologically responsible way with the apparently contradictory concepts of continuity and change? Especially is this problem a burning one today when we must struggle within the light of the so-called "ecumenical question." Here the issue is posed in a peculiarly clear form. Two or more Christian traditions seek to converse with one another about their common claim to be disciples of Jesus Christ and their conflicting definitions of what that loyalty means. Each of them, because each is a church tradition, has undergone change in the course of its history. Perhaps one of them may argue in favor of change, declaring that the Holy Spirit has been particularly guiding its movement. Perhaps one tradition or both will argue rather for the unbending faithfulness with which it keeps repeating the biblical words. Yet even this claim to preservation without adulteration will likewise assert that it has been guided by the Holy Spirit. This preservation of an unchanged heritage itself constitutes as well a change and a development, for to say the same thing in a different place or time is to say something different.

As these two (or more) traditions claim each to have been led by the Spirit of God, each appeals nevertheless to a standard of faithfulness. Each appeals to a common tradition which is above or below or beyond both of them, on the grounds of which it claims the other should listen. This common tradition may be simply the text of Scripture. It may be more than this, as with those churches committed to the standards of later dogmatic developments such as the Apostolic Creed or the Symbol of Nicea. Or perhaps the common court of appeal is less than the whole Bible, if for theological or historical grounds one enters critically into determining what it is within Scripture which is of final binding quality.

As soon as we have taken stock of the fact that we find ourselves in this ecumenical situation, we have passed the point where we could have asked the question, "Is there a development of doctrine worked by the Holy Spirit?" The affirmative answer to that question is presupposed by the very fact of our being here. But the burning question is how we are now to proceed when various developments, each claiming to be inspired, collide. We must permit ourselves to over-simplify the choice of possible procedures to which we now can resort.

1. One position, which traditionally most churches have taken, is to hold that there is one particular inspired correct tradition. This is the one to which God has led the organized church, and since the church has always been organized, we can tell which church is bearing the correct tradition by the simple criterion of succession. This answer has traditionally been given in the most radically consistent way by Roman Catholicism. In case of "collision" or contradiction with other developments in other traditions, the others are simply wrong. When the attempt is made to apply this clear answer to the ecumenical problem, however, we find that it is impossible by definition to test or to support this claim. Since the only reason for being right is that we are in the right organization, we have no basis for imposing this claim upon those who are in other organizations which (at least in the case of some other Catholic churches), have an equally ancient succession behind them, or which (like Protestants) deny that succession proves anything. Nor is such a position acceptable when tested by the scriptural

demand of faithfulness. If not every spirit is of God, then not every development in unbroken succession is necessarily faithful.

Nor is this position acceptable from the perspective of world mission, for it gives no hope for a renewal of that genuine spiritual unity which the world will see and believe. If there is to be any ecumenical conversation or cooperation at all, then Christians must recognize as brethren, or as sister churches, others who do not stand in the same line of succession. Thus the ecumenical problem only exists because the criterion of institutional succession is insufficient.

la. It is only a minor variation of this kind of claim when one holds that one particular correct tradition is defined not by an organization but by a creed as, for instance, the Augsburg Confession and the Book of Concord define what it means to be faithfully Lutheran. We might welcome the fact that in such an approach it is possible to evaluate a particular development as unfaithful. A negative application of this criterion is possible. Anyone who teaches otherwise is condemned, as the Reformation creeds condemn the Anabaptists and the Catholics. But the creedal test is ultimately of the same character when it is claimed as a definition of faithful Christian unity for all times and places. For that creed is just as bound to a time and a place as is the bishop of Rome. It is just as incapable of carrying on a conversation, and less capable of continuing development.

lb. A much more refined form of the "one correct development" conception might be found in a more "dialectical" view of things. Since there is to be development, we could say that truth is identical with the course of history. History is truth unfolding itself. What is now right (for now) will in time become inadequate, will call forth contradiction. Then the original thesis and the new antithesis, the past affirmation and the present contradiction, will move history forward into a new synthesis. Thus the fact of opposition and judgment is recognized. Opposing positions are both given their place. Each right position can at the same time become a wrong position in that it calls forth its own antithesis. Each counter position, although negative, is also right, in its place, before it is swallowed up in a new resolution.

Thus the difference between contradictory positions is itself a work-ing of the Holy Spirit. The meeting of opposites is indispensable for the development of truth. In the age of Moses, Jahweh was the only King of Israel; but with time this kinglessness called forth criticism, and the new solution was the anointing of Saul and David as kings. At this point, kingship was the true form of the covenant; but then later it needed to be left behind in the age of captivity and replaced by the promise of the Suffering Servant. In the time of Ezra and Nehemiah, Judaism was the right form of the cov-enant but then Jesus, both fulfilling the hopes of Judaism and rejected by it, brought history one step farther. For its time the New Testament church was the true form, then the medieval church, then the Reformation, then Enlightenment, then the missionary movement and revivalism, and now the "world come of age." Then the concern of ecumenical study is to discern in good time what the present critical thrust must be and what the coming resolution will have to be.

But whether we see this kind of vision classically exemplified in the phi-losophy of Hegel, or in the many modern thinkers who unwittingly follow his pattern of thought, or in the very different but somewhat analogous form of the "dispensational" heritage of John Nelson Darby, this position is no help. Although there is conflict and judgment, there is not really any criterion of right or wrong, but only of timeliness. Every position is right, but only in its place and time. Every position may be wrong, but only by being premature or obsolete. Each age criticizes the age before it, but there is no over-arching appeal beyond the flux of history to a normative revelation whereby some synthesis might be measured and found more right than others.

Nor is this kind of vision of progress subject to conversation or testing. Ultimately each position must have its own "pope," its Hegel or Tillich or Robinson, who decrees at a given time and place where the top of the pin-nacle is, rejecting all other positions as outworn and incapable by defini-tion of criticizing the novelty of his own position.

But before we leave to one side these varied forms of the claim that there is "one true tradition," let us be reminded that in one way or another this is the position which we all take. At some time, in some types of discus-sions, every Christian and every Christian group appeals to the criterion of dogma or of succession or of progress, in support of his own position.

2. The second type of approach to our problem is the pluralistic. Here all positions are somehow correct. This may be a serial pluralism,

according to which each position is right for its time and place; or it may be a cumulative pluralism, according to which all the various positions need to be added up and to correct and to complement one another in order to get the "richness" of the "whole truth."

Even apart from the fact that it radically renounces the responsibility to test new developments, such a position as this is not ecumenically acceptable. It begins by denying one thing which all historic Christian bodies have agreed on, with the New Testament, namely that there is such a thing as wrong teaching, as heresy or apostasy or anti-Christ. Now it may be possible to affirm that everyone is in some sense standing for some element of truth, or that in everybody which claims to be Christian there is some vestige of the character of the church. But it cannot responsibly be held that every position formerly held by everyone is equally right. Some of these positions are mutually incompatible and cannot possibly be set side by side as both somehow true.

And yet before we leave this lazy solution of pluralism aside, let it be remembered again that all of us use it at some times and places. Every Christian tradition has somewhere or other made use of the distinction between essentials and non-essentials: non-essentials are the points at which contradiction is either good or at worst unobjectionable.

3. A third possibility, logically speaking perhaps the only one left, is to conclude that all the traditions are wrong. Since development is sure to lead to diversity and to conflict and therefore certainly to error at least at some points, the only development that we can accept is that which took place before the closing of the canon of the New Testament. The only purpose of theology is to return to the New Testament norms for doctrine as well as for church order.

a. One logical application of such a rejection of all traditions is then the "restitution" theme which was so prevalent in the Reformed and Anabaptist wings of the Reformation. All human traditions being under judgment, the church should be restored according to our New Testament motto. Now as a matter of fact no Reformation churches did claim finally to have established this New Testament model in its detail. Probably the closest examples were when Ulrich Zwingli claimed that the city council of Zurich was the equivalent of the elders of the New Testament church, or when John Calvin claimed clear New Testament precedent for his form of the four-fold ministry.

This "restitution" position has great strength; it has given to the age of the Reformation, and to Free-church Protestantism, their great moral power. Yet as we have already seen, such a position very easily tends to be blinded to the fact that it is itself also a tradition: that going back to the New Testament in sixteenth-century Zurich or nineteenth-century Kentucky is not the same as living in New Testament times, but is itself a particular doctrinal development.

b. But it would be just as possible to argue that since all development of tradition is wrong, we should have no forms at all. The hardening of forms, whether of organization or thought, is itself a loss of the vitality of New Testament faith. We should have no organizations, no visible church, we should reject the temptation to form orderly structures and to let faith take shape within history. This is the position traditionally identified as "spiritualist."

Although it is enjoying periodic popularity in ages of cultural confusion and criticism, it is by definition not theologically and ecumenically responsible; one cannot converse with it.

c. But it is just as possible to hold that since all forms are wrong, therefore it makes no difference in what form we express our faith. We cannot get away from the need for one shape or another but it is immaterial which shape a church takes, for such matters are *adiaphora*. Anything we choose to do or to believe is all right. The only thing we shall object to too strenuously is anyone else's claiming to have one right form. If by alliance with the State the church can survive and get a hearing, that alliance is good. If in the modern Western world all society becomes a computerized, centralized bureaucracy, the church structures should do the same. If in another age the church is a persecuted minority, we can stand that too. Doctrine too should adjust freely to the needs and tastes of every society.

Such a position has all the theological weaknesses of the "pluralism" we mentioned, with the additional one that the "adiaphora" argument is almost always used to justify accommodation to the prestige and power structures and the philosophies of a given age; i.e., to undercut the elements of judgment and mission in favor of identification. It is likewise incapable of conversation; all it can reject is decisiveness.

What Then?

Perhaps this brief listing of the number of ways, all unsatisfactory, in which Christians have felt they could relate faithfulness and change, will have led us to the conviction that the task is hopeless. But rather than seeking simply to mix or to alternate these various traditional strategies, let us first take account what all of these positions have in common.

All of them, we may observe, begin by assuming the concept of a "tradition" or a "denomination" or "confession." Hereby is meant a major stream of church history, with its particular doctrines and church administration. This "confession" can relate to others as a unit. In meeting them it can take a clear position, one of the positions indicated above. It could if agreement were reached and the problems were all solved, be reconciled, as a whole, with that other tradition or confession with which it was in conversation, and then the two together would form one new confession or "church." It is this assumption, the picture of large denominational units expressing distinct traditions, which we must learn to reject on the basis of the facts. Let us first test this concept of "traditions" by asking whether denominational fellowships really do have this character. We shall discover that no group is bound to the creed which it professes. We shall find that those groups which teach in principle that the possession of bishops and apostolic succession is necessary to be a church are ready in practice to admit the real Christian faithfulness of non-Episcopalian congregations. We would further observe, if we studied critically, that most traditions do not have a clearly qualified organ of conversation and commitment whereby it would be possible for them to be reconciled with some other tradition.

The questioning is just as fundamental if we begin on the level of the congregation. We discover that no congregation is fully within only one tradition. Whatever be the formal denominational affiliations, all Christians have learned something from outside their own groups. And not only do Methodists respect Francis of Assisi and Catholics listen to Billy Graham: on every level and in every way every Christian and every congregation are broader in their loyalties than the concept of the monolithic tradition would permit. Not only is this the case factually: it is also proper that it should be so. No Christian and no congregation *should* be exactly like the next one. Every different place and every different time pose their own questions. To the extent to which answers to those questions are correct, every faithful congregation must be different from every other one.

We have been exploring simply the logic of what it means to say that the church is called to be faithful in development. In summary we may say that it is not a meaningful possibility to say that "everyone is right"; for such a claim to development would be that there is no longer such a thing as a concept of right. *We must* therefore, as in New Testament times, *be ready to "test the spirits."* We must be able to discern precisely (because development is real) where there might be genuine rebellion or apostasy.

Similarly on the other side, it is not meaningful to deny, a priori and in general, that there is such a thing as valid development. Every Christian, every congregation, *must affirm*, with regard to his or her own testimony, *that such development* has taken place and must confess that this *is the work of the Holy Spirit*. Then the issue is not "Is there development of doctrine through the work of the Holy Spirit?" but rather "How shall we proceed in conversation between or among several Christian bodies, each claiming to stand faithfully in the path of Jesus, but who disagree?"

Thus our question has become one not of general principles or truths but of correct procedure. It is to this point that the earliest reformers spoke with their doctrine of the Christian congregation. We may turn for instance to Balthasar Hubmaier, as he laid out the rules of proper disputation in September, 1524:

> I. Every Christian is obligated to give account of his hope and his faith and the faith that is in him, to whoever asks it.
>
> II. For whoever confesses Christ before men, not fearing those who can kill the body, the same Christ will confess before his Father.
>
> V. But the judgment, which of two is of the more correct opinion, is conceived in the church by the Word of God and born of faith. "When you come together, each of you contributes . . . of the prophets, two or three may speak, while the rest exercise their judgment upon what is said" (1 Cor. 14:26, 29).

VI. Nevertheless so that order might be maintained and disorderly babbling avoided, three or four men may properly be chosen from the congregation . . . not that they might sit in judgment on the truth of the Word which is eternal and unchanging, but to determine which party understands more nearly the intention of the divine work.

XIV. The judgment of the moderators shall be as follows: One who is seated, to whom something is revealed, shall have the right to take the floor, and then the former speaker shall be silent.

XV. But when the mass of the church is silent, then the judgment of the experts is confirmed by the silence of the congregation.

XVII. All men may teach individually, so that everyone might learn and all might be edified.

XVIII. Therefore God has subjected the spirit of the prophets to the Prophets, so the spirit is a teacher not of division but of peace, as in all the congregations of the saints.

We have here a classical statement of the position which had already been advocated by Huldrych Zwingli in January and October, 1523, namely that any local Christian gathering is authorized by God and empowered by the Spirit to discern the true meaning for that time and place of Scripture. This is the same claim which was made in February, 1527, by those brethren who gathered in Schleitheim and testified under seven headings how they had "been brought to unity." It was the position in the somewhat later document, of "several who are called Anabaptists, answering the question, why they do not go to churches." Here the Anabaptists, citing 1 Corinthians 14 as did Hubmaier, explained their avoidance of state-church services by the fact that the congregation was permitted only to listen, not to speak.

The challenge to free-church ecclesiology is to apply this congregationalism of the earliest Reformation to the conversations of our day. It must suffice here to propose some bare theses to indicate how this might be done.

I. The nature of the unity we seek is congregational. It takes place where disciples of Jesus Christ gather, where all listen and all may speak.

II. In the gathered congregation there must be exercised the gift of the teacher, transmitting to the present members of the congregation the tradition of God's people in the past. The nucleus of this tradition is Scripture and the nucleus of Scripture is the person and work of our Lord Jesus Christ. It is thus in the congregational process that the concern of *sola scriptura* and of apostolicity is realized.

III. In the gathered congregation there must be exercised the gifts of prophecy in the discerning of contemporary truth and error. Not all "insight" or "development" is divinely given; the prophets' speech must be *weighed* (1 Cor 14:4-29).

IV. The gathered congregation is constituted of believers. Not every gathering is a Christian church, even where the word of God is preached. It is in the constitution of the congregation that the baptism of believers is indispensable.

(If we were discussing whether the unbaptized may be saved from eternal perdition, or whether the faith of the adult candidate for baptism is always genuine, we could not argue irresistibly against infant baptism or against the disuse of baptism. The cruciality of baptism is not that it guarantees individual experience but that it constitutes the covenanted congregation.)

V. The gathered congregation may be served by agencies of liaison and government relating several or many churches, whether these be called conventions, commissions, bureaucracies, or bishops. The authority and the legitimacy of these agencies are derived from the congregation, and not vice versa.

VI. A congregation may gather which is "in one place" for only a limited time. (Ecumenical conventions, assemblies, synods, task forces.) In such a gathering may be discerned the marks of the church inasmuch and insofar as it does the work of the congregation in proclamation, in sharing word and sacrament, and in discerning the will of God. The authority and legitimacy of that gathering as congregation are determined by the faith and covenant of its members and the quality of their fellowship and not by juridical links to bishops or synods claiming authority there or elsewhere.

VII. Congregations may be served by verbal statements of what other congregations have testified to be the meaning of faithfulness in other times and places (confessions, epistles, declarations). A faithful congregation will listen with great earnestness to any such communication from another congregation. The authority and legitimacy of such statements is determined in their being received by the local congregation, not by their age or by the juridical authority of the person or group which wrote them.

VIII. A congregation, like an individual Christian, may fall away from the faith and leave the communion of the church universal. Such apostasy may involve wrong teachings or actions on the part of its members, but the criterion of unfaithfulness is not the doctrinal or moral standard which other churches uphold, but rather this congregation's failure or refusal to receive fraternal admonition and counsel from sister churches.

IX. But since apostasy is a decision of a congregation, so is the promise of renewal made to every congregation. Just as no church is indefectible, so no fallen church is beyond the divine possibility of renewal. It is not possible to condemn forever certain communions or certain ideas on the basis of their fathers' or their founders' disobedience or error.

Thus the promise of the Spirit to lead the Church "into all truth" has led us to examine not faith or order, doctrine or organization, in their own right, but rather to seek their rootage and their legitimation in the reality of the believing, forgiving congregation. It is because that Spirit is a permanent Presence in the church that bishops and synods, creeds and councils may be used of God; it is because the congregation is the locus of that presence that no creed or council, synod or bishop may stand in judgment over the congregation as in each age and in each place men gather around the Bible and confess that Jesus Christ is Lord.

ABOUT THE EDITOR

JOHN C. NUGENT is a Long Island native and Professor of Old Testament at his alma mater, Great Lakes Christian College. His Ph.D. is from Calvin Theological Seminary, where he wrote a dissertation on John Howard Yoder's appropriation of the Old Testament for ecclesiology. He holds additional graduate degrees from Duke Divinity School (Th.M.) and Emmanuel School of Religion (M.Div.). John has published articles in books, academic journals, and popular level magazines in a wide variety of areas including Bible, theology, Christian ethics, church planting, Yoder studies, and Stone-Campbellite history. John regularly writes Bible lesson commentaries for Standard Publishing, and he has also been involved with youth ministry, associate ministry, camp directing, campus ministry, church planting, and house church ministry. John, his wife Beth, and their three girls are committed members of Delta Community Christian Church in Lansing, Michigan.

LaVergne, TN USA
18 August 2010
193741LV00005B/1/P